P9-APA-618

BIG CHUCK!

BIG CHUCK!

My Favorite Stories from 47 Years on Cleveland TV

Chuck Schodowski

WITH TOM FERAN

GRAY & COMPANY, PUBLISHERS

CLEVELAND

Photos are courtesy of Fox8 TV or the Chuck Schodowski
collection except where otherwise credited.

Gray & Company, Publishers
www.grayco.com

Library of Congress Cataloging-in-Publication Data
Schodowski, Chuck.
Big Chuck! : my favorite stories from 47 years on Cleveland
TV / Chuck Schodowski, with Tom Feran.
p. cm.
ISBN 978-1-59851-052-2
1. Schodowski, Chuck. 2. Television personalities—United
States—Biography. 3. Television broadcasting—Ohio—
Cleveland—Anecdotes. I. Feran, Tom. II. Title.
PN1992.4.S29A3 2008   2008541914

Printed in the United States of America

10 9 8 7 6 5 4 3 2 1

I dedicate this book to all the wonderful people who watched and enjoyed what we did. It's because of you that Ernie Anderson, Bob Wells, John Rinaldi, our large and talented cast, and I compiled "the longest run" in television history—in the world! I love you all. God bless you.

—Big C.

CONTENTS

BIG CHUCK!

INTRO

Hi, gang! Thanks for buying the book. Here's how it came about: Back in October of 1997, about eight months after the death of Ernie "Ghoulardi" Anderson, a book titled *Ghoulardi: Inside Cleveland TV's Wildest Ride* was published by Gray & Company. It was written by TV columnists Tom Feran and R. D. Heldenfels. I helped them with it. After eleven years, the book is still selling. Following its initial release, Tom Feran asked me, "When are we going to do *your* book, Chuck?" I said I'd like to start working on it soon.

The book you hold in your hands was published in October 2008. I didn't want to wait until the last minute.

While working on this book with Tom, I found that we have a lot in common. We were both born and died in Cleveland. (I figure neither one of us is going anywhere.) We both like the traditions and history of Cleveland, and we are both big Cleveland sports fans. Tom and I both have large families. He has four children, and I have five children and fourteen grandkids. Christmas costs me a fortune—that's why I worked so long. Tom and I are both Catholic, and we are both graduates of Harvard. He graduated from Harvard College in Cambridge, Massachusetts, in 1975. I graduated from Harvard Elementary School, on East 71st Street and Harvard Road in Cleveland, in 1946.

Now here's Tom to tell you more.

Thanks, Chuck! (I should object to being killed off in the first chapter, but it's too late now. Chuck killed me off in a skit about twenty years ago. He'll get to that later.)

Most people know Chuck Schodowski as Big Chuck—the comic TV character whose career spanned five decades at WJW Channel

8 in Cleveland, where he began work as an engineer in 1960. He started his on-air career with the Ghoulardi show in 1963, and he won early fame as handsome, debonair, downstairs neighbor Jerry Kreegle in a series of *Peyton Place* spoofs called "Parma Place." The stories he tells of Ernie Anderson and Tim Conway in this era will make you laugh out loud.

After Ernie headed out for Hollywood in 1966, Chuck teamed up with Bob Wells, TV8's Hoolihan the Weatherman, and *The Hoolihan & Big Chuck Show* was born. It ran for thirteen years, featured many local and national personalities, and of course provided its own store of very funny happenings, both on and off the air.

John Rinaldi, known as Lil' John, joined the guys about 1971. When Bob Wells left the show in 1979, John took over as co-host on *The Big Chuck & Lil' John Show*. It lasted an incredible twenty-eight more years.

But there is more to Chuck's career. In his early years, he was involved in countless telecasts of Indians and Browns games at the old Cleveland Stadium. His behind-the-scenes stories are hilarious and sometimes eye-opening.

Storer Broadcasting promoted Chuck to producer-director in 1969, and over the years he wrote and produced hundreds of shows whose numerous awards include twenty-eight local Emmys and three international film festival medals. Several of these shows were seen nationally. He also directed two made-for-television movies, *Heartsong, U.S.A.,* with Brock Peters, and *The Wandering Muse of Artemus Flagg,* starring Burgess Meredith.

In the hours and hours we spent gathering stories and information for this book, one thread from beginning to end ties together Chuck, Ernie, Hoolie, and John: They're all fun-loving pranksters, as you will learn as you read on, and they entertained themselves as much as they entertained the people who watched them on TV or just happened to encounter them in real life. It helps explain why the four of them combined to produce the longest-running local show in television history. Starting in the days when TV was live and in black-and-white, and finishing in the era of high-definition digital color, it celebrated forty-four years at Chuck's retirement in June 2007.

Me at age two, entered in a "Beautiful Child" competition.

One other thing stands out: Chuck brought innovations to Cleveland television that were influential—and sometimes copied directly—from Hollywood to Europe. He's been called a television genius, using a word that gets tossed around too casually in television, but evidence backs it up.

If it ever sounds like he's bragging, don't believe it. He is justifiably proud of his work and achievements, but he remains a modest, generous, and self-effacing man who is most proud of his family and credits hard work for his accomplishments. Very few people have worked in TV as long as he has, and his stories will interest, amuse, and even amaze readers of all ages. Let's get started.

The story starts on June 28, 1934, when Charles Mitchell Schodowski was born in the Polish neighborhood at Harvard Road and East 71st Street on Cleveland's southeast side—not in poverty but in the next thing to it, at a time when the effects of the Great Depression were still being felt.

He was a skinny, blond-haired kid, and he remembers his early childhood as "very sickly." A bout of scarlet fever led to rheumatic fever and a heart murmur when he was only six years old, and it kept him going in and out of the hospital for about ten years. His physician—fresh out of medical school (the only doctor they could afford)—was a short, stocky man named Edward R. Rinaldi. He remained Chuck's doctor for more than thirty years, delivered his first two sons, and—in the sort of coincidence that Chuck relishes—turned out to be the uncle of the other Rinaldi who'd partner with Chuck for another thirty years.

Being sickly was bad enough. Worse for Chuck, who was shy and worrisome anyway, it meant he wasn't allowed to take gym class. It irked and embarrassed him deeply. He tried every year to get permission but never did, and worrying that his classmates would find out plagued him all through junior high and high school.

He also remembers being "extremely nervous" about doing book reports in front of a class. "I was so worried," he says, "it would affect me physically for two weeks before I did it. I can't tell you how hard it was, and how relieved I was after it was over. To this day, people who were my classmates and knew how hard it was, knew that I was ready to pass out, will see me on TV and say, 'How the heck do you do that?'"

He was a long way from being Big Chuck. But he was getting there. And he can tell you the rest.

CHAPTER 1

LITTLE BIG CHUCK

ODD JOBS

Being from a poor family, I always had jobs, beginning with a *Cleveland News* newspaper route at eight years old. I had what seemed like five customers spread out over about ten miles. Every *News* route was like that. Later I carried the *Press*. I never did deliver the *Plain Dealer* because delivery was early in the morning and I had evening jobs. I worked in a soda parlor, worked at the Food Town on Broadway all through high school, and I set pins at Marcelline Tavern on East 71st Street.

That job started when I was about twelve. We were paid two cents a line. No one wanted to work the ladies' league on Saturday afternoon, but being one of the youngest there I got stuck with it. It'd take forever. They'd take three hours to play a game that guys would play in one. When you set pins, there's a wall between the alleys and a pit where the pins fall. You'd have to jump in, pick up the pins, look at the ones standing, and put the knocked-down pins in the rack above the lane. You'd pull the thing down to set the pins. Then you had to sit on the ledge between lanes and hold your legs up as high as you could. Guys would throw fastballs, and the pins would really fly. The kids in the pit would try to push each other in the way, and it was sort of fun. The good thing about women bowlers was that the pins fell so softly you could stand in the pit. Sometimes they'd just fall over on the alley and you'd have to crawl out to get them.

I was standing in the pit one Saturday, figuring that, having watched the first three or four bowlers, they'd take all afternoon. All of a sudden—*boom!*—pins were flying and hitting me all over. I

Nine years old, in knickers for my First Communion photo.

bent down and looked, and it was Stella Walsh, the Olympic gold medal sprinter. She really had an arm, too. I thought she broke my leg.

She lived in my neighborhood. I didn't know her, but everyone knew who she was. You'd see her and nod your head. I raced her a couple of years later, when I got over being sickly. I was playing softball, she was watching, and some of the kids told her I was pretty fast ("Bet you can't beat him!"). I didn't want to do it, but they egged me on. We ran the length of the field next to South High School field. The tale afterward was that I demolished her, but I'd say it was a tie—and she was about forty.

When she died in 1980, the funeral was at Komorowski Funeral Home. They called Komorowski "the Digger," from Digger O'Dell, the undertaker on *The Life of Riley*. On Sundays, when I was a kid, the men would go to each others' houses and listen to the ballgame and drink. Everyone was in walking distance. When they ran out of booze, they'd send the kids to the Digger. He always had booze, but he didn't sell it. He'd give you a bottle you had to replace. I'd see all my school buddies, going to the Digger to get booze for the guys. At Stella Walsh's funeral, everyone edged up to him and said, "Man? Woman?" Everyone wanted to know, and the word was *man*. The autopsy showed she had mosaicism—male genitals and male and female chromosomes. They tried to hide it from us when we were kids, but she looked like a guy.

I worked as a caddy, too, at Sleepy Hollow in Brecksville. It was a private club then, and I thumbed rides to get there until I was sixteen or seventeen. One afternoon I was really tired after doing thirty-six holes and just wanted to go home. But the caddymaster, a guy named Carmen, said, "You gotta caddy another time. It'll go real fast—you only gotta do nine holes." When they gave me the clubs, there was a big leather bag with everything in it, which usually meant a good golfer, and a little canvas bag with three clubs in it. I said, "Holy crap, he's got a kid with him. It's gonna take forever." Carmen said, "I told you, it'll be fast." We went out. The guy nailed a drive right down the middle. Then the kid got up, seven or eight years old, and I thought, here we go. But—*bam!*—the kid hit it straight, walked to the ball, and hit it straight again with the same club till he got it on the green. They were done in no time, and it was the easiest round I ever had. The guy's name was Weiskopf, and the kid was Tommy Weiskopf, who had a pretty good career and won the British Open in 1973. Even as a kid, he had a great swing.

GETTING BIGGER

By this time, I was over being sickly. My last attack of rheumatic fever was in junior high school, and an amazing transformation took place when I was fifteen. I began to feel healthy, grew more than a foot, gained weight, and became unusually strong for a kid my age. Kids who used to push me around suddenly got pushed back. I became so athletic that, without telling my parents, I started tossing and catching footballs on the sidelines as the South High School football team practiced and was noticed by the coach. I wanted to play, but when the time came to sign up, my parents wouldn't let me do it. Doctor's orders. I was really down because the coach, Gene Wolansky, sent an assistant coach to tell them I probably could win a college scholarship. I wasn't going otherwise.

I also didn't tell my parents when I started sparring with a friend, Ray Cieslinski, who was in Golden Gloves. I could hit really hard. Without telling anybody, even Ray, I went down to the Y, started boxing, and got good at it. Maybe not good enough. I was skinny but weighed 178 pounds, so I had to

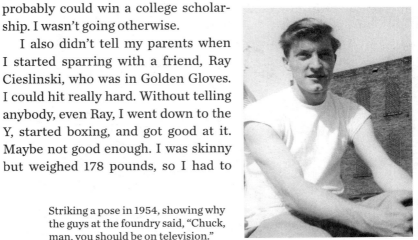

Striking a pose in 1954, showing why the guys at the foundry said, "Chuck, man, you should be on television."

fight heavyweight. I was sixteen or seventeen, and they brought in a man against me, thirty years old, 215 pounds, and punchy as hell. He just beat the crap out of me. I never told anybody about it, not Ray and not my high school sweetheart, June. She'd see cuts on my cheek, and I told her I got them working at the foundry.

HER NAME WAS JUNE

I had just turned seventeen when I began my senior year at South High in September 1951. Because I couldn't play sports, I desperately wanted to get involved with something else. I thought about taking the drama course, but being an introvert, I was much too chicken to get up on stage. My close friend Ray Uzell—an excellent trumpet player in the marching band who later played in the U.S. Navy Band and then for the Harry James Orchestra—talked me into becoming a trumpet "faker" in South's very small marching band. I also joined the German Club with him, and we were both hall guards.

A hall guard's biggest job was to direct new tenth grade students, or "flats," to the proper classrooms. In January of 1952, a brand new flat caught my eye. She was very attractive, with strikingly beautiful eyes. After several days of nervous flirtatious glances, I got the guts to talk to her. Her name was June, and she was fifteen-and-a-half years old. I had very few dates up to that point. I was very clumsy and naive with girls (and, to some degree, with women in general as

I got older). We had a few very awkward dates before I got to know her better.

She lived in the Broadway–East 55th Street area of Cleveland. I lived in the area now known as Slavic Village. Dating was no problem because I had a car—a '39 Ford convertible with a rumble seat. Everyone loved riding in the rumble seat, winter or summer.

June and I had a lot in common. We

My senior photo from South High School, Class of 1952. Many of the guys in the yearbook had the same tie.

were both Polish (her name was Kolec-
zek, shortened to Kole). We were both
from less-than-average-income families, she more than me. Both her parents worked, like mine, and she pretty
much had to raise her three younger
brothers. I had to care at times for my
younger brother, Paul, and sister, Mary-
ann. She had a job working at Cole's
Shoe Store on Broadway. I worked just
down the street at Food Town. We were
both Catholic. She went to St. Hyacinth
Church, and I went to Holy Name
Church. (Its high school was South's
archrival.)

June Kole, South High School Class of 1954—the future Mrs. Schodowski.

June was busy with schoolwork,
working her part-time job, and the
cooking, washing clothes, and other
jobs that went with taking care of her young brothers. She had a
sister, Pat, two years younger, who shared the chores with her.

She lived on East 66th Street, just off Bessemer Avenue. Right
across the street from Ferro's foundry, and I mean *right across the
street*—only fifty feet from her house, with forges pounding away
all night. During the night shift, June told me, the men would come
out to eat lunch on the railroad tracks, and they would sometimes
leave empty pop bottles that were redeemable for two and five
cents. She and Pat would run out and collect them, using the money
to buy a quarter pound of ground meat and tomato paste to make
spaghetti for themselves and their brothers.

It was not an easy or happy home life for her. She could never
remember getting Christmas or birthday presents. Her life was not
like that of the kids depicted on *Ozzie & Harriet*, *Leave It to Beaver*,
or other 1950s TV shows.

Whenever I picked June up for a date, she was always just finishing washing dishes, housecleaning, or washing clothes. It was hard
to find time for dating. In June of 1952, I took her to my graduation
prom. Then I started working six days a week in the foundry. We

dated a few times that summer. I liked her and she seemed to like me, but . . .

I started thinking maybe I shouldn't get involved with someone with such a complicated young life. I really felt like I didn't belong there, and didn't need to be part of her hardships. So I decided to break up.

I was working the second shift. One day I left a little early for work, and drove over to her house to tell her what I had decided. As I pulled up to her rundown old house, I saw her in the back yard, carrying a heavy basket of clothes to hang on the line. It was very hot; she was sweating, and she looked very tired. She was surprised and happy to see me. And she never stopped working as we talked. I felt this was not the time to tell her about breaking up and left for work.

I thought about her all that night and did a whole lot of soul-searching.

Ever since I was a kid, I wanted to get married, have children, have a home of my own, and provide for my family. And as dumb as I was back then, I knew the girl that I married must share my desire for a close family life. She must be a good and loving mother. My parents were very stoic with me, and I didn't like that. June's parents were not very loving either, yet June had so much love to give to her brothers and sister. And she cared for them faithfully—a trait she got from her Polish grandmother, I later learned.

There I was at 4 a.m. in the filthy, dirty, smoky foundry. Thinking about my girlfriend who, at age sixteen, knew more about cooking and taking care of a family than most grown women do. One who openly cared and loved her family. And she actually liked a jerk like me.

On that hot summer night in 1952, I decided not to break up with June. Instead I would get even more involved with her and seriously try to be of some help. Was I lucky, or what?!

We dated, and made a few serious plans. June graduated South High School in January 1955 and went to work full-time as a wait-ress at Stouffer's restaurant on Euclid Avenue. She also moved in with her grandmother in the East 123rd Street and Miles Avenue area. We got engaged about a year later, and got married on September 22, 1956. If you do the math, that's fifty-two years ago.

Of all the good things that have happened to me in my long and eventful life, getting married to June was the best thing ever—by far. Yes! I am lucky! She raised five children without much help from me. I was always working. All of our children, our daughter- and sons-in-law, and our fourteen grandchildren worship and adore her. Everyone loves to come to Grandma's house.

For over fifty years I worked two jobs, I figure an average of sixty hours a week, and I never took a sick day.

June worked twenty-four hours a day, seven days a week, for over fifty years, caring for me, the kids, the grandkids, and our home. And she never took a sick day either.

After all this time, I'm still stoic and do not express love and appreciation as often as I should to June. But I take solace in that I know she knows how very deeply I love her. I'm still working too much. And so is she. God has truly blessed us.

GOOD TIMES IN A TOUGH JOB

I was only seventeen, in my last semester of high school, when I began work at the foundry, Alloys & Chemicals, down in the Flats behind Alcoa. I worked full-time on the midnight shift because I wanted a better car. I was always pretty independent. I stayed at the foundry after I graduated. College was out of the question because my family could not afford to help me.

I started playing sandlot football and baseball, and gained some neighborhood notoriety for being a home-run hitter. But I still wished I could have played high school sports. I still love sports. I became an avid Browns fan when they started in 1946, and it affected my whole week if they lost. To this day, I don't think I've missed a game. I went to a lot of Indians game, too, and was behind home plate when Herb Score got hit in the eye in 1957. It still amazes me that I got to work with him years later, especially because I always idolized pitchers. When I was a little kid, my grandmother had a farm in Independence, and we would listen at night to games on the radio. When Bob Feller pitched, I'd write down every strikeout because he was always flirting with a record—never knowing that someday I'd work with him, too, and get to know him.

My younger brother, Paul, became All-Senate quarterback for

Showing off the Ford ragtop I bought while working in the foundry after high school. Note the white socks on the clothesline.

South High in the fall of 1956. I had a vicarious thrill watching him play. I was so into the games that it was like I was playing myself. He was good enough to win a scholarship to Kent State University, but he blew out his knee. It hurt us both.

Still wanting to participate in athletics myself, even though I was working at the foundry, I went to the owner who let me organize a company team in the industrial basketball league. It was known as commando basketball–rough! No blood, no foul. We were good enough to get the state finals in Columbus.

I was the only white guy on the team, so my teammates gave me a nickname. They called me Spot—like white spot—which was typical of the attitudes and camaraderie we had. If you've ever been in a foundry, you know it's not a place you want to work. The work is hard, and it can be dangerous. For me, it was both a crappy time and a great time. The people make the difference. Because I was only seventeen when I started, I felt the men in the foundry sort of raised me. I learned about "man things" and more from them.

They gave me my love of rhythm and blues. Most of the time, I was the only white guy on the shift; they had the radio on, and R&B was all I heard every night for eight years. It was the Moondog show with Alan Freed, the father of rock and roll. The bluesy music Ernie Anderson first used on *Shock Theater* came from my records—songs that I heard on the Moondog show. To this day I love that stuff.

I also developed an appreciation for black humor, especially from the countless pranks we'd pull. There was something almost every day. They'd pull stunts on me, and I'd think of funny stuff to pull on them. It could get pretty elaborate.

I was going into work one night and saw a big, nasty, stray cat that looked like he'd been in a hundred fights. He wouldn't let me grab him, so I threw my coat on him because I knew what I was going to do. I worked in the spectrographic lab at that time, and it had to be kept clean. There was an airlock between the lab and the foundry. They'd put in metal samples from the foundry side, ring a bell, and I'd blow the air out before taking them into the lab. That night, I unscrewed the light in the airlock, threw in the cat, closed the hatch, called for a sample, and went out to see what happened. By now, the cat was really mad, hissing and scratching. A little guy named Brown no sooner opened the door than the cat flew out with all four legs right on him. Brown was a guy who used to wear discarded clothes because he didn't want to buy them, so they were really baggy. He had enough room to pull the cat away from him and go running through the foundry, with the cat still attached. Guys were crying from laughter.

Things happened at night that didn't happen during the day. At night, we'd refine molten metal by boiling chlorine through it. This sent big clouds of poisonous gas over the neighborhood. We weren't supposed to do it, but there was no OSHA back then, and at night no one knew. This was what the foundry could get away with.

When we set up to do it, I would carry over a big cylindrical can, and one of the guys would have to take a washer out of it. It just so happened that at that time, my mother had a wrap with a fox's head on it. I "borrowed" her stylish accessory and turning it into a glove, stuck my hand into its head. Then I took the bottom off the washer can, put my hand inside, and waited for the moment when the foundryman needed a washer. I took the can over and, as he opened it, I made a hissing noise while popping my gloved hand up. He didn't react right away but stood staring like Stan Laurel, holding a hand on this can with a head popping out of it. Then he slammed down the lid and took off running.

We planted rubber snakes and hooked up plates to deliver electrical shocks. I'd come home in the morning with tears in my eyes from laughing, and I usually couldn't sleep right away, so keyed from what we just did. I was married by then, and June really thought I was nuts.

They'd tell me, "Chuck, man, you should be on television."

I had a good friend there, Bill Strass, who was an artist. I liked cartooning, so we'd draw four-panel cartoons of all the guys in the plant. We'd post them, and they were always a hit. The owner of the plant was a guy named Noah Butkin. We'd draw him by accentuating his big nose and having him smoke a cigar. It really looked like him. One day he heard about the cartoons and called me to his office. *This is it,* I thought—*I'm getting canned.* Noah was real gruff, but he was so cool. He put aside his cigar.

"So you're doing these cartoons of me and everybody. You have time for that?" he asked.

I told him that I tried to squeeze it in on my lunch hour, which was bullshit.

"How much time does it take you?"

I told him about a half hour, though an hour was more like it.

"I'll tell you what I'm gonna do," he said. He gave Strass and me an hour whenever we wanted to draw the cartoon. He thought it was good for morale, and it really was. It gave everybody a good laugh. I realized I liked doing stuff like that.

LOOKING FOR MORE

I was always looking to improve myself—to somehow get a better job and make more money. So during my years in the foundry, I booked tickets for football games and the treasury balance, which was printed every day in the newspaper and worked like a lottery number. This was illegal. I hope the statute of limitations applies.

I never actually bet; I just booked the tickets. Guys on my shift would play, and one actually hit it big. One Sunday I went to Smoker's Bar off Union Avenue. Bars weren't open on Sunday, but cops were drinking there, and guys would come in before football games. The guy who handled the bets told me that someone hit the number, and I had to take him the money. Six thousand dollars. It was a rough neighborhood, and I thought I was going to have to do it alone. I was sweating it for days. When the time came, I thought, *What am I gonna do?* I was afraid I was going to get killed.

The bookie said, "Don't worry about it! These guys are gonna go with you," gesturing to three guys sitting there smoking cigars. It looked like a scene from *The Godfather*. They grabbed hold of me and took me to the car. Two of them sat in the back while the third drove. I was so relieved. It felt like I just finished a book report in junior high school.

In 1956 my wife became pregnant, and that was a huge emotional thing to me. I was both elated and worried, because I was twenty-two and not making much money at the foundry. So I got a part-time job driving a Yellow Cab. I thought I knew Cleveland, but every time I had a fare I'd get lost. I quit pretty quickly.

On a vacation with friends, around 1955

Then, to my shock, I got drafted. I went to see Dr. Rinaldi to see if my heart was OK for military service. He said, "It sounds fine. I think they'll take you." Feelings of regret immediately went through me. Maybe it was fine in high school and I could have played sports after all. I might've won a scholarship. "*Now* you tell me," I said—just in time for the draft. But because June was pregnant, I got a six-month deferment. I'd stay at the foundry.

CHAPTER 2

THE TV LIGHT IS LIT

One summer night I found myself sitting in my car at a light at State Road and Pleasant Valley Road in Parma, looking up at the Channel 8 transmitter tower. I'd gone out to get a Manners' Big Boy for dinner, and I just sat there, thinking it must really be nice to work at a TV station. I don't know why. Maybe it was because I was out in the fresh air, watching the tower lights blinking in the night sky, and had to go back to the dirty foundry. But the thought stayed with me. It must really be nice.

I remembered that as a kid, I used to take bed sheets, hang them up on the garage to make curtains, and get my buddies to act in some simple play I'd written. Never, ever having the guts to be one of the actors myself, I even popped popcorn, which I sold for a penny a bag, and figured out a way to draw the curtains open. I did a lot of that as a kid, and I completely forgot about it. But it flashed through my mind while I was sitting at the light.

There were no malls or anything like that when I was growing up. Every community had its own stores. The Polish community had its own grocery store, hardware store, shoe store, and movie theater. When TV first came out, we used to stand in front of the furniture store and watch the television sets in the window, even though they only showed a test pattern. It always seemed like it was snowing. We'd watch it for hours, kids and grownups, hoping something would happen. I never did. We'd go back the next day and watch again. It fascinated the hell out of me from the very beginning.

Maybe someday I could get a job as a cameraman in TV. The thought kept bugging me, so I went downtown to Channel 3, KYW, on East 6th Street, and asked for an application. The chief engineer happened to be in the lobby, and I asked him what kind of training I would need to be an engineer. I had none. He said it was pretty complicated. I'd need a first-class FCC license, which I'd never even heard of. Maybe he was just trying to get rid of me, but he was good enough to tell me about a school in town, National Radio School, that would train you for the FCC test. It was a three-year course. Three years seemed like an eternity, but I went and signed up for classes—one night a week for three years. The first year-and-a-half was learning how to repair TV sets.

After three years of night classes, I got my certificate from National Radio School in 1960.

My son Michael was born about then, on June 26, 1957. I was elated to have a son. He's now fifty-one and a very successful dentist. I was still working in the foundry, but things seemed to be picking up for me.

I thought about becoming a cop. I talked about it with my uncle Bert Wiglicky, who was a Cleveland police detective. He said, "You're really built solid, you're pretty smart. I'm sure you could do it." He told me of a school run by a Cleveland patrolman, Don McNay, that would train you to pass the police entrance exam. It was a six-month course, one night a week, and I signed up. I was actually going to two schools at the same time. Then Uncle Sam called me again—and, after finding out I had a child, deferred me again.

I finished training for the police academy exam. I scored first in the mental testing and second in physical to a bodybuilder who later won the Mr. Ohio title. Our instructor, Patrolman McNay, was elated. He knew I would score well when I took the police entrance exam, and it would give his school a big name.

I was excited, too. My son Mark was born on May 4, 1959, and I was really eager to get a better job.

I finished radio school early in 1960. Rather than wait for the test to come to Cleveland, I drove to Detroit, where I could take it immediately. I knew I passed it right away. A week later, three things happened the same day: (1) I was called for my appointment to take the police academy entrance test. (2) The draft board notified me they were no longer interested in me now that I had two kids. (3) I went back to KYW, asked for the chief engineer, and showed him my FCC license.

There were no openings, and I don't think he really had room for me. But he was so impressed that I'd come back after three years that he said he could put me on as a summer replacement. I probably wouldn't have a job in September, but he promised he'd try somehow to keep me.

I don't do things like this easily. I waived my appointment to take the police academy test, which really ticked off McNay, and quit my job at the foundry—while making them assure me I could come back to working second shift in the lab, just in case. And off to Channel 3 I went.

FAMOUS AT CHANNEL 3

I told them I was glad I knew radio-TV repair because I could at least fix monitors. I had no training whatsoever for everyday live production in a TV studio. So where do you think they put me? Production operations, of course. But my first day was really easy. I was in film projection, and I was supposed to spend a whole week with engineer Ron Manolio, learning to thread commercials and rack up filmed programs. No one had videotape yet.

The next day Ron called in sick. I was alone, and I knew very little. I was ripping film and messing up so badly I thought I was going to get canned right away. That's when I first met Bob Soinski, a film editor. He came in between his other duties to bail me out. I was a nervous wreck by the end of the day.

At four the next morning, the chief engineer called to tell me to get in as soon as I could. A studio cameraman called in sick. I told him I'd never even seen a studio camera. Don't worry about it, he said—somebody'll be there to teach you everything you need to know. They gave me about five minutes of instruction. I got through the morning news all right because it was a steady, static one-camera shot. It was easy. Just focus.

Then Big Wilson's movie show came on—another one-camera show. But there was one problem. Viewers would send in postcards that Big would pull out of a hopper. He'd hold up the card, and we were supposed to zoom in and focus on it. So I followed him when he started talking and walking to the hopper. It's easy to focus when you're far away. Then he held up the card.

Cameras used to have turrets with different lenses for close-ups. This one had a new Zoomar lens, which could get tricky. You'd zoom in and focus with your left hand by pushing a handle in and out and twisting a knob at the end of it. You'd wide-focus, or rack focus, with the handle in your right hand that steadied the camera.

I was really nervous. I pushed the handle in slowly. The director shouted, "Pop it in there!" in my headset. I did, thinking the focus position was preset. It wasn't. Everything in the viewfinder was a blur. Instead of focusing with my left hand, I started focusing with the right—which left everything out of focus when I pulled back to start over with a wide shot. I heard laughing in the headset. Everything was live. All the mistakes were aired. They went to a commercial, and I got focused again. The show resumed, Big pulled another postcard, and again it was a blur. Luckily Big laughed, because that's the kind of guy he was.

After they cut to another break, he was supposed to pull another postcard. "Wait!" he said, starting to laugh again. "Don't move a thing! Don't touch a thing!" He came out from behind the desk and started walking slowly toward the camera, almost tip-toeing, holding the postcard in front of him and watching the monitor as I slowly kept focus. He saved the day with that. I thought they'd die laughing in the control room.

I was a wreck. I couldn't even eat lunch. And I was still facing Linn Sheldon's afternoon *Barnaby* show for kids. It at least used two or three cameras. To my relief, the director said he'd give me only one shot, the easiest one.

The show opened, Linn started talking, and the director told me to "get a shot of the parrot." I pulled away from the viewfinder and looked around the room in terror. Parrot? I didn't see a parrot.

I could hear the director getting frantic, shouting in my headset, "Get it, goddammit! Get the parrot!" Barnaby was talking about it, and I was wondering where the hell it was. All I could see was an empty cage—not knowing the cage was where I'd find Longjohn the Invisible Parrot, a famous Barnaby bit with Linn throwing his voice. I'd never watched the show.

I couldn't wait for it to end at five o'clock so I could go home. The whole control room was screaming all day, and it was always because of me. But at the end of this long day, more than eight hours, they told me I had to stay and run a camera on the six o'clock news because something had come up. *Then* I could go home. The director knew I'd been screwing up all day, and he assured me I'd have "the easiest shot," which I'd heard before—"just a stationary shot of the news people."

He also told me they had a new sponsor, a beer company, for which they'd set up a sign and a pyramid of beer cans on a card table, against the wall on the other side of the studio.

"Get a shot of it," he said. "When we get off you and go out of news, truck across the studio, boom down, and get in focus. You'll have plenty of time."

I'd never done any of that. They showed me how to do it. I practiced over and over. Then the news started. It was live and fast-moving, and I thought, "I'm big-time now." The director told me to get my shot. I got it. "All right," he said, "go for the beer shot." I carefully started trucking the camera across the studio, booming down at the same time. "Get it!" he repeated after a few seconds, starting to shout. "Get it! Get it, get it, *get it!*" To him, apparently, a lot of time was seven or eight seconds—and it is. Sometimes you have to get a shot in two seconds. But this was my first day. I was still coming into the shot, pushing the camera faster than I should have, trying to stay in focus. They took the camera while I was still moving. The shot was jiggling. I heard the announcer start talking.

Ernie Anderson was the announcer, reading voiceover copy. I didn't know him then. He started to chuckle. I pulled back on the camera to stop and focus. But the old cameras were huge and heavy, and I couldn't believe how much momentum built up. The camera hit the table. The cans tumbled down. Ernie was breaking up, trying to read copy. People in the studio were laughing, and all I could hear was laughter in my headset. The news anchors were shrieking.

In two days at Channel 3, I was famous. Everybody knew who I was. But I got better, and I got fast. I liked it.

One day there was a fire in a building down the

In 1960, long before minicams, I set up a news lead-in during my first TV job, as a summer replacement at KYW.

street from TV-3, and we got a call to set up a camera on the roof for a live shot. Minicams weren't invented yet, so we ran to get a spare studio camera on a tripod. The elevator didn't go all the way to the roof, so my coworkers and I sent it to the basement, opened the first-floor door, put the camera on top of the car, and rode up with it amid all the cables. It was like something out of a James Bond film. This was getting really exciting. We stepped out onto the roof from the little shed holding the elevator mechanism, set up the camera, and got the shot. But the fire was disappointing by our standards—just smoke. We started to break the camera down. Then, on another roof below us, we saw a woman walk out in a bikini, all by herself, carrying a blanket. She lay down and took off her top. We set up the camera. Knowing the tape machine was offline in the hallway downstairs, we called that we had to make a test recording. We must have shot for an hour.

Word got around the station of what we did, and people started telling me about things they'd done. Most of the pranks, it seemed, involved distracting talent on the air. It worked on most of them, except for two guys who were considered unflappable: sportscaster Jim Graner and announcer Paul Bedford.

Linn Sheldon and Joe Finan, the disc jockey and TV-3 weatherman, always tried to bust up Graner without success. The two

Videotape later made images available instantly, but news footage for City Camera in 1965 had to be run through a film-developing machine. A print could be struck for broadcast in thirty minutes.

of them used to go to the Roxy burlesque theater down the street, where they'd sit backstage and eat lunch. They got to know the strippers, and one night they talked a girl into going back to the station with them. Wearing a fur coat, high heels, and nothing else, she stood between the cameras during the news until Graner started talking, then dropped her coat and started dancing around. Graner kept doing sports. Joe said, "Whaddya think?" Linn said, "I wasn't sure, but I thought I saw him blink."

Graner used to do a live commercial for Manner's Big Boy during the sports segment. I love Big Boys. They were all I ate from age sixteen until I was married. But Graner hated them. At the end of the commercial, after reading his copy, he had to take a big bite out of a Big Boy, smile, and go "Mmm-mmm." They'd cut away to another commercial, and he'd spit it into a wastebasket next to him. One night they didn't cut away. He spat, looked up at the camera, looked at the monitor, and took another bite. "Mmm-mmm," he said.

Paul Bedford would do the news on KYW radio every half hour during Big Wilson's morning show. Big used the time as a chance to step out for a smoke. But one morning, Big intro'd the news and didn't leave the small studio. While Paul started reading, Big dropped his pants, sat down on a wastebasket, and started grunting, really taking a dump. Without hesitation, Paul took a sheet of copy he'd finished reading and handed it to Big to wipe with. Instead of Paul cracking up, Big was howling with laughter in the background.

I was really enjoying my new career, living down my first-day fame and doing very well in various jobs. I liked the people. Linn Sheldon was teaching me how to play the ukelele, which I kept up over the years, and I was becoming good buddies with booth announcer Ernie Anderson, an ex-deejay from the East Coast who found we had something in common as pranksters.

But as summer came to an end, I knew there was a chance I'd be let go. When the chief engineer called me into his office, my heart was in my throat. He said he had bad news and good news. "The bad news is, we have to let you go," he said. "The good news is, I persuaded the chief engineer at Channel 8 to hire you. It's a temporary position, but they'll be telecasting both Indians and Browns games, so it'll be a good chance to stay on—they'll need remote crews, at least for the next couple years."

I was elated. I was staying in TV. On October 1, 1960, I moved from KYW, on East 6th Street, to WJW, on Euclid Avenue in Playhouse Square. For the next forty-seven years, I would experience things that I couldn't have imagined in my wildest dreams.

Please stay tuned.

CHAPTER 3

LIVE AND LOCAL ON TV8

PERMANENT TEMP

Being hired on temporary status at Channel 8 was a big concern for me. I'm a worrywart anyway, and I was less than six months since I left the foundry. I became paranoid about it once in awhile and asked when I would know I was permanent. I learned that the labor contract required both management and the union to inform me within six months. That was supposed to be written in stone. It's good I didn't lose sleep over it. In forty-seven years, through promotions, job changes, management turnover, and five station owners, I was never told I was permanent. Maybe it kept me on my toes.

I started on October 1, 1960, mostly working the midnight-to-8 a.m. maintenance shift. We'd finish airing the late movie, run the late, late movie, and sign off about 3 a.m. Then we'd eat lunch and prepare for the next day by changing tubes and fixing anything broken. We signed back on about 6 a.m., ran a filmed public service show, and then ran Jack LaLanne's exercise show. *Captain Kangaroo* came after that, which meant I could go home. His theme music became my favorite song.

If you've ever worked the night shift, you know there's a point where you get tired no matter how much sleep you get. Even after eight hours, a full day's sleep, around 4 a.m. I just couldn't stay awake. Maybe we were punchy near the end of the shift, but we'd die laughing at the way Jack LaLanne chirped "Students!" in every show, the same way every time. I saw him at the station on a promotional tour and laughed to myself about it. I didn't meet him, but he was the first actual celebrity I saw.

The first celebrity I met, not much later, was Raymond Burr. I was working an earlier shift, and between the six and eleven o'clock newscasts we filmed promos of him plugging *Perry Mason* and Channel 8. He sat talking and telling stories with the cameramen after it was over—really a nice guy, and that impressed me more than anything. Cameraman Cook Goodwin asked to take a picture, and Burr said sure, then told him to wait. He put out the cigarette he'd just lit—everybody smoked then—and took out a pack from the brand that sponsored his show. "I'll tell you a story," he said. He smoked Kools, which had a little penguin on each cigarette. One time, after he let someone take a picture, somebody blew it up and saw that he was smoking Kools. CBS told him they'd lose the sponsor if it happened again and even put it in his contract. For the photo, he made sure had the sponsor's pack in his hand and not the Kools with the little penguin.

SATURDAY AFTERNOON WRESTLING

I soon realized I liked operations and live production much more than maintenance. I worked both in the early years of my career, and being the new kid on the block, I had to work weekends a lot. I was actually excited about that, however, because Channel 8 was about to begin a live Saturday afternoon wrestling show, and I'd been a huge fan of wrestling on TV in the 1950s. "Nature Boy" Buddy Rogers was my favorite because he was a bodybuilder. I was no kid, but I still wished I looked like Nature Boy. His arch-enemy was Argentina Rocca. I hated him because Rocca beat him in the only match I ever went to see at the old arena.

My live introduction came while I was working the four-to-midnight shift one Friday. Because the security guard left at 10 p.m., the night shift had to answer the door and phone calls. Right after the eleven o'clock news, the bell rang at the back door, which opened to Brownell Court, the alley behind the station. I used to call it "Studio C" because we ended up using it so often in skits. I opened the door and found myself looking right into a man's chest. I looked up at the biggest guy I'd ever seen: Lord Layton, the wrestler and wrestling commentator. He was about six feet six or seven, and he had boots on. He had to bend down and turn sideways to get in the door. In a wonderful accent—he was Australian and known for signing off with "Cheerio to you all!"—he introduced himself and said they were there to set up the ring. Behind him, a few shabby, grumpy guys were hauling poles and mats from a beat-up old truck. From the way they were throwing stuff around, I could see they were very strong.

The next day, after I went home and doubled back early to televise the show, I recognized them as the wrestlers. It was like the circus. The performers, even Layton and old Baron Gattoni, were the same guys who set up the ring. And they really put on a show.

They usually didn't tell us what they were going to do. We'd try to follow the action and wing it, which added to the excitement. The Gallagher Brothers were in the ring for one tag-team match, and a supposedly Japanese tag-team sat in the audience, provoking them in heavy accents—"We kill you at Cleveland Arena Monday night!" The Gallaghers yelled back, calling them "Japs," and a big argument started. This was standard. The Asian guys tore off their suits and climbed into the ring. Lord Layton tried to break it up. The wrestlers took his microphone, ripped his shirt, and hit each other with chairs. I was shocked. They paid for everything, but they really tore the place up. I knew it was staged, but it was so realistic that people in the audience were screaming, terrified.

As the next bout began, one of the Japanese guys walked down the hall into the studio behind me. I was the switcher at the control board, switching between cameras and breaks. He looked around and in perfect, unaccented English, said, "Pardon me, do you know what time it is?" I found out later he and his partner were both from California. Fritz Von Erich was like that, too. It was all part of the show, which sort of impressed me.

I got over hating Argentina Rocca. He was known for his tremendous leaping ability. One time they were betting he couldn't kick the ceiling in a dressing room downstairs. He did it, not knowing there was a low-hanging light behind him. He put his head right into it. They had to stitch him up minutes before one of the live bouts.

They were nuts—real characters. I was grateful I had the chance to work with them because I felt I was witnessing an early TV art form that soon would be gone—never realizing I was working with the pioneers of what has grown into a billion-dollar TV attraction. They weren't the end of something; they were the beginning, but these great guys never knew any of that big money. My education in things like this was just beginning.

REX HUMBARD, ALL SHOOK UP

The live wrestling shows lasted about three years on Channel 8. I felt they were starting to fade, and I was sorry to see that. But I got another taste of live production in 1961, also on weekends, when TV8 started to carry Rex Humbard's show from his Cathedral of Tomorrow in Cuyahoga Falls. We'd have to get up real early on Sunday morning for it. I didn't mind because I thought it would ensure my future on the remote team. I knew the Indians and Browns were coming, and I still hadn't been told I was permanent.

Rex bought the time for his shows and paid enough to cover production costs. He came to the station for some shows, but we went to Cuyahoga Falls every Sunday for the services he sent all over the country for broadcast on two-inch videotape. I hit it off with him and got to know him and his wife, Maude Aimee, pretty well. I got a kick out of them. He had a control room that was way better than ours at Channel 8, much better equipment, but he'd cry for money on the air, pray over the videotape, and then take us all out to lunch.

I worked as the switcher on the Cathedral of Tomorrow shows, running everything but audio. The guy who did the audio, Ed Guild, would not do things logically. Instead of putting microphones on the control board in order, corresponding to their location below, he arranged them in a way only he could understand. They had a powerful amplifying system, which made sense because The Cathedral of Tomorrow was huge, like an arena. Ed got sick one Sunday. I had to run audio, which I had never done. I raised the level on a mic—the wrong one, because it was on Ed's system—and got the loudest feedback I ever heard in my life. Feedback happens when you open a mic near a speaker that feeds back into itself, causing continuous screeching. Even through thick glass inside the control room it was loud. I could see people on the floor holding their ears and hunched down on the stage. Kids were screaming. The Cathedral of Tomorrow also had a cross bigger than an airplane hanging from the ceiling. People would come in and gawk at it as it changed colors. The feedback was so loud that the cross started vibrating. Dust cascaded down from the top of it, almost like it was snowing. After what seemed like an eternity, I found the right switch and stopped it. A miracle.

WOODEN LEGS AND WAR NICKELS

I worked extra hard. Television sure beat the smoke and fumes of my eight years in the foundry, even though I did miss the guys from those days. But I was starting to make new friends. One was Jim Doney, who became one of my early influences. Jim at the time was a recovering alcoholic. He told me his addiction was so bad that he'd drink a pint of gin every morning on his way to Channel 8. When they started getting ready for the news, he'd run to the Biscayne Lounge or Pierre's next door and drink right up to air time. He was sober by the time I met him, yet he would still go to Pierre's for lunch and sit at the bar playing dominoes with his friends, like he did when he was drinking. He became very active in Alcoholics Anonymous, and he sponsored many other TV and radio personalities, some of whom helped others in turn. He was a major Cleveland TV figure, and he and I were becoming good friends. I was awed by that and realized I liked it very much.

I was becoming better and better with on-air operations. If you're good in local TV, you get punished by working the four-to-midnight shift. The six and eleven o'clock newscasts go on in those hours, and news is local TV's biggest moneymaker by far. Between newscasts was almost all CBS network time. We did station breaks and occasional cut-ins, ate lunch, and talked a lot.

The nighttime technical director was Clyde Freeman, an elderly man who was a pilot in World War II and would tell the most outrageous war stories. True or not, they were moving, and when I found out that some of his stories really happened, I decided to believe the rest. He could show the medals to back them up.

A newcomer was engineer John Sweeney. A hard worker who'd been a Korean War paratrooper on a bazooka team, Sweeney would sit with us in the studio and listen to Clyde's war stories. Only he knew enough about wartime to pull Clyde's leg and badger him about his tales—saying stuff like, "They didn't have that plane then!" They'd argue about it. Later, when we started working remotes from the old stadium, I found out how tough and strong Sweeney was. They didn't have elevators to get cameras to the roof, so you had to carry them up a ladder and lift them through a trapdoor only one guy could fit through at a time. These weren't minicams, either; they were studio cameras. The only guy who could do it besides me was Sweeney, who was a lot smaller.

One night when we were eating lunch, Sweeney started arguing with Clyde while cutting slices from an apple with a big switchblade.

"Goddammit, Clyde," he shouted, "you and your bullshit get me so mad!" He suddenly slammed the knife down into his own leg! The room got silent. I couldn't breathe.

"Goddammit!" he said. "Now look what you made me do!" He seemed to start crying. *Holy crap,* I thought—this guy's got a knife, he's a combat vet, he's crazy, he's going to kill all of us. Then I realized he was laughing, almost crying from laughter. He had a wooden leg. No one knew until then, and no one suspected.

"Ever pull that before?" I asked.

"A couple times," he said.

Another guy on that shift was Bill Demeter, who taught me all the Hungarian swear words I know and, like me, was a practical joker. He saw the night crew coming to clean out the big sand ashtrays in the control room, take out a ten dollar bill and stuff it in before they got to it. "Wait a minute," he'd say, putting out a cigarette and pulling out the bill. "Geez, look at this! How did that get in there?"

He was always looking for get-rich schemes, and one was saving "war nickels." Nickel was diverted to military use during World War II, so the Mint issued the coin using a silver alloy, which worked in phones and vending machines that detected slugs by electrical resistance. When the price of silver rose and the Mint started recalling them, they became really rare. Bill said, "Save all the nickels you can. Put them away for twenty years. You'll be amazed how much they're worth." He took it a step further. He would go to the bank and buy five rolls of nickels, look through them, find one or two distinctive war nickels in each roll, replace them, and exchange the rolls for more nickels. The bank hated this. It was a nuisance taking up their time.

I was embarrassed to do it, so I would go to banks where they didn't know me. There was one I had never been to on Snow Road in Parma. There were no customers, so I went right up to the teller and asked for five rolls of nickels. She looked at me, really mad, and started going on about how she knew what I was doing—"You guys exchanging war nickels," she grumbled. Suddenly, I heard a commotion, looked at the door, and saw a cop with a shotgun pointed at me and another on one knee pointing a handgun. They told me to freeze. Terrified, I froze. They ran up, jumped on me, twisted my arm behind me, and shoved my head down. There were five cops on me. After about thirty seconds, somebody said it was a false alarm. The cops apologized. I said I was all right, and a few minutes later they left.

I was scared, excited, and out of breath. The teller was shaking. I walked up to her and said, "I know you don't like exchanging war nickels, but that was ridiculous." She was still mad and didn't get it right away, but then she started laughing and crying at the same time.

"You ought to be on television," she said. After that, I always went to that bank and waited for her. There was no hassle. She'd always laugh and greet me. I'd made the joke more for the teller than for me, but it helped us both. It worked. After that I started concentrating on thinking of ways to be funny.

The odd thing about the war nickels is, I still have a box of them. The first time I went to Las Vegas, years later, I started playing nickel slots while waiting to see a Glen Campbell show with June. I won, and I couldn't believe my eyes. The tray was full of nickels, and everywhere I looked there were war nickels. I pulled them out and kept playing and winning—filling a plastic cup with them, and hoping my wife would take her time getting ready. It was all I could think about during the show. I marked the machine because it was paying off, and I couldn't wait to get back to it.

"We come all the way to Vegas, and you're collecting war nickels," June grumbled. When she went to bed, I said I wasn't really tired and raced back downstairs. All those years of finding one or two nickels, and now I was finding dozens. Then it hit me: Vegas was built during World War II, and all these coins never left town. Winners cash them in, and they go back into the machines until collectors get them. I got so many war nickels that night I had to split them up to have other people in our group put some in their luggage.

My wife still gets mad about it.

ERNIE'S PLACE

Things began to change at Channel 8 in 1961, when my pal Ernie Anderson and Tom Conway came over from Channel 3. Ernie was going to be the new booth announcer and producer and host of a daily movie show called *Ernie's Place*. Tom was going to help him write the show and direct it. At least, that was the story. To get him hired Ernie told everyone Tom was a director. So Tom sat in the director's chair next to me in the control room but didn't know how to direct. I worked as switcher on the show and would oversee everything. Ernie told everybody, "Whatever Tom tells you to do, do it only if it's right. If it's not right, do the right thing."

It wasn't your typical movie show, to say the least, but Ernie wasn't your typical host. After coming to Channel 8, Ernie and Tom were still calling all over the country to book guests for TV-3's *The Mike Douglas Show* and getting a fee for it. Ernie made his own rules. On his own show, he was beginning to do some real interviews but couldn't get enough guests. He wanted to do some comedy anyway, so Tom said he'd be the guest. They worked up skits where they introduced him as everything from a karate instructor to a bullfighter. No matter what he was, usually his name was Dag Herford.

Not only did Tom *not* know how to direct, he didn't know how to backtime a movie, or how to run it to finish by the end of the show with breaks and commercials. I *did* know because I had to do it whenever there wasn't a director working. What you can do, when a movie is running long, is burn film during commercial breaks—just let the film keep running, without going on the air, to pick up a few minutes. But Ernie and Tom were using so much time hosting the show that there was still too much film. We'd have twelve minutes of show left and twenty-two minutes of the feature. So they just cut off the ends of the movies. People liked the show with the skits but they were annoyed they couldn't see the end of the movie. Ernie said, "I'll fix it." On Fridays, they'd show the ends of all the films we showed that week.

The show was doing pretty well, and the station liked it. The guys on the crew were laughing at the bits, which was a good indicator that it was going over. Ernie also owned Cleveland radio when it came to doing voice spots, and he talked BonJour Coffee into being a sponsor. It was a unique arrangement because he and Tom were to write the thirty-second commercials as comedy bits and be in them. The ads were so good that they seemed like part of the show. And that was good for the sponsor because viewers kept watching. It was good for Ernie and Tom, too. Especially Tom.

Networks at that time would send stars to affiliates around the country to record local promos. Rose Marie from *The Dick Van Dyke Show* came to Channel 8. Tom went to the studio to direct, threw out some funny lines, and took her and Ernie to lunch. While they were out, I racked up the BonJour spots in the tape room, which Rose Marie took back to Hollywood for Steve Allen. At that time he was doing for Westinghouse the same kind of late-night program he'd done for NBC with *The Tonight Show*.

Steve liked the tapes. He said, "Bring me the short, fat, bald guy. I can take the other guy's place." Rose Marie told Tom, and they set it up for him to get a shot doing a little stand-up comedy thing. I don't think anyone but Ernie and I could tell, but he was really nervous—it had to be tough going on a national show considering he'd never done it. Allen liked him, though, and wanted him to come back to join the "man in the street" segments he did with Tom Poston, Louis Nye, and Don Knotts.

I was excited. It was a terrific show, way ahead of its time, and every opening was different. Once it started with Steve playing the piano, which was all you could see until the camera pulled out and you could see he was hanging from a crane. He'd try anything.

Tom went out reluctantly, partly out of loyalty to Ernie and partly because, like me, he was a Cleveland guy He kept coming back to Cleveland, though, and Steve kept calling him back to Hollywood. The station manager Joe Drilling told Tom it was a great opportunity for a young guy, but Tom was still hesitant. He was really loyal to Ernie. Finally, Drilling said, "I'm gonna fix it. You're fired. Now get out." Tom thought it was a joke, but Joe officially fired him so he'd have to go.

Out in L.A., Tom changed his name to Tim, because there was a British actor named Tom Conway, and landed a role on a major series, *McHale's Navy,* which premiered in the fall of 1962.

EXPANDING THE FAMILY

My life had other changes. Our third child, Marilyn, was born in March 1962. We call her our miracle child because she weighed only one pound, thirteen ounces when she was born at St. John's Hospital. Preemies back then had almost no chance. She was in the hospital more than a month and had developmental problems from which she was classified as mildly retarded. We took her to a special school, and she started to regress among kids who were more challenged. So with the extra dough I earned making public appearances, I had her tutored so she could attend regular high school. I'm so glad we did. It was a big part of her life, and she still talks about it. She's forty-six now, and she's been a blessing to us. She lives with me and June, and probably always will. She's a big help to us, especially as we get older.

But with three kids, we were growing out of our space—upstairs in my parents' old three-family home on Indiana Avenue on Cleveland's southeast side. I started looking for a small, inexpensive home where I could raise a family and maybe have a small dog.

Ernie lived in Willoughby, which was still very rural, and took me there to look.

"We're wasting our time," I told him. "I can't afford this—I can barely afford the homes I'm looking at."

"Bullshit—afford it," he said, "everything'll be fine." Those were his exact words, all his life. "Everything'll be fine. It'll be fine." He'd say that, and I'd know right away that it wasn't going to be fine. I'd have to go behind the scenes and find out what I could do to make it fine. He was a day-to-day person who never worried about anything. You could tell him, "Something's gonna happen." He'd ask when. "Wednesday." It'd be out of his head. "I might never make it to Wednesday."

That's why it was no setback when *Ernie's Place* was canceled in 1962. Ernie didn't want to do it without Tom and told the station he couldn't. He needed a partner who had the time to write. Otherwise, it would become just a straight interview show, and no one was going to watch that. I think the station was actually relieved, because Ernie and Tom were getting pretty wild and Storer Broadcasting was pretty straitlaced.

ERNIE BREAKS THE STATION

Ernie had a two-year contract, so he stayed as a booth announcer and picked up more voiceover work. Working the sign-off shift left his days free. It also had him reading a statement before we rolled the national anthem: "Storer Broadcasting now concludes another day of telecasting with entertainment, education, and information." One night I was working audio, and the switcher was Dom Lolli, who was local president of NABET, the National Association of Broadcast Engineers and Technicians, and always grumbling about labor negotiations with the station. Ernie started reading the statement with a small change: "Storer Broadcasting now concludes another profitable day of telecasting . . ."

He did it so naturally, in that beautiful voice, that we almost missed it. He did it for his entertainment and ours, and he started doing it every night. I got nervous, because if you have a first-class FCC license you're sort of responsible. You're supposed to be squealing. I was sure it would leak out. But no one ever caught on, or maybe people thought that was how it was supposed to be. That happens when you do something so well. When I worked with actor Burgess Meredith years later, he said that if he ever came to a line he wasn't sure of, he'd say it with all the authority in his body rather than blow it. The audience would buy it.

Ernie could really sell it. He'd slip the names of Channel 8 staffers into the movie credits during breaks, and he'd flirt with trouble by talking to me on the intercom during movies—making comments like, "Look at the cans on that broad," which was really dangerous, because the keys to talk to me and to go on the air were next to each other.

He never swore on the air, although he used profanity in abundance at other times, but once in awhile something on the edge would slip out. Then he would calmly hit the button to go on the air, and in that voice of authority say, "KYW ... TV-3 ... Cleveland."

It could be duller than hell at night waiting for sign-off. Everybody would be smoking and staring at the monitor while the late movie ended. I started sneaking in sound effects. One movie had a love scene, with syrupy music playing and a woman professing her love, and suddenly you heard "rowf" in the background—a dog barking. Ernie, who was smoking and watching the monitor, got a puzzled look on his face. I played the dog louder and louder until Ernie saw what I was doing and started laughing. Another time an old Western was on, and I got some World War II sound effects. The cowboys would shoot, and you'd hear a machine gun in the background. But I'd sneak it in so subtly, you'd just barely hear it. It'd take five minutes and get louder before Ernie noticed. I'd do that about once a month. He'd say, "It gets so lonely here at night."

GHOULARDI MAKES HIS ENTRANCE

Late in 1962, the station picked up a package of horror movies for a Friday night *Shock Theater*. Howard Hoffmann, an announcer and weatherman, was originally considered to host it. But Bob Buchanan liked the way Ernie emceed the station Christmas party, knew his work anyway, and asked him to do it. Ernie agreed.

They gave him a fake Vandyke beard and mustache and told him to talk about the feature in the Bela-Lugosi-typical-of-every-horror-host style back then. Only his face appeared on-screen, lit from below with one light. It was January 1963, and Ghoulardi was born.

Or almost born. That first version lasted about two weeks. Then

Ernie started talking about anything. He'd knock stuff you never knock on the air, talking about celebrities and politicians and personalities on other stations. His Lugosi accent slipped into something more like a beatnik, and he made the sort of comments on the air that he usually made on the intercom.

I came in one night and told him I finally got a home.

"Oh, great!" he said. "Where is it?" It was in Parma. I found out later that he lived in Parma. He never cut his grass and had weeds everywhere. The neighbors hated him. They'd get on him and he'd argue. "I'm not gonna be picking dandelions," he said. "If it's green, it stays." To me, he said, "Parma! With all the shitholes in the area, you go there."

On the show, he said, "Chuck Schodowski finally got a home. You'll never guess where he moved. Parma! I took him to some neighborhoods, and he goes to Parma! Where they put plastic pink flamingoes and chrome balls on their lawns!"

My neighbors did have them. They're really nice people, friends to this day. I told Ernie they'd resent me if he didn't stop knocking Parma. He said OK, he'd cut it out. Naturally, at the first opportunity he did it again, and kept it up. I said, "If you say Parma again, I'm going to cut your mic." I was a little mad and he was a little mad, but I was the only person who'd argue with him like that. I think everyone else was intimidated. I was, too, but we were friends, and he wouldn't put me down like he did everybody else. He said, "Oh yeah?" I had threatened him, but he knew I couldn't cut him—it's a cardinal sin to put out dead air.

Then it hit me like a ton of bricks. He talked about people doing the polka. Polish people do the polka. I'm Polish. I cued up Frankie Yankovic's "Who Stole the Kishka?" because it's got that crazy opening. When he started to say *Parma*, I cut his mic and played it. He was genuinely surprised the first time, and he started laughing. He liked it so much, he'd say *"Parma?* Did someone say *Parma?"* just to do comic takes off the music. It became a big thing.

"You know what?" he said on the air. "I feel bad for Chuck." I was at the bottom of the scale, not making much money. Ernie said, "I'm gonna get him a pink flamingo. Or if you want to get him something, get him a pink flamingo."

That was on a Friday night. On Sunday morning, they started showing up. Before the next show, there must have been fifty pink flamingoes on my front lawn. Kids must have stolen all the flamingoes in the neighborhood. I didn't know whose they were, so I brought them in to the station. Ernie had a wall of them on the set. And for maybe a year, one or two or a bunch of flamingoes would show up on my lawn.

Now there are businesses that will put flamingoes on lawns as a surprise gag for birthdays, anniversaries, or other occasions. But that's how it started.

It was the beginning of Cleveland TV's wildest ride.

A publicity photo showing Ernie Anderson as Ghoulardi.

CHAPTER 4

GHOULARDI AND ME

BUILDING A SENSATION

The Ghoulardi show was booming in a matter of weeks, and Ghoulardi was a household name throughout northeast Ohio. Ernie made TV history. No Cleveland TV personality was as popular before or since. The show drew such a large audience that Cleveland police noticed a drastic drop in crime rate Friday nights, which was usually one of the worst. The show was such a sensation and made such an impression that I'd need another book to describe it all. Fortunately, I don't have to, because *Ghoulardi: Inside Cleveland TV's Wildest Ride* is still in print. It's all there, and I recommend it.

Being relatively low in seniority, I was still rotating all three work shifts, as I would for a few more years. But Ernie was working 4 p.m. to midnight, and he wanted me on that shift, which would mean no more switching back and forth. He argued with the chief engineer, Gil Anderson, to keep me on his shift. Gil told him that he'd put me where he wanted, and I could see scheduling would become a sore point. It was the union steward's job to make out the work schedule, however, and he didn't like doing it. So I volunteered to be the union steward and organized the schedule myself. I fixed things like that all through Ernie's show. It kept him from alienating me from coworkers.

Ernie's personality and inventiveness made Ghoulardi work, but he did get help with the show. It gave some of us a new creative outlet.

Bob Soinski, the film editor who helped me on my first day at KYW, had moved to Channel 8, and he came up with the idea of

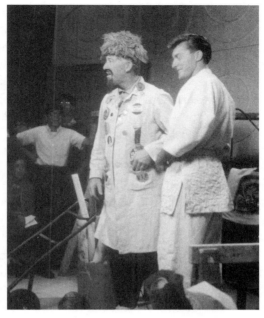

My skits as a pitching and batting coach did so well in 1964 that Ernie made me play a karate instructor with Ghoulardi.

using drop-ins—interrupting the movies with film clips, which was something I hadn't seen done before. He scoured old movies, newsreels, and network footage for material, and I helped him look for audio drop-ins. We dropped in train wrecks, car crashes, and the most famous one, the "Papa-Oom-Mow-Mow" guy. Bob found him in footage of a "gurning" facial contortion contest in Britain. It cracked me up, and I had the perfect audio for it, "Papa-Oom-Mow-Mow" by the Rivingtons, which got a lot of radio airplay as a result and became a local hit. Ernie cracked up at the drop-ins. He never planned anything, but our additions would spur him to do something else good for the show.

CBS would send features to use on the news, usually for the off-beat "kicker" story at the end. I was working videotape in 1963 and saw one about a weird group from England with goofy haircuts—the Beatles. We didn't use it on the news, so I told Ernie about it.

I forget what song they were playing, but we put "Who Stole the Kishka?" behind footage of them performing, and it fit. Ernie said, "There's this weird group in England you'll probably hear about. They're getting real popular," and showed the footage on his show with our audio. As far as I know, the first time the Beatles were ever seen in Cleveland was on Ernie's show, which was likely the *only* time they were seen "performing" a polka. Ernie got Beatle-style wigs after that, and the whole news team put them on when they tossed to Ghoulardi after the news the next Friday night. They got chewed out for that.

One of my jobs was switching the six and eleven o'clock news. Before a newscast, we had to have the art department type onto cards the names of everyone who was going to be identified on-screen. The cards were black with white type and we'd put them on a big board in the studio, where a camera shot each name. I could then superimpose the shot of a person's name over the corresponding story. I told Ernie, "I think if you wore all-white clothes, I could key you into movies." He wore khaki and tennis shoes all the time anyway, but this comment led to the white lab smock and white fright wig.

Soinski and I would watch the movies for long scenes with no edits, where they used one camera and the same shot, with no zoom and no tight shots. If we put Ernie in a scene that zoomed in, he'd be out of proportion. Cheap movies had a lot of long scenes because they didn't want to do much editing. They'd just roll the cameras and keep following the actors. Some would go on for seven or eight minutes.

Being in those scenes is hard. It's not like looking in a mirror, which everyone is used to. When you move your right arm and look into a TV monitor, you see your left arm moving. Ernie was really good at being keyed into scenes, which made it really funny. We found a scene in *Attack of the 50-Foot Woman* that was absolutely perfect. The actors go into a cave and just keep walking and talking. We put Ernie in there, walking with them, and the whole crew in the control room was dying because it was so funny. We had a clock running on the sequence to get him out before the scene changed, and we started yelling to the studio that time was coming. But before we got him out, the scene changed to a tight shot of the fifty-foot woman. Ernie, who was leaning on a cave wall with his arm outstretched, now had his hand right on her boob. It fit so well that it looked like it was done on purpose, but it wasn't. Ernie saw it on the monitor, yelped "Whoo!" and pulled his arm away.

STARRING WITH THE GHOULARDI ALL-STARS

Soinski and I were big on stuff like that. Ernie kept trying to put us on the show, but I wanted nothing to do it. I was happy to be a big part of the show behind the scenes, and to join activities like the Ghoulardi All-Stars, which is where I got the name Big Chuck.

The All-Stars started because Channel 5 had a softball team, and Ernie wanted to play them. He goofed a lot on Captain Penny, Channel 5's kids' host, who was Ron Penfound, a pretty good ballplayer. We put together a team and went to a practice field where the outfield went up a hill to a highway. Ernie told me, "Get up there and whack away." I'd played a lot of softball, and I told him the ball would end up on the highway if I hit it as hard as I could. He was surprised and maybe didn't believe me. He said, seriously, "You know, you shouldn't brag like that." And he wouldn't back off on telling me to whack away. It was a practice game, but he wanted to win. I tried to hit line drives.

Then we played Captain Penny and the Channel 5 team, and I hit four home runs. It was a close game, and the home runs won it. Ernie showed highlights on the show, and said, "Big Chuck swung the big bat and won it." After that, it was always "Big Chuck." I'm not all that big, but it was an affectionate term, and it stuck.

Ernie was a sports fan who wanted to be a jock. He was as serious about the All-Stars as he was about anything at the station, maybe more. He loved being an athlete or feeling like it. He would have us play anybody and one summer booked fifty-six softball games. The season stretched way into fall, May to October, way too long. Then we played football, basketball, and even hockey. We played the old Barons a couple of times at the arena. I played goalie. I could skate, but not that well.

Football was flag or touch, but there was downfield blocking and

I earned the name "Big Chuck" from Ernie for hitting four home runs when the Ghoulardi All-Stars played Captain Penny and his team from Channel 5.

no pads or helmets. It was brutal, and we did have some pretty bad injuries. The team was unbeatable. Ernie insisted on playing quarterback, and he surrounded himself with the whole line from my brother's South High team, including the three Arslanian brothers, two of whom were also state heavyweight wrestling champs. My brother, Paul, the All-Senate quarterback, was another ringer for us. Ernie would keep us in the game, but he knew just when to put in Paul, the last possible few minutes, to pull the game out.

Ernie would brag it up on the show about how we were undefeated, so other teams gunned for us. They were all-star teams, too. In a lot of small towns, they'd bring back every old high school player who was any good—really rough-and-tough guys. It got harder and harder. But we went undefeated through Ernie's three seasons, and then for another eight with Hoolihan and me.

Had this not happened, I might have been bitter about all the years I never got to play sports. With the All-Stars, I got my fill.

To warm up both team and the crowd before softball games, I hit fungoes to our guys. When I knew the crowd was paying attention, I would flex a little bit, toss up the ball, swing with all my might, and miss. I turned it into a little routine, and it cracked Ernie up. When our 1964 season came around, he told me he wanted to use me on the air. *No way*, I said. He asked, "What size pants do you wear?" I asked why he wanted to know. He said, "What size shirt?" I said, "I'm not doing whatever it is you're thinking."

He wanted me to do the routine, swinging and missing, as the batting coach of the Indians, newly arrived from the New York Mets. I said I wouldn't do it. He got the uniform and enlisted three or four of the biggest guys at the station. They were going to pants me, put me in the uniform, and make me do it. I finally agreed because it'd be easier than fighting with Ernie and the guys. I did it, and that was the first time I was on the air.

Ernie and I wear jerseys from the old Cleveland Barons at a hockey game between the Ghoulardi All-Stars and Channel 5 at the old Cleveland Arena.

I sort of enjoyed it after that. It got easier and easier, as long as Ernie was calling the shots and was there to tell me what I was supposed to do. He ad-libbed everything. Conway could do that, too, but I'd always write something for myself. I had to know exactly what I was going to do and say.

But playing with the All-Stars helped me be prepared for anything. You never knew what would happen in a lot of places we played. After one football game, Ernie and I came out of the shower and saw a kid standing in the locker room. I asked if he belonged there. "I'm just taking towels," he said, and then he turned around and snapped a picture of us, bare-ass naked. It's probably out there somewhere, and I suppose it could turn up on YouTube someday— maybe with its sequel. A few years later, after the team became the Hoolihan & Big Chuck All-Stars, we stopped at a nightclub called Red's, as we usually did whenever we played near Akron. I went to the john, and a kid came in and stood at the next urinal. All of a sudden he stepped back, pulled out a camera, and took a picture.

He flew out the door, and I heard a woman's voice say, "Didja get it?" I'll wait for that photo to turn up someday, too.

FRANZ JOINS THE ALL-STARS

We got some new people at the station, Franz the Toymaker and then Hoolihan the Weatherman. Both of them wanted to be on the All-Stars. Ernie was dying to get more celebrities on, so they automatically made the team.

Franz was a character. He went to South High School, too. We're about the same age, but I didn't know him there. His real name was Ray Stawiarski. He was a huge guy who probably could have been on the air a lot longer if he did a little bit of work. But he wouldn't prepare the show at all. Most days, this big Polack in lederhosen with hairy legs and a bad accent would go on the air and say, "Kids—you know what?" And he wouldn't know what. Music would play in the background, and we knew what he was thinking. Sure enough, he'd say, "I think it's time for a cartoon!" They were trying to get away from always running cartoons on the show but always had them as a backup. During the cartoon, Franz would think of something to do or talk about. The show had good ratings, so they brought in Raggedy Ann as his sidekick, mainly because she was interested and prepared craft segments. Franz wouldn't prepare anything, and you knew you were in trouble when he said, "You know what?"

He'd go right from the show, at ten in the morning, into Pierre's bar next door and drink until late afternoon—still wearing the lederhosen costume. One evening the All-Stars were going to a big game at Firestone Stadium in Akron. It was an annual event with a lot of local celebrities. Guys were going from work, so they sent a bus for us stocked with sandwiches and a keg of beer. Franz stayed in Pierre's until it was time to leave. Ernie fetched him, and Franz sat up by the beer on the bus.

We had a police escort into the stadium, and the bus pulled right onto the infield. A guy came aboard and said we were all going to be introduced in sequence. First out was going to be Franz, for the kids. He went to the front of the bus and down the two steps to the

door. We all got in line behind him. Franz was quiet.
He rested his head against
the door. It probably felt
good—cool and solid. Out-
side, the announcer started
his intro: "OK, for you kids,
let's hear it for the kids'
favorite from Channel 8,
Franz the Toymaker!"

The door opened. Franz
was out cold. He fell out
like a sack of bricks, flat
on his face, and the infield
dust came up around him.
The crowd thought it was a

Franz the Toymaker in a parade in front of
WJW's old studios on Euclid Avenue at East
16th Street. He even wore the outfit into bars
sometimes.

stunt. They gave him a standing ovation. Ernie jumped out right
away to grab him, and as we helped him to his feet, Franz was waving to the crowd. He was tough! And a real trooper.

He usually came late to games. Ernie used to nag him merci-
lessly, and Franz wouldn't fight back. He was like a big bear. Ernie
really got on him one time the station was doing a big Franz promotion with one of our games in Ashtabula. Ernie said, "I'm telling
them all week, 'Bring your kids,' so get your ass out of Pierre's."
Game time arrived, and Franz was nowhere to be seen. Ernie was
mad the whole game. We finished the game, did the Franz promotional giveaway, and plugged his show as the lights were going off
on the field. We were loading our cars, getting ready to go to a bar
for the party that always followed games, and here came Franz's
sports car, racing in at eleven p.m., driving right onto the infield in
clouds of dust. He jumped out triumphantly, like "I made it!" He
had gone to Ashland for the game, a good hour south of Cleveland,
and then drove all the way to Ashtabula, an hour east, thinking he
was going to get there in time.

My whole life was changing, and it was really exciting. I was on
with Ernie, playing sports, and beginning to get recognized on TV.
It hit me that I was a buddy of Cleveland's hottest celebrity. People

in the business knew I was doing stuff behind the camera. I liked it.

At the same time, I got on the remote crew for Indians and Browns games. It took me to places I never dreamed I'd go.

CHAPTER 5

WITH THE BROWNS
AND THE TRIBE

IT WAS LIKE I HAD MY OWN VENDOR

Looking back, I don't know how I did it—the work, messing around with Ernie, and working games.

Doing the Indians, I worked days except Fridays for a while. I'd work a full day at TV8, then at four or five go to work the ballgame that night. I got to know everyone at the stadium—at least, everyone who worked there. Nobody else was there. It was like I had my own personal vendor. "Chuck, you need anything?" I'd buy something even if I wasn't hungry. I'd grab all the foul balls nearby because there was no crowd scrambling for them. My kids were in Little League, and I was supplying three teams with baseballs.

They used to do doubleheaders on Sunday, and we'd telecast one or both of them.

I set up cameras, ran cable, worked a camera or audio, and would have to stay until everything was off. The camera positions were in slings, open platforms hanging from the upper deck along the first- and third-base lines. I also worked for the Sports Network out of New York on a lot of games, especially if the Yankees were in town. They'd bring a behind-the-plate camera and director, and pick up a local crew from stations. I ran audio for them or ran a camera. It was a good view.

I was running a camera for Sports Network on one night game when the Yankees were in town. Mickey Mantle was coming up, about to reach some milestone, and I got a tight shot of him looking at the pitcher. They were both laughing. Mantle stepped out of

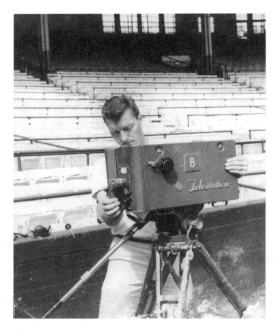

Setting up for a pregame interview with Indians announcer Harry Jones and slugger Rocky Colavito on the field at Cleveland Stadium.

the box, and the ump told him to get back in. He did, still laughing, and I looked at the pitcher. He was gesturing like. "Where do you want it?" I guess he wanted to be in the record book. He grooved it. Mantle crushed it and circled the bases with a big grin, talking to the pitcher. The manager hit the field, chewing out the pitcher.

I was running visitors' audio when Cleveland played Detroit one afternoon. There was a rain delay, and I pulled down the canvas canopy over the open sling. You didn't go back to the station on delays in those days. The announcers had to fill the time. They could talk and talk, and that's why a lot of them got hired. George Kell, the Tigers' announcer and Hall of Fame third baseman, started telling about the first time he batted against Bob Feller. I was really interested. It was at the stadium, and he said the pitcher really had an advantage there at a certain time in the afternoon. The pitcher was in the sun, the batter was in the shade, and it was hard to pick up the ball. He'd never hit against Feller and had heard stories about how fast and wild he was. He said Feller probably encouraged the stories so guys wouldn't dig in against him. Feller went into his motion, delivered, and Kell did not see the ball. He heard it hit the catcher's mitt like an explosion, and the umpire said, "Strike!" Kell was no longer thinking about hitting. He was thinking about picking up the ball and wondering what he would do if it came at his head. He swore he could hear the ball but couldn't see it. *Boom.* Strike two. He was scared to death. Feller really loaded up on the next one. Kell listened to the loudest bang he ever heard from a catcher's mitt. The ump yelled, "Strike three!"

Without thinking, he turned to the ump and said, "Come on, that sounded low"—immediately realizing what he'd just said.

The rain stopped. The grounds crew started taking the tarp off the field. The director told me to tell Kell to stand up by the railing so they could get a shot of him from the opposite sling. I pushed the tarp back. It had filled with a big pocket of water that came down at an angle into the old wooden amp that should have been in a museum. I handed Kell a microphone, and he turned to face the sling across the field. I cued him, he started to talk and took hold of the railing, and I guess that's when he grounded himself. I heard something snap, and Kell got shocked and yelled, "Owww, goddammit!" It went out on the air, everything was live, but he knew better than to apologize—don't ever apologize, you just draw more attention to it. So he just went on.

While the grounds crew was setting up the batting cage before games, I'd set up a camera for interviews on the field. I was running the camera one afternoon for announcer Harry Jones, who seemed sometimes naive in some ways.

He got Rocky Colavito out there, and I was watching through the viewfinder. Colavito had a bat, and Harry said, "OK, Rock, I want you in that famous pose you have, pointing your bat right at the pitcher. I want you to point right at the camera and give the people at home an idea what it's like if you were pitching to Colavito."

Colavito didn't seem too sure if he should do it, but he went into his stance, put his bat out, and stood there holding the pose. Harry didn't say anything. He just stood grinning and nodding his head.

It was like a skit, with Colavito never losing his stance while his eyes slowly went to the side to look at Harry and then back to the camera, then slowly back to Harry, who stood smiling. It went on for a good ten or fifteen seconds. I no sooner got to the truck than I said, "Save that tape for me." I had that piece of tape for years.

RUNNING THE PARAB ON THE BROWNS

Football was different from the start, beginning with the crowds. Bill Demeter, who got me saving war nickels, said to always bend down and look between the fans' feet if we were going past concession stands at halftime. Guys are drunk and reaching into stuffed pockets to pull money out. He was right. Every time I did that, I'd find money—bills. You ease your way toward the bill, step on it, pick it up, and leave. Try it sometime. It works.

Mostly I was on the field. I worked the parabolic microphone, or parab mic, which is a microphone mounted inside a dish. It's directional and good for recording relatively faint sounds at a distance. They used it to pick up kicks and quarterback calls at the line of scrimmage. It wasn't on all the time because the crowd noise was too loud, but it was always on to my headset.

I stood right on the sideline, a little bit in front of the line of scrimmage. A Jim Brown sweep would run right at me, and I'd hear a lot of him grunting and the sound of growling and pads smashing. I told the guys in the truck they ought to use the parab on the sweep; it was incredible. They did, and it became standard practice. I can't say I invented it, but everybody started using it all the time.

I wangled my way onto the sideline for halftime one game, right on the Browns' bench. What a great job. I would have paid them to let me do this every Sunday. After a few games the players started to say hello to me. We stood shoulder-to-shoulder on the sideline. It felt like I was playing. I never felt more like part of a team. I got to know some of them well.

Gary Collins got used to stopping by me coming off the field. He was a friend of Ernie's, a great guy, did all the punting, and was a tremendous receiver. Frank Ryan, the quarterback, was a mathematician who could read defenses like something out of science fiction. He'd always find something to do. One time Collins ran his post pattern, a goal-line post move where he'd run the defender into the pole or lose the defender behind him. He was wide open in the end zone, with nobody near him, and Ryan threw way behind him. It was muddy as hell, but Collins contorted his body, dove, put his hand under the ball, and held it up as he slid in for a touchdown. It was a sensational catch. The crowd went crazy.

Collins trotted back to the sideline. As he passed me, taking his helmet off, he said, "Man! That guy can really throw a ball." He'd do something like that all the time.

I flash a CBS "eye" tag at Cleveland Stadium, as part of the TV8 remote crew shooting Browns and Indians games. That's the sweater the Certain Ethnic character later made famous.

One time Collins dropped what looked like a sure touchdown. He had earlier hurt his ribs, which caused excruciating pain when he twisted, but the crowd booed. Lou Groza trotted out to try the field goal, and Collins passed me, taking his helmet off and mad as hell.

I heard the director say, "Stand by to open parab," to catch the thump of Groza's kick. Collins walked right up, stuck his head inside the parab dish, and shouted "F***!" Real loud. He no sooner said that than the director said, "Open parab!" We just missed it. One second later and it would have been the loudest F-bomb ever telecast—although it was so loud it would have been distorted. Collins was joking around, but he was mad. He was sensitive to the crowd, and I don't blame him.

The center was John Morrow. I got know him after I got a dog from Ernie, a Rhodesian ridgeback that didn't develop properly and had to be put down after six months. The kids felt so bad that I had to get another, but no one even knew what I was talking about. I told announcer John Fitzgerald, and he said, "I think Morrow raises ridgebacks." Morrow came to me on the sidelines and said he didn't have any, but he did breed them and could get one. Getting a ridgeback is like adopting a baby—they check into your background and make sure it's a good home. Morrow and I got to be really close because he would come over to the house to see the dog. June and I had supper with him and his wife a few times, and I still have the recipe for Swedish stew his wife made with beer.

When Collins heard I knew Morrow, he said, "Oh—Mandrake," for the cartoon magician. "He holds on every play and he never gets caught."

Clifton McNeil was called Sticks. He was tall and so skinny that I don't know how he was one of the gunners. I'd always laugh on kick-offs, where he stood right on the sidelines and I stood as close as I could to him. Huge guys would whisper in his ear, "I want you to kill somebody when you go down there, Sticks. Punish 'em, Sticks. Punish 'em."

UP CLOSE AND BLOODY

Linebacker Mike Lucci was the handsomest guy I ever saw—dark hair, really striking light blue eyes, perfect teeth. He was another of Ernie's friends. I was running the parab on a goal-line stand for a game against the Giants when he jumped up to meet the runner. The guy's facebar pushed his helmet back, hit him right in the mouth, and shaved off four teeth. Lucci came back to the bench bleeding, and I was almost sick to my stomach. All I could think of was his perfect teeth.

Almost the same thing happened to Lou Groza, making the tackle on a kickoff against the Redskins. His facebar broke, and a helmet hit his nose and broke it.

He was bleeding like a faucet, blood just pouring out, and swearing continuously. He sat with his head down, helmet off, and Vic Ippolito, the team doctor, kept saying, "Shut up, dammit," while he stuffed cotton in the nose with long tweezers to stop the bleeding. Ippolito gave him a shot in the nose, probably Novocaine, and Groza, still swearing nonstop, now had a big wad of tape and cotton on his nose. They just about had the bleeding stopped. Then the Browns got the ball back in field-goal range, on a delay-of-game call against Washington, just before the half ran out. Lou had to go in. They pulled out the cotton, and he put on his helmet and trotted onto the field. He kicked the field goal, blood streaming from his nose, and trotted off. He never stopped swearing.

I got to know Groza pretty well after he retired. He liked the show and was at the station one time when John Rinaldi and I were going into the studio. He was a big guy, and his back was to us. John walked behind him and pinched him on the ass. He does that to me sometimes when I don't know he's there. He's really strong and can pinch hard as hell. The first couple of times, you wheel around and don't see anything. It's a shock. Groza whirled, started laughing, and ran after John down the hallway, yelling, "Come here you, little shit. I'm gonna drop-kick your ass down the hallway."

My daughter and wife became friends with Groza's daughter and wife years later, who told them how much he liked me and the show. I wish I'd known that when he was alive. I really liked him but didn't want to push it. Typical of those days, he didn't make enough money playing football to make a living, and he had an insurance business. He'd go to his downtown office after Sunday games and work until he fell asleep on the desk.

SNEAKING ONTO THE FIELD

Players came in for Saturday practice at ten or eleven in the morning. We'd be there, too. The guards knew us, and we had passes. But when Walt Roberts came, brand new to the team, he looked like a hanger-on. He was called "The Flea" because he was so small and fast. A big cop grabbed him, shook him, and told him to get out. Roberts started to explain who he was. The cop said, "Yeah, I play for the Browns, too. Get the hell out. I'm gonna bust you, man." I thought the cop was right; the guy was too small. He had a hell of time getting in until somebody saw him and said, "Yeah, he does play for the Browns."

It was easier when I used to sneak my brother, Paul, into games. I'd give him stuff to carry. Everybody knew who I was, so I'd take my pass off and give it to him. My goal was somehow to sneak him onto the field to tell Ernie. I tried it for a big game that had extra security, which meant we had to have field passes, tags wired to an eyelet on a lanyard. I kept the eyelet on the lanyard, tore off the pass like someone had grabbed it, and gave it to Paul. He had a headset and walked on the field behind me, carrying stuff.

A cop said to me, "Chuck, some asshole took your tag! They're taking everything. Be careful." I thought, *Uh-oh.*

I told Paul to keep his headset on at all times and stay with me. I put a cable between him and me, so it looked like he belonged with me. But he was by the bench, and I was way down the field. A new cop I never saw before was on the field. He saw Paul and said, "You doing something for the game?" Paul is such a liar. He said, "I'm the guy who tells them when to take a commercial." I don't know where he heard that one. The cop said, "Come on! Get out of here." Paul said, "You know how much commercials are for this game? You want to be responsible for losing that spot?"

It worked, but after that he stayed with me.

Ernie was jealous I was working on the field. I had one up on him, which no one ever got. I'd say, "Where you gonna be during the game? I'll wave to you." He'd grumble, "Get outta here." Then one day he wangled a field pass. He couldn't be near the bench but had to be out where the photographers were. Collins caught a touchdown pass, and Ernie ran onto the field into the end zone to congratulate him. The cops dragged him away and threw him out.

MODELL GETS AN EARLY REPUTATION

I used to think Art Modell was a pretty nice guy, but he was really a pompous jerk. He had to stick his nose into everything. We'd do the *Countdown to Kickoff* show on Saturday, and he'd be there holding the ball for Groza. That's why he got rid of Paul Brown. He'd make suggestions, and Brown told him he wasn't coaching. I think Blanton Collier was getting sick of him, too. He was a pain in the ass during practice or warm-ups.

The Browns were doing so well in 1964 that Modell resodded the whole field, even the grass next to the stands. Every time he spent money he was on the field. I had to set up the field camera, so I'd drag cables we'd tie to the rafters, which was pretty dangerous, and drop them down to the field. I was dragging an extension from the stands over the grass and across the track. Modell said, "We just put sod on here." I said, "I can see that." It was nice—I was nobody.

"I don't want you guys tracking across this grass," he said.

I'm not a smartass, so I just said I had to cross somewhere, and there was no break in the grass. He could see I had to get the cable across, and he said, "You guys are the last of the wood-burning TV stations"—a line he probably heard somewhere. Afterward I heard him telling his cronies, "last of the wood-burning TV stations," looking at me. It ticked me off.

We used to set up his booth. Before luxury loges, it was built of wood and looked like an outhouse. It had a window in front and a door on the side, and was on a sling reached by a ladder from the upper deck. Dick Lorius usually ran the camera next to the booth on the sling.

Modell used to drink a lot before he gave it up. Guys told us he wouldn't drink for a half hour, then would take a water glass half-filled with gin and chug it. He wouldn't drink for another half hour, then he'd chug another glass. You've got to be a real drinker to do that.

We'd be starving after a game, so during teardown we'd hit the half-full bottles of booze and the snacks and sandwiches that Modell and his guests left behind. That continued until someone found out the guys in Modell's booth never left and didn't have a toilet. They peed in the empty bottles and left them there. I don't know how someone found out, but it was obvious what was in those bottles. So we'd only take the peanuts and snacks after that.

KEEPING THE NETWORK EYE ON

Maybe it was the last of the wood-burning stations. The game TV director from CBS came up before one game, saw we were from TV8, and said he was looking for the remote truck. "This is it," we said. He started laughing and said, "No, no kidding. Where's the truck?" Then he got upset. It looked like a junk truck, full of boxes of headsets that didn't work. We were sitting there trying to piece together working sets.

One engineer was a big, soft-looking, fat guy we called Candyass. I was switching for the first time on a coast-to-coast feed, and I was nervous as hell. We were ready to go on the air, and the network was checking in: "L.A. OK." "Chicago OK," "We're here; Cleveland OK." "Standby, forty-five seconds to air." Candyass came in and took off his coat. The racks of amplifiers and tubes, which are usually covered, were open, and he hung his coat on the edge of a rack by the power supply. "Twenty seconds to air." The coat slipped off and on the way down turned the power-supply switch off. The whole truck shut down. You couldn't come right back on because the equipment had to warm up, so we were off for about a minute. Candyass calmly put on his coat and left. The director collapsed. We all thought he had a heart attack. He hated the Cleveland gig after that.

CBS had stickers of the CBS "Eye" that they put on everything to make sure they had all their stuff going back. Big stickers for big stuff, little stickers for little stuff. Ed Bates, one of our news reporters, had a glass eye, though you'd never know it because it would move naturally. Ed took out the glass eye, stuck a little CBS Eye on it, and put it back in. Then he'd go talk to the guys.

When one of our dogs, Rowdy, got real old a few years later and had to have an eye out, Ed consoled me. I told him how bad I felt, and he said, "Believe me, you get over that so fast. Hell, he'll be walking around fine in no time at all." He had me feeling better. Then he turned and purposely walked into a door frame.

KEN AND CASEY

Ken Coleman was the Browns announcer when I was working the games in the '60s. He would come down to Saturday practice at the stadium and bring his little kid, Casey. I'd throw a football to him, never knowing I'd be a colleague some day, directing him on TV8 news and in a number of skits on our show.

DESPERATE SITUATION, DESPERATE MOVE

I got along really well with the guys from New York. In 1964, they told me there was a new guy on the field who looked a lot like me. I was flattered. It was Pat Summerall, the former Giants kicker, who was a new color commentator for CBS and a nice guy from the start.

He was on the field and really quiet. I was running audio for him. The director told me we'd go to a commercial as soon as he did his color, and then we'd go to halftime in the TV room. All I had to do was stay on the field and link from that shoot to the truck.

The TV room in the old stadium was an old restroom with everything torn out. They put up a set with a backdrop behind the announcers, and it looked great on camera. But the room was terrible—all cement, no heat, wet, damp, and dirty. One toilet had been left, and I knew it worked because we would use it sometimes when we ran cable to the field. It was near the tunnel to the field, and they wanted us not to go into the stands. It was too crowded and there wasn't time.

Summerall was pale as a ghost. He said to tell the director he felt bad. "I can't do it," he said. The director said, "Bullshit, you tell that (bleeper) hell no." I said, "He says he'd really like you to try to do it."

I'd heard these guys had gone out the night before and really got torn up. I didn't know if he had diarrhea from drinking too much, but I knew exactly how he felt. He was in bad shape. He said, "I don't think I can do it." The director said, "Bullshit. Tell him stand by."

Summerall finished his commentary, and said he had to go real bad. It was halftime at Cleveland Stadium. "You can't get close to a bathroom," I said. "But I do know . . ."

"Tell me! Tell me!"

I tried to explain to Summerall that the toilet was in the TV room, but he begged me to take him there. "Just hang on," I said. "Take shallow breaths."

I opened the door, and they were on the air with the halftime show. The room was real quiet. I pointed to the toilet. Summerall looked at the announcers talking, looked at me, and looked at the toilet. The announcers were facing our way, with the camera in between. He walked to the toilet. I had to get back to the field, figuring the director was probably screaming for me. Summerall started to take his pants down. The technicians cracked up, and the announcers started to laugh. The director was screaming so loudly I could hear it through the cameraman's headset—"What's going on there!?"

I split. The announcers couldn't believe what they were seeing. They probably thought it was a joke, but they were about to find out it wasn't.

It was a good thing everybody smoked in those days.

From that rather shaky start, Pat Summerall went on to one of the longest and most illustrious careers in sports broadcasting. Nice guy—and we still look somewhat alike.

YOU CAN'T BELIEVE YOUR EYES OR EARS

We used to do *Countdown to Kickoff* on Saturday with CBS. They had a five-minute segment on every game being played the next day. We put a camera in the locker room to interview players coming in from practice.

Monte Clark was on this team, a really big lineman with skinny legs. He used to wear three or four pairs of socks to make his legs look thicker. He studied TV production in college, watched us setting up a live shot, and asked me to wheel the camera by the shower door to pretend we were shooting.

One of the Browns was in the shower—a linebacker famous for a very large endowment. "It's legendary," John Fitzgerald said. I once saw Paul Brown, as stoic as he was, end an interview in the locker room and say, "Stay here for a second, Fitz; he's coming out of the shower now."

Clark, who had pants on and a towel around his neck, stood by the door holding a hand mic. When the linebacker came out, he grabbed him and said to the camera, "Ladies and gentleman, it's true! This man is the best hung man in the NFL."

I stood at the camera looking dead serious, with the light on. The player tried to pull away, and Clark kept talking. "We're so proud, ladies and gentlemen. Yes, it's true . . ."

They were almost fighting before he realized it was a joke.

Blanton Collier, the head coach, was very hard of hearing and wore two hearing aids. We used to do a midweek phone-in show with him, *Ask the Coach*. One time no one called in, and the show was a bomb. I told my son Mark, who was a big fan, to call in a question.

Mark was nervous as hell, and his voice was shaking. He asked, "When the quarterback goes back to pass and runs past the line of scrimmage, can he run back behind it and throw a pass?" A good question.

"Well, Mark," Collier said, "we plan to pass a lot this year." He went on to talk about the receivers.

SOMETIMES YOU HAVE TO HOLD BACK

I got so close to the field and the team that I almost went too far a couple seasons later. The Browns were playing Green Bay and were ahead by six points with about two minutes left. Green Bay had the ball on fourth down. They were too far for a field goal—it wouldn't have done any good anyway—and they had Jim Taylor and Paul Hornung in the backfield.

I was at the line of scrimmage with the parab mic. The ball was snapped, and it looked like a screwed-up play. It took a lot of time, and I knew if the Browns stopped them they'd win. All of a sudden, Taylor broke loose, and he was coming around end right at me. It was incredible the way Jim Brown would run up to the sideline, full tilt, then plant his leg and turn. Taylor was coming, and he had even bigger thighs than Brown.

I looked to see who was defending. Ross Fichtner, the safety, tried to turn him in, but Taylor blew past. Safety Erich Barnes, who we called a dirty player with New York but physical when he got here, clotheslined him, but Taylor stopped, and Barnes's legs flew around him. Jim Houston, the linebacker, was unblocked. He fired right in front of me and grabbed Taylor, who gave him a juke and slipped off. Taylor stumbled, recovered, and started to run off.

I had the most tremendous urge either to hit him with the parab, like I was falling onto him, or to jump on him. I was so into it, at that split second, I honestly don't know how the hell I didn't do it. He was right in front of me, and I don't know I stopped myself. It would have been the most played thing on highlights that week, and I would have been out of TV. And Taylor probably would have carried me into the end zone anyway.

I was out of breath from the adrenaline. It was like I had actually done something, and I was mad for weeks. Taylor scored, and the Browns lost. And honest to God, to this day, when I tell that story, my heart rate and blood pressure go up and I tremble. No exaggeration. I don't know how I stopped myself, and I will never forget that tremendous urge.

A STRANGE SECRET BEFORE THE BIGGEST GAME

The NFL championship game, on December 27, 1964, was magical. The night before it was surreal.

There was way more media than usual, so we had to run extra phone lines at the stadium. The basic CBS crew had everything in place, but Hap Hallas and I still had to wire eight more headsets for a crew from Canada. It was 7 or 8 p.m. on Saturday night, cold as hell, dark as could be, and deserted. We were sitting in a sling, working with flashlights, and bats were flying around.

Suddenly a bank of lights came on, then all of them. This never happened before. We kept working, and there came the Cleveland Browns onto the field. It was a secret practice. It wasn't long, maybe forty-five minutes, but they ran through plays. And for whatever reason, one play that they ran maybe ten times was Jim Brown taking a pitch and running to the right like he always did. Every team in the league knew it was coming, but they couldn't stop it because of the fast line we had.

In this play, however, Brown rushed to the right, stopped, and drop-kicked the ball. He made half of the dropkicks. I wondered: Why would they do that? It's three points, just like a field goal, and they had the best kicker in the NFL in Lou Groza. To this day, I would like to know why they practiced this play. They wouldn't have done it over and over if they were just screwing around. Please, somebody, tell me why.

CBS brought in key people for the game and would use us from the affiliate for the full crew. We had a call at the stadium at 6:30

a.m., as we did every time CBS came in. There'd be nobody there, and everything would be in place, but they'd insist on it. The stadium would be in complete darkness. We couldn't even find each other. We'd go into the stands, and the rats would run right over your feet. It was spooky as hell. We'd sit listening to them run around for a good hour until it got light enough to do anything. But there'd be a guy waiting to check us in and give out passes. The nice part was the network would buy lunch. They'd send out for shrimp and stuff we usually never ate.

MAGIC TIME ON THE LAKEFRONT

If you ever go to Disney World with little kids, you know there is some kind of magic there. Walking to the stadium for the 1964 NFL championship game was magical. The Browns were seven-point underdogs to Baltimore at kickoff, but I knew the Browns were going to win. It wasn't like, "We're going to kill them, woof woof," but everybody knew. They would not be denied. I got it from the players and got it from the bench. Everybody in that stadium at the same time got the feeling the Browns were going to win. I don't know why.

The first half was scoreless. But on the bench, working the parab mic, I could tell the mood of the players, and it was like they were ahead and the game was in the bag. I felt that way, and I think the entire crowd of eighty thousand did, too. We were cheering when they went to the locker room. It didn't show on the scoreboard, but they were manhandling the Colts. They seemed to dominate every stage.

On their first possession of the second half, Groza kicked a forty-three-yard field goal for the Browns. For a straight-on kicker, forty years old, that's a long kick. It hit the crossbar and went over. The stadium went nuts.

If you're in the stands during a Browns game, you only hear the cheers close to you. If you're on the field, you hear it all. That's why quarterbacks are not faking it when they call time because of noise. You can't hear someone next to you talking. And that's how it was.

From that point on, the Browns were off and unstoppable. The Colts were double- and triple-teaming Jim Brown, which is why other guys were open. He ate up a lot of defense and a lot of ground—114 yards. He ran wild. Groza kicked another field goal, and Collins set a title game record with three touchdown passes. Browns, 27–0.

At the end of the game, it was euphoria. People started bustling over the stands onto the field. It's really dangerous—you can get trampled and killed. I've seen it happen at personal appearances, where even a crowd of kids becomes a powerful force that can pin you against a wall.

The cops were battling, trying to hold them back. I told the director I had to get out, and he started yelling at me to leave everything—"They're going to try to get souvenirs. They'll kill you! Leave everything!" I took off my headset and looked at the parab. A real expensive mic plugs into the dish. I took it out and put it in my pocket. No sooner did I do that than a wave of people came pushing and running.

If you fall, you're dead. No one behind can see, and they keep coming. So wherever that crowd wanted to go, I went. I was pushed this way, then that way. It was like the current in a river. They grabbed the goal post, which was thick steel. They crowded around and started twisting it to break it off. People were getting cut by the sharp metal edges. They didn't get reported like they do now, but there were several injuries.

I was lucky to get out. I just happened to have a little bit of experience, having seen many crowds pushing, and I got pushed the right way.

CHAPTER 6

ERNIE AND ME

WHEN GHOULARDI OWNED CLEVELAND

Downtown was booming and bustling in the big Ghoulardi days. We were part of it on Playhouse Square, where we could walk to everything, and it was fun. Groups of guys in suits, obviously corporate cats, would see Ernie and give him the Flash Gordon salute, the Ghoulardi "hi" sign—thumping your hand against the middle of your chest with your thumb, fingers pointing up. Some would do it with exaggerated furtiveness, like it was secret code, and others made a big show of it. Either way, they'd always shout, "Hey, Ernie!"

He enjoyed it, but he was insecure and kept his head down so no one would recognize him. One time we were walking and I put my head down, the way he did, and started toeing in more and more, imitating his pigeon-toed walk. He finally noticed and pushed me into the street. I had him on that one, and there wasn't anything he could say.

He and I were doing things together daily. I don't know if he didn't want to be alone or what, but he always wanted me to go with him. He was in demand as both a personality and a voiceover commercial announcer. I got to meet a lot of people that way because he knew everybody, and it was always interesting. Once we walked out of the station lobby and saw a couple of nuns sitting on a bench. Ernie stopped, lit a cigar, and said, "You know, you two look enough alike to be sisters."

We'd go to a bar and everybody would want to buy Ghoulardi a drink. He'd say, "No, thanks a lot, I gotta run, but here, I'll just take

At Chippewa Lake Park for a Channel 8 company picnic. Ernie and I in front; cameramen John Jackman and Carl Szubski behind.

seventy-five cents"—and then scoop up some of the change they'd left on the bar. That would kill me. We'd leave, and the guys would be left at the bar with a funny and confused look. And Ernie actually kept the money. He was a guy you'd either want as a friend or someone you'd never want to see again.

We started pulling a lot of pranks on each other.

Ernie drove a little two-seat sports car, an A.C. Ace convertible, and he'd leave it in a no-parking zone in front of the station. There was even a bus stop there. Ernie didn't worry about it, and he'd leave the keys in the ignition. I know I worried. I'd take the keys out, and I told him someone was going to take the car. "Bullshit," he said, "that's that Parma thinking." Two or three days later, when I saw he left the car and keys again, I jumped in and drove it around to the alley behind the station. Eventually, as I expected, he said, "Come with me," walked out front and saw the car was missing. "Son of a bitch!" he said. I told him I took it. "You know, that's really a Parma joke," he said. "It's not funny. Funny is funny."

Another time, knowing I couldn't do the same thing again, I drove the car around back and put in the Frankenstein dummy from the Ghoulardi set—stuffed coveralls with a mask as a face. Ernie went out the front door, saw the car wasn't there, and then went around back, swearing to himself. He saw the dummy, and said, "That's really not funny. That's the difference between funny and not funny," and went into a long explanation.

So I did the same thing again, but this time I dressed up as the Frankenstein dummy. I heard Ernie coming, muttering and swearing to himself. He reached to move the "dummy," and I grabbed his hand real hard. He screamed and immediately shouted, "You didn't get me!" I said I got him good, and he was unbelievably scared, but he insisted I hadn't got him, and it wasn't funny. This went on constantly.

CATCHING A BUS THE HARD WAY

One Friday afternoon in 1964, I came to work a bit early to help Ernie prepare for that night's show. Ernie said, "Before we get started, come on with me. I have to record a radio spot."

The recording studio was several blocks east of our station on Euclid Avenue. Ernie drove the A.C. Ace. It was a hot day, so he had the top down. As we drove up Euclid, he startled me by yelling, "Holy shit! There it is!" and pointed to a Cleveland Transit System bus going the other way. He made a wild U-turn, yelling, "There it is! I got to have it for tonight's show!"

"You gotta have a bus?" I asked.

"No!" he said. "Look at the sides."

The sides of the bus, which usually carried advertising posters, had big green public service posters from the mayor's traffic safety education committee that read: "Don't jaywalk . . . live longer." Next to the slogan was a drawing of Ghoulardi.

"I forgot to tell you they were going to do that," Ernie said as he pulled directly behind the bus. "When the bus stops, jump out on the curb and see if you can get the poster off."

"How?" I said. "What if I get caught?"

"Don't worry, trust me!" he said—a favorite expression of his. "Just do it. I'll keep the bus driver occupied. He won't notice you." He then pulled his car slightly to the left, behind the bus, so the driver could see him and not me. He waved to the driver. The driver went *nuts,* as everyone did when they saw Ghoulardi in person. The driver was so excited and laughing so hard he almost missed a stop. When he stopped to pick up people, he stuck his head out the window, looked back at Ernie, and said, "Ghoulardi! I watch you every night, man."

While he and Ernie talked, I jumped over the door of the car and surveyed the poster. It was enclosed in a metal frame with a lock on it. The frame was tight against the poster. I couldn't get my fingers in to pull at it. The bus started up, and I jumped back over the door into the car as Ernie followed the bus.

"It's not going to work," I said. "I can't pry it loose. The metal frame is too tight."

"Look in the glove compartment," he said. "There's a screwdriver in there, I think."

There was a little three-inch one, very old and rusty, with a split wooden handle. The bus stopped. The driver stuck his head out the window and excitedly continued flattering Ernie. Out I went, knowing I only had about fifteen seconds of time to work. I slammed the screwdriver into the corner of the frame and pulled down on it hard. I heard a snap. I hoped it was the poster board popping out of the frame. No luck! It was the screwdriver busting in half and the handle cracking off. The bus started. I jumped into the now-moving car.

"Well?" said Ernie. I held up half of the screwdriver and a piece of the handle. "The other half is stuck in the frame," I said, now noticing that my thumb was bleeding.

Ernie scooted toward me. "Here, in my pocket," he said. "A knife." He wanted me to try to pull it from his pants pocket while he drove. "Here, you steer," he said, twisting himself the opposite way and almost standing up. He managed to pop the knife out of his pocket, along with some coins, bills, and business cards. The knife was a tiny pocketknife about two inches long, but it was very sharp. The bus stopped. Out I jumped and began jabbing away at the bottom left-hand corner of the poster, finding that it was made of some very tough material.

The bus took off. Back in the car I went, telling Ernie my strategy of digging a hole in the corner of the poster so I could get a couple of fingers under it to pry it out of the frame. For the next two stops, I put my plan into action. We were now back in front of TV8. I figured it would take at least five more stops before I dug a hole big enough to get my fingers in. Ernie told me he thought the bus driver was getting a little suspicious. So, the next stop I tried very hard, jamming one finger into the hole and getting a just under the corner of the poster.

The bus started. I tried to pull my finger out. It was stuck. I

started running with my
finger under the poster.
I jerked my arm back as
fast as I could. My finger
popped out, raking my
knuckles against the edge
of the frame. I jumped into
the car. Ernie was laughing
hysterically. Now both of

my hands were bleeding. I told Ernie I didn't think it was so funny.
But my aching hands now made me more determined than Ernie
was to get that poster. I was mad. Which, of course, made Ernie
laugh even harder.

We had now traveled through Public Square and on to the Near
West Side. The bus driver's fascination with Ghoulardi following
his bus seemed to be fading. He was probably wondering why Ernie
was following him.

Ernie kept smiling, shouting wisecracks, and waving, but we
knew the next couple of stops would be critical. A few stops later, I
had most of a corner of the poster out of a slightly bent frame. We
were well into the West Side now.

The bus stopped. I was pumped. Now, with a huge surge of
adrenaline, I jammed my whole left palm under the poster, bent
down, and pushed up until my whole hand was in up to my wrist.
I reached my right hand over, grabbing the corner, and with both
hands made a superhuman effort to pull the poster out. I could feel
the frame bending as the thick, sturdy poster board was forced out
with a big pop. I fell backwards against the curb. People getting on
and off the bus were now telling the driver that some "nut" had
taken the poster.

Holding the prize under my arm, I jumped into the car. Ernie
let out a triumphant cheer, laughed, and pulled up beside the bus.
He waved to the driver, said, "Thanks, man. Be cool," made another
frantic U-turn, and headed back to TV8.

We had gone all the way to Lakewood. We had been gone for
over an hour; Ernie had missed his voiceover gig, and I was late
for my engineering shift. It was worth it, because in the car we had

our subject for the entire show that night. Then a worry crossed my mind. I said, "What if the bus driver sees the show and tells the cops what happened?"

"Rat on Ghoulardi?" Ernie scoffed. "It'll never happen. Don't worry, trust me."

He was right. We pulled into the alley behind the station and hurriedly walked in the back door. We apologized for being late, and I started for the men's room to wash my hands.

"Hey!" Ernie said. "When you're done, bring in the show mail from the lobby so we can go through it."

The show mail was all in one box. As I started to take it to Ernie, our receptionist, Marge, said, "Here! This came in for Ernie, too." She handed me a three-by-two-foot, half-inch-thick package, wrapped in shipping paper. The writing on the outside read, "Ernie, thanks for everything. Maybe you can use this on your show. The signs will be on the buses today!"

Ernie and I must have laughed for an hour after we unwrapped the "Ghoulardi—Don't jaywalk" poster from the mayor's traffic safety education committee.

Ernie had a great show that night, and the poster became a permanent fixture on his set. And I still have the one I took off the bus—it's a permanent fixture in my rec room. Even today, more than forty years later, each time I see it, it reminds me of how Ernie and I both enjoyed telling the story of how we got it. I still do.

BLACK AND WHITE AND COLOR

Channel 8 had one color camera in 1964. You obviously couldn't use it on a show where you change cameras, like the news, so it occurred to them that there were only two shows we could use it on: Jim Doney's *Adventure Road* and *Shock Theater*, Ernie's Ghoulardi show.

Doney is a great guy. He was our public service director, quite a big-time broadcaster, and he pitched on the Ghoulardi All-Stars softball team. His *Adventure Road* had guests talking about their travels and showing some of the films shot on their trip, and it was a perfect late afternoon program for kids coming home from school

"Holy pierogi, look at that!" In the TV8 in tape room with engineer Pete Kneffel.

or to watch while eating supper.

Jim's most memorable "guest" was one that viewers didn't see—a big black bird that Ernie used on the Ghoulardi show and named Oxnard. Ernie told me a priest gave it to him. He got the name when he got lost visiting Conway in California, drove through the city of Oxnard, and thought it was the funniest thing he ever heard.

The bird—a raven or a crow—got loose after the show one night. We were there until two in the morning trying to coax it down with poles. When it finally came down, it flew through the hallway and into the next studio, which was Doney's, and perched right above the set. It stayed there a week or ten days, way longer than you'd think it could survive.

Jim was pretty cool. He'd sit talking on camera, unperturbed, while the guest would look up nervously. Every so often, a big ball would plop down from the rafters and splat on the set. In color or black and white, it looked the same. The show was live, and it was funny as hell to see the guests keep looking up all through the show.

Then the station wondered if we could use the color camera

on another program I used to do, the *Mass for Shut-ins* on Sunday morning. Yeah, I said—you could zoom, pan, or pull out. One color camera would work. So they made a big to-do about premiering the show on Channel 8 in color, and the diocese was really going to dress it up. Instead of having lay people in the congregation, they filled the entire audience with nuns. I looked at the monitor as they filed into the studio in their habits, and it still looked like black and white. The priest was in black and white vestments. The only color was the Mass book he held up!

I don't know if Ernie really got Oxnard from a priest. But I once got a request from St. Stanislaus parish, in my old neighborhood, to bring the Ghoulardi All-Stars there.

Ernie said, "Oh man, St. Stan's? Catholics? Play in a church?"

I said, "Ernie, this is a Polish Catholic neighborhood. It's going to be cool." He was still skeptical when we got there and was sort of quiet in the locker room when a priest came in. I introduced them. Ernie was cordial. The priest opened his coat, and he had a bottle of booze and some glasses.

The game should have started, but he and Ernie were having a few and talking. Ernie looked at him and said, "I think you're gonna convert me."

THE WET AND WILD WEST

You had to be there to know *Mass for Shut-in*s was in color, and you had to be in on the joke to understand a long skit on *Ghoulardi* that parodied *Gunsmoke*.

Ernie had a small part in *Gunsmoke* in 1964, a reward for being a big star on a CBS affiliate, and he came back complaining how dull and slow-moving it was. The show had expanded from a half-hour to an hour, and they did it by lengthening every scene so they could use the rest of the half-hour scripts already written. I was a big fan of the show, and it was noticeable.

So Ernie did a filmed take-off called "The Stranger." He played Marshal Dillon, I was the Stranger, and Bob Soinski and actress Patty Rowe were in it, too. All he did was have long, dead pauses in it, with no real set-up or explanation.

"Ernie," I said, "no one's going to get it."

He didn't care. *Eff it,* he said. He'd do it anyway.

He also came back with a story about James Arness wanting a raise after *Gunsmoke* got really popular. He was turned down and told it would be considered when he got his next contract. Arness decided to play hardball. So they gave him the script for the next show, and it had Marshal Dillon getting killed. That was the last of that dispute.

It might have been *Gunsmoke* that inspired Ghoulardi to use a squirt gun on the show one night. We got dozens in the mail the next week, and everybody in the station had one. They'd be reloading and shooting so much, it was like the Old West—with ambushes and people coming around corners. Water eventually got squirted in the switcher in the control room, which is dangerous but didn't put an end to the shootouts. Union president Dom Lolli, who you *think* might be calming things down, was in the thick of it, squirting everybody.

Curly Maska, a serious and great guy who worked in the tape room, got mad about it. Dom decided to get him. He went creeping down a hallway—this is a grown man—and peeking around corners to sneak up on him. But Curly knew he was coming. He got a bucket of water and went up one flight of stairs. When Dom came around the corner, Curly poured the water on him.

Dom got mad but went back to work. He went into master control, took off his shirt and hung it up over the power supply to dry, and sat smoking a cigar, all hairy and wet and shirtless. It was just then that Ken Bagwell, the general manager, walked in with a group of men and women who were touring the station.

We used to call Bagwell "Daddy Bags," which was a take-off on Leon Wagner of the Indians, who was nicknamed Daddy Wags. He was always arguing with Dom because Dom was union president. One sore point was eating and drinking in the control room, where Dom would knock his coffee into the switcher about once a month. So Bagwell finally put it in writing: *No more eating in the control room, and violation would be grounds for dismissal.*

I was working the sign-off shift one night after that. After the eleven p.m. news ended, Dom told me to pick up a pizza for the

Running the switcher at TV8 in the early 1960s. I once saved several people's jobs by knowing there was room to hide a pizza underneath the controls.

control room from New York Pizza on East 9th Street. Bagwell's memo didn't worry him. After I came back and put the big pizza box next to the switcher on the audio console, Dom told me to get some coffee.

I went down the narrow hall facing the front of the building, heading for the basement. It was about midnight. To my shock, Bagwell and a group of people, probably coming from Pierre's, were headed right toward me in the lobby. If I went back to the control room the way I came, he'd see me. My only shot was to go back downstairs to the basement, where I was going for coffee, run the width of the building, go up the other side stairs, and get back into the control room that way.

I just made it. Bagwell and his group were close. Dom was sitting there smoking a cigar. I don't how I thought of it, but I grabbed the switcher console board. It lifted up in case we had to work on the parts and relays underneath, and there was a small space under it to allow the heat to escape. Bagwell was right at the door. I put the pizza box under the switcher, set down the board, and sat down. Dom looked baffled. He'd no sooner said, "What the?" when Bagwell walked in.

The control room reeked of pizza. There was no doubt it was in there. Bagwell stopped talking and looked around. We had to keep the control room clean, and everything was spotless. He walked around the room, resumed talking, and went behind the console in front of the monitors, looking around at the ceiling and floor, trying to find the pizza as he continued his tour of the station. I couldn't have put it anywhere else except inside the switcher. Only maintenance engineers knew the space was there. But Bagwell didn't think to look there, and we kept it hidden there after he finally left, not sure he wouldn't come back.

The pizza was still there when John Mahoney, the booth announcer, walked in a few minutes later and sniffed the air. "Christ, it smells like an Italian submarine in here," he said.

"STOP SCREWING AROUND WITH ERNIE"

Bagwell liked me. He was a good guy. He put me on the air after Ghoulardi ended and eventually made me a director. He complimented me on my work. But he periodically warned me about the pranks and other stuff that Ernie was usually at the center of. One time when he was chewing me out, instead of naming the other guys who were involved, I said, "We shouldn't have done it." He let everyone know I didn't name names, and his secretary told me later that he said, "There goes a real man." Things got a lot easier for me at the station after that.

But that was later. Earlier on, Bagwell threw a real scare into me by sending an official memo that said: "Stop screwing around with Ernie. You're a good guy, and you're going to get in trouble. Stop it." He also sent a copy to the union.

That was on my mind the night Ernie said to me, "Come on, I'll take you for a ride around the block," wanting to show off the motorcycle he just bought. I told him no because I'd miss the half-hour station break. So would he. "Come on," he said. "What's going to happen?" He talked me into it. I climbed onto the motorcycle, hanging on to him. He took off and turned onto the Shoreway, going probably one hundred miles an hour. He was brand new on a motorcycle but acted like he'd been on one all his life. I started yelling to turn around, we were going to miss the break, but he kept

Golfing with Ernie at Manakiki, the course where Ernie's wicked slice had us running for cover.

going until I knew we'd passed the point of no return. *This was it,* I figured—*I'm going to get canned.* I was glad I left the foundry on good terms.

He drove all the way to his house in Willoughby. "Come on inside," he said. We went downstairs to his musty basement, which had a mud floor and was full of cobwebs. He pulled out a big wheel of cheese and Ballantine beer. He always drank Ballantine's, it still reminds me of the old days when I see it. He cut the mold off the cheese, and we sat at a wooden table with a light on it, eating cheese and drinking beer. "Don't worry about it," he said.

I was really down when we walked in the back door at the station. I didn't know what would happen. Dom was waiting with the rest of the crew.

"Jeeezus Christ! Schodowski, where the hell were you?" he said. "Bagwell's calling, we were in black for two and a half minutes! What the hell!" I was sick.

Then they all started laughing. The guys who supposedly went to lunch had stayed at the station and ate there. It was a set-up. They did it because I was so worried about the memo from Bagwell. I'm a prankster, but that one really scared the crap out of me.

BLOWING UP THE STATION

Ghoulardi got boxes of mail, and I helped Ernie go through it. Kids sent all kinds of junk, including firecrackers. One day he picked up this thing with a wick on it. I said, "Oh man, I don't know what this is, but you better not light it. It's too heavy. I don't know explosives, but it's dense, man. It could be half a stick of dynamite."

As soon as I said it, I knew it was the wrong thing to say. You didn't tell Ernie not to do something. He put it aside. When he did his Saturday afternoon show, it was next to the ashtray on the little coffee table beside him.

He drank some coffee, put it down, picked up this thing, and said, "Big Chuck doesn't want me to light this." As soon as he said that, I told everyone in the control room to turn away from the window if he lit it because I didn't know if it was plastic explosive or what. "Sure, yeah," they said, waving me off and laughing. *No,* I said—*seriously, turn away.*

Ernie lit a cigarette, then put on a helmet and safety glasses. Then he lit the thing and leaned away.

The glass between the control room and studio was thick and soundproof. When the thing exploded, the concussion pushed it inward like a piece of plastic. Bob Soinski, farther away in the projection room, said his ears blocked. You could not see in the studio. Smoke was everywhere. The camera guys ran down the hall holding their ears. When the smoke started to clear, I saw flames. The drapes were on fire.

We didn't want to call the fire department because everyone was immediately worried about lawsuits, fines, or other trouble. We grabbed every fire extinguisher we could find to put the fires out, but the drapes kept smoldering. Eventually we had to call the fire department since we used up all the extinguishers. Later we them by the front door to be refilled.) Ernie never mentioned it on the air, and TV8 kept it hushed up pretty well, but you could smell the smoke for days. It was scary, really bad, and I'm still amazed nobody was hurt. I don't know what that little bomb was, but Ernie was told to seriously cool it after that.

YOU CAN'T TAKE THE CONWAY OUT OF CLEVELAND

Tim Conway came back frequently from Hollywood even though he was on *McHale's Navy.* He was a real homebody, and he loved Cleveland. "Every day is just like the day before," he complained about southern California. "I want to see rain, snow, fog, clouds." Before he got used to the West Coast, he visited often enough to be a regular playing football and softball with the All-Stars.

One time he came back and went golfing with Ernie and me at

Tim Conway was a star on *McHale's Navy* but still came home to play with the Ghoulardi All-Stars—and to attend postgame parties.

Manakiki on SOM Center Road in Willoughby, near where Ernie lived. Ernie was the second worst golfer I ever saw. Conway tells about him getting a seventeen on one hole. Most hackers slice the ball, but Ernie's swing was unnatural—more like a baseball swing—and he hooked it. This time, teeing off on a little hill, he hooked a drive that went pretty far across SOM to a row of homes where a guy was cutting the lawn.

I don't know if the ball hit him or came close, but the guy went nuts. There was going to be some kind of confrontation. He came running across the street right at us, yelling and swearing, really screwy. I could see the guy was pretty old, panting and out of breath. I was in my prime and figured I'd just grab him and hold him to cool him down. I turned around to tell Ernie and Tim, but they were running away into the woods, laughing. The guy was getting close, and he was uncontrollably mad. I decided I could outrun him, so I followed Ernie and Tim.

The guy was still coming, swearing and panting, so we went farther into the woods and crowded behind a bush to hide. We were stifling laughter. I even had my coat in my mouth to muffle my laughs. The guy got so close we could hear him gasping for breath. He could hardly breathe and started coughing. Finally he left. We kept quiet, and I figured it was over.

Then I saw Conway had left us. He circled around behind the guy, started jumping up and down, shouted "Hey!" and started it all over. Ernie and I crouched behind the bush, watching the guy chase Conway. We probably stayed there twenty minutes, occasionally sticking our heads out, probably enjoying ourselves more than if we were playing golf.

Our bags were still on the tee. Ernie said the guy was probably hiding, waiting for us to get them, so we made a dash out of the woods and walked back to the clubhouse for the car. We drove down SOM toward the hole, all crouched down when we passed the guy's house, and saw no one was there. We jumped out of the car, ran like hell, grabbed the bags, and drove off.

Tim Conway and Ernie visited Hoolihan & Big Chuck to promote their comedy album *Are We On?* They never got to plug it in the sketch because Hoolie and I kept interrupting when they'd start to talk about it.

Conway always kept us entertained. He'd talk about whatever we saw in passing, keeping it up non-stop and never running out of stuff. Once we were driving past a raggedy-ass used car lot, with a beat-up old trailer that said "Office" on it. Conway immediately said, "Yes sir, Williams Used Cars. You know we're in business to stay because our trailer has cement steps!" And it did. And that's how his mind works.

I've never heard the same message twice on his answering machine. One time it was, "I don't really care about your message. I'd appreciate if you didn't say anything." Another time it was, "Harvey, if this is you, stop calling my house. You're a sick man"—aimed at his good friend Harvey Korman. When I call him, it's usually to relay a message from someone wanting something. Once, after I hadn't called him for probably a year and a half, his wife answered the phone. I heard her say, "Honey, it's Chuck." He picked up the phone, gave a long sigh, and said, "Now what?"

ESP: ERNIE'S SPECIAL PERCEPTION

Ernie wanted to do a prime time special in 1965, reuniting him and Conway to do the sort of bits they did on *Ernie's Place* and on a couple of comedy albums. Patty Rowe, the singer and actress, would also be in the show, and Ernie wanted me sing in it. He had heard me sing, and I was pretty good, but I didn't want to do it. He

I went to Kelleys Island to escape Ernie's 1965 prime time special, but Ernie somehow found me—and made me sing "You Made Me Love You."

interviewed me on all the stuff I'd done before that, which meant I was working with a partner. I still get nervous if I have to do something by myself.

I had vacation time coming and figured I could go somewhere when the show would be taping. I asked John Fitzgerald if he knew of a place I could go that was nearby and not expensive. He said, "Ever go to Kelleys Island?" I'd never even heard of it, but that's where I took the family. Back then it was desolate, and you really felt isolated. We could take the kids fishing and swimming at the beach like we owned the place.

There was a cop there named Norby, who called himself the chief of police and later made me a deputy because I had police training. He drove up to the house where we were staying on this first trip and said, "Chuck Schodowski? Ernie Anderson wants you to call the studio." I was stunned. No one knew where we were going. I hadn't told a soul, not even my brother. To the day Ernie died, he never told me how he found out.

I called the studio, did the show, and it got good reviews—and I now have a home on Kelleys Island. It's another thing I wouldn't have done if Ernie hadn't prodded me into it one way or another.

DEALING WITH A MAD DOG

He kept getting me in trouble, too, or at least brushing against it. Whenever football season approached, he'd want to practice passing in the parking lot or the alley behind the station. He'd throw way too far or way too short and hit cars. The owners would complain to the station. When I told him that Bagwell had called me into his office to warn me, he said, "Oh bullshit." And out we went to the alley.

He threw a pass that hit a railing and ricocheted right through one of the small windows on the garage door of a car repair shop. The ball had "Ghoulardi All-Stars" on it. We had to get it out, more to keep me out of trouble than anything, but it was out of reach. So we got a studio pole that was used to push overhead lights around, put a wad of duct tape on the end, and tried to snag the ball.

I thought we had it when the biggest German shepherd I ever saw came out barking and charging, biting the pole and scaring the crap out of us. Ernie went down the alley into Pierre's and came back with a ball of cut-up raw steak. He tossed it to distract the dog. It worked, but the dog came charging back. Ernie tried again, and the same thing happened. Now the dog was expecting more steak. Ernie went back for more and started tossing it farther and farther from the football inside the shop. Finally, it worked. We got the ball out, and Ernie made good on the garage window the next day. I just didn't want it to get back to Bagwell.

DON'T MESS WITH GHOULARDI

Ernie's nemesis was program director Ted Baze. They just hated each other. Baze was crafty; he had just so much power, and he would find ways to irritate Ernie. I can't stand bickering like that; I'd have to have it straightened out. But Ernie would taunt him, referring to him as *Ted Buh-zay* on the show and writing him into skits as a heavy. Baze struck back by taking away the cameraman who came out to shoot the Ghoulardi All-Stars. He could get away with it by saying the station couldn't afford it.

Ernie relied on that film. He'd start the show with nothing prepared, hoping something would happen, and make the film a whole segment. Very seldom did he see it ahead of time. He'd follow it on the monitor, make stuff up, and most of the time it was hilarious. It pulled viewers, too, because tremendous crowds came out to see the All-Stars. We outdrew the Cleveland Indians some nights.

After Baze took away the cameraman, Ernie spoke on the air to "all of you who came out to the game." He said he figured they'd each told somebody they were at the game, which meant thousands of people were hoping to see the highlights film—"but you're not going to see it because program director *Ted Buh-zay* said we can't do films anymore."

He played it up that the films were a public service. The games were all for charity, the people who came out were supporting the charity, and that we wouldn't draw big crowds anymore without the films. Charities would suffer. He just ate Baze alive. "It's out of my hands," he said. "We'll continue to do the games, but we won't be able to show them anymore. So if you have any complaints, here is his home phone number."

He showed it on a card. Baze really got harassed. He had to take his phone off the hook and change the number. The station manager told Baze to cool it. Ernie won.

FORGOTTEN GAMES AND A NEAR-MISS

The Ghoulardi All-Stars were going strong, and Ernie was booking so many games he forgot some of them.

I was going home one day and saw a charter bus parked in front of the station. Nobody parked a bus there unless we were doing something, so I went back inside and asked if we had a game. Oh, yeah, Ernie said—he forgot. None of the team had been notified. We had nobody. He sent me all over the station, and I was only able to grab three or four guys. "Don't worry," Ernie said. "It'll be all right."

Maybe half a dozen of us left for the game. Every time the bus stopped for a red light, Ernie would see somebody waiting at a bus stop and stick his head out. Inevitably, the guy waiting for the bus would yell, "Hey, Ghoulardi! How you doin'?" And Ernie would shout, "What are you doing tonight? You want to play ball? Come on!"

We picked up about fifteen guys that way, telling them we'd get them home later. They played in street clothes and said it was the most exciting night they had, playing in front of a large crowd for the Ghoulardi All-Stars. We got a couple of really good players we kept on the team from that. They all wanted to stay.

Ernie called me at the station another time for a basketball game he forgot. "You gotta come out to my house right away," he said, explaining the game was near where he lived. We'd meet everybody there. I arrived, and we jumped into the A.C. Ace. He had the top up because it was chilly. Because we were late, we were just flying along country roads. And it looked like we were going to get delayed because a train was coming, heading for a road crossing ahead of us where there were lights but no gate.

Right away, I knew. I said, "Ernie—don't try it, man." He didn't say anything. I looked over, and his expression was dead serious. There was still plenty of time to stop the car, but the train was getting close. The engineer could see us, and he was just laying on the whistle. I figured this was it. We were either going to make it or we weren't. I just shut up.

The tracks were up on a rise in the road. We hit them in the little A.C. Ace, went airborne, and the train roared by, so close I could feel it behind us. It was like a movie. I was so elated that we were OK; for a split second I didn't even realize we were up in the air. Then I knew we were going to hit. I put up my arms in front of my head and hit the dashboard hard. Ernie cranked his nose on the steering wheel and started to bleed. He should have had stitches. We made it to the game and played the whole thing in bandages, with blood all over. It was crazy.

After we beat the train and hit the ground and knew we had made it, Ernie was bleeding and I was emotionally spent. I couldn't talk. He lit up a smoke, took a big breath, and said, "I always wanted to do that."

Looking back now, that pretty much summarized the story of his life.

CHAPTER 7

THE FORTUNE COOKIE

TAKING IT ON THE CHIN

The great film director Billy Wilder came to town in the fall of 1965 to shoot the comedy *The Fortune Cookie*. It featured the first pairing of his favorite star, Jack Lemmon, with Walter Matthau. Lemmon plays a TV cameraman who gets run over by a player while shooting a Browns game, and Matthau plays his brother-in-law, a shyster lawyer who wants to ride the accident into big money.

Ernie told me they were looking for extras. I went down to the tryouts at the stadium. It was a thrill just seeing a big Hollywood production.

A big group of us lined up to be looked over. The guy doing the initial screening said we were going to be in the background, if we made it, and began asking us what we did. I told him I actually ran the parab mic during games, right there on the field. He said, "OK, you're in."

He cut the group in half. I was in the group on the field, and the rest would be part of the crowd in the stands. An assistant director, who could have been cast as a lisping, effeminate film snob, announced they were looking for someone to do a speaking part.

I wasn't saying a word. The idea of a speaking part scared me.

About twelve of us lined up. The A.D. came up to us and started asking more questions. The other guys rattled off their credits, puffing up backgrounds in little theater. When he came to me, I didn't say anything. I really didn't want a speaking part. I was already nervous about it, and I was happy just being there. The A.D., who never smiled, cut the group down to six, then three.

Finally it was down to me and another guy, who gave his credits

With Jack Lemmon (puffing a pipe) and some of TV8's Browns crew—Rolland "Hap" Hallas, Carl Szubski, and John Jackman—during a break in shooting of *The Fortune Cookie* at Municipal Stadium.

and experience. I still wasn't saying anything. The A.D. looked at me and said, "You—out."

I started to leave. As I walked past him, I said, "Was it something I said?" I thought he'd laugh. But he snapped, "We don't need any Kirk Douglas types in this movie."

GOING HOLLYWOOD

All of the movie's good scenes were not on screen.

One came when Ron Rich, the actor playing Boom Boom Jackson—the player who knocks down Lemmon—showed up before the shoot in what looked like false eyelashes and eye shadow. When it was time to start filming he came out in a sparkling clean uniform. It just didn't sit well with the real Browns in the scene. They grabbed him and said they'd have to dirty him up.

He was not what you'd call a real he-man type. "You can't do that!" he shrieked. They dragged him through the grass by his ankles and started piling on him. He was screaming, "Quit it, stop it!"

but smiling and laughing like hell, just having a great time.

One Sunday when they weren't shooting and the Browns were playing, Jack Lemmon came to the stadium to be a guest in Art Modell's booth, the wooden shed on a sling.

Modell was still drinking then; Lemmon hadn't yet stopped, and the booth was well stocked—at least with liquor. At halftime, Lemmon emerged to go up to a restroom, and he was plastered. He started to climb the vertical ladder to the stands. As soon as his head got to where the crowd in the upper deck could see him, they started to clap and cheer.

Lemmon took both hands off the ladder to wave and fell dead backwards. Dick Lorius, the big Channel 8 cameraman, was standing behind him. Dick grabbed him. If he hadn't, Lemmon would have been gone.

GETTING TO THE BIG SCREEN

Even though they didn't need any Kirk Douglas types, I still got a part in the movie. I'm a news photographer on the sidelines. When Jack Lemmon gets knocked down, I run over to take his picture before a Cleveland cop grabs me and pushes me away. In a two-page picture that ran in a movie magazine about that time, you can see me holding a camera behind Lemmon.

When *The Fortune Cookie* came out, in 1966, it had a one-day premiere showing in Cleveland, at a theater on the West Side. I was really excited. Not only was I on TV, now I was going to be on the big screen, too. I wanted it to be a special night, so I took June, my brother Paul, and his wife to the Stagecoach Inn in Brecksville. We'd have an early supper and then see the movie. I told them we'd have to watch the time because I was in the movie's very first scene, where Lemmon gets injured, and I didn't want to miss it.

There was a clock in the restaurant, and I saw we had plenty of time—even though the waitress told us they had some kind of problem in the kitchen, so it would take about twenty minutes to get served. We had a drink, talked, and got our food. Midway through the meal, I looked at the clock and realized it showed the same time it had before. It wasn't working, and it was stopped at about the.

time we arrived. I looked at my watch in alarm and said we had to fly. There was no time to finish eating.

We jumped in the car, and I drove like a maniac to the West Side. I ran to the box office and asked if the movie started. "It's just starting now," the woman at the window said. We dashed into the theater, looked up at the screen, and there was the ambulance pulling away from the stadium.

I was really bummed out and figured I'd have to wait until the movie went into general release in theaters. But I missed it again because it didn't have a long run. I figured it would be on television in a year or so. It was. But I had a personal appearance that night, and

My Kirk Douglas–type pose. I gave this photo to Hoolie as a tongue-in-cheek Christmas gift.

there were no tape machines back then. So I'd have to wait for the movie to reach the drive-in circuit. That came during a week we were on vacation on Kelleys Island.

Now I was really frustrated. Movie rentals were still years away. Then June called me at work and said it would be on the late show that night on TV. I came home and saw it was the movie after that— the late, late show. I had to double back at the station to work the next morning but figured I'd tough it out. I didn't make it. I woke up in front of the TV to see the end of the movie but missed the rest.

Finally, twenty years after the movie's release, it came out on video. I was thinking about having a party, but it was just as well that I didn't. I rented it and found it had been edited down. I was cut out.

People who saw it in theaters said they saw me in it. But I never did see it, and probably never will. I was left on the cutting-room floor.

CHAPTER 8

FROM GHOULI TO HOOLIE

ERNIE WINS WITH "PLACE" AND GOES

I got to be a part of TV history on the Ghoulardi show thanks to "Parma Place." It was a take-off on *Peyton Place*, the prime time soap opera, and only three characters appeared in it. Ernie and Gena Hallaman played a Parma couple named John and Janet, and I played "handsome, debonair, downstairs neighbor Jerry Kreegle."

It was outrageously funny, filled with white sock and pink flamingo jokes and all the funny Polish words and references I could work in. It became the talk of the town in a very short time, and it brought the sort of attention to Ghoulardi that the show enjoyed in its red-hot early days. Everybody in Parma loved it.

Almost everybody, anyway. Parma mayor James Day said it was a slur on the community, and he led a contingent to the station to complain. People took sides, and the controversy heated up. After thirteen weeks, in March 1966, "Parma Place" went off the air.

Ernie was ticked off, but he used the controversy on the air, talking about how chicken the station was. Because he was live, the station lived in mortal fear of him every week. But "Parma Place" turned out to be his last big shot.

By the summer of 1966, I could sense he was tiring of it. The ratings were down, if still good, and he was going through a hard time personally. He was going through a divorce, dating Edwina Gough, who became his second wife, and trying to keep the family together. His wife came down to the station with his clothes and threw them in the lobby.

Maybe that was the turning point. He decided to leave. He didn't give me any notice. It was out of the clear blue.

Tim Conway, who kept urging him to come out to Hollywood, set him up with a voiceover audition. It was rough for Ernie, and he told me afterward how ticked off he was about it. He was in his forties, and his great voice owned Cleveland, which was then the country's ninth-largest market. But in L.A., they didn't know who he was. So he had to sit in a lobby and wait to read for "some punk A.D." who wouldn't know if it was any good anyway. It bummed him out. But Ernie won the audition.

Handsome, debonair, downstairs neighbor Jerry Kreegle makes a gift of white socks to slicker-clad John (Ernie Anderson) and Janet (Gena Hallaman) in a 1966 episode of "Parma Place."

Channel 8 was still making money on Ghoulardi, so they wanted him to try recording shows to keep it going, even after he left. He came back every few weeks to do two or three weeks of shows. But he wasn't up on things happening in Cleveland, and that was half the show. It wasn't current, it wasn't the same, and anyone could tell. Ghoulardi ended officially in November 1966.

A SIDEKICK BECOMES A PARTNER

A lot of big name disc jockeys tried out when the station had auditions for a replacement. Most of them tried to copy the Ghoulardi model, which was a mistake. Ernie was original. They looked like copies.

Bob Wells wanted the show, too. He was an actor who did a lot of community theater, and he was looking for more to do at the station. Ted Baze, the program director, had hired him as Hoolihan the Weatherman to go up against Channel 3's Wally Kinnan the Weatherman. Then Channel 8 got Dick Goddard, who wanted to come back to Cleveland after a short time in Philadelphia, and

Ernie, me, and and Bob Wells, "Hoolihan the Weatherman" during a photo shoot for *City Camera*.

Hoolihan was moved to the noon news and weekends. He understood, but he didn't like it. He didn't like being Hoolihan either, and he still doesn't like it because his real name is Bob Wells and nobody knew it.

Bob—Hoolie—knew I'd been helping Ernie, and he asked me to help with his audition. I told him not to copy what Ernie did, and I wrote three or four skits that we recorded. He introduced them in the old Ghoulardi format, with a light bulb under his face putting him in a circle of light.

I thought it would be great if he won. I'd still be on TV, but as a definite sidekick without the responsibility or pressure Ernie had. When Hoolie did win the audition, I was elated. But the station said they wanted us to be co-hosts, and I thought: *Wrong.* No way could I do that. I'm nervous on live TV, and I didn't speak well, especially next to a pro like Hoolie. But I found out years later that Ernie had a talk with Ken Bagwell before he left and told him they had to find a way to get me on the air. And Hoolie had won because of the skits. So we were partners.

The first thing I told Hoolie was to take the lead: "Don't think if we're partners that you can't go ahead and jump in. Really." I meant it off-camera as well as on. But he was busy as an announcer and weatherman, had outside voiceover sessions, and knew I helped Ernie. So he didn't really do much for the show. The trouble was, Ernie had done a lot. He'd think of bits and dig up material. I helped, but I wasn't running the whole show. Now I had to. And I had to create something.

THE ODDER COUPLE

Hoolihan & Big Chuck went on for the first time on December 16, 1966, running a movie and a promo we made. It was live TV, and I was terribly nervous, stammering and stuttering. I figured my family would be embarrassed. Sitting next to Bobby made me seem even worse. I really felt inept.

Our real show debuted a week later, on December 23. I was searching for a format for us and knew you couldn't have two guys side-by-side with light bulbs under their faces. I thought of us being roommates in an apartment, like *The Odd Couple*. It was the worst idea I ever had. It seemed even worse when Hoolie called me "roomie." I never told him, but I really hated that.

Ernie came back a lot to visit in those days, and I asked him to do a live walk-on. I outlined a bit where he'd ring the doorbell and apologize for accidentally backing over our pink flamingo while turning around in the driveway. I gave him and Hoolie their lines in a run-through. I'd given Hoolie maybe one line, and he said, "Is that it? All I have is this?"

Ernie said, "And don't blow it!"

They didn't like each other. They both had strong personalities. It was easy to like or dislike either one of them.

Ernie didn't say anything negative, but having him there made me more embarrassed about the format. We even started getting calls about it, that Hoolihan and Big Chuck were "fags." It only lasted about a month before I changed the format to both of us sitting behind a desk—a poor man's *Tonight Show* without any guests. My only consolation was knowing the show wasn't going to make it. I didn't think we'd last thirteen weeks, and my ordeal would end. I shut up and leaned on Hoolie when I started to stammer and choke. Hoolie has the incredible ability to talk for several minutes without really saying anything. If you weren't paying close attention you'd swear he was saying something, but you couldn't remember what it was later. He was calm and collected. I'd shut up and he'd run with it. He was a pro's pro.

GUTS IT, BABY, GUTS IT

It got easier as the weeks went by. Then we had our first national TV star as a guest: Imogene Coca. I was a huge fan from when she was on *Your Show of Shows* with Sid Caesar. I was so nervous I couldn't sleep. Next to her on live TV, I thought I was really going to look like a schmoe.

She was very likeable and sort of shy, which knocked me out because of all the goofy parts she played. I started explaining the little skit we planned, and she seemed nervous. She said she hoped she didn't forget her lines. It struck me that someone I watched and admired was more nervous than I was. How could that be? She had an elderly traveling companion who took me aside and told me Imogene was very shy and nervous; to help her be comfortable I had to make sure she knew exactly what she was going to do.

I said, "Would she like to have cue cards?" Her friend said, "That would be wonderful!" So I frantically made cue cards and found myself telling Coca, "This'll be easy. There's nothing to it." And I couldn't believe how calm that made me.

It made me think of a letter I just got from Ernie, with everything he wanted to tell me:

"Chuckie sweets: I hope the show is going well for you. Hang in there and do it your way as often as you can. Remember if they knew how to do it they

Imogene Coca (left) was very shy, despite all the goofy roles she played.

would be doing it. The very people who are telling you how to do it have tried themselves and failed in the past. If you fail you want it to be because your way was wrong. You already know their way is wrong. They have proved it. Guts it, baby, guts it. Say hello to anybody I know. Tell them I'll be around sometime this summer. Lov from the tinsel city."

I kept the letter in my briefcase. Every time I'd get in a bind, I'd take it out and read it. It got me through. After getting it, I began to take control. I was going to do it my way—if it fails, that's it, but I stopped worrying about it.

FUNNY THINGS HAPPEN

Andy Griffith was one of our first guests after Imogene Coca, and he was really easy to work with. I wrote a skit saying we were interviewing "new and upcoming talent for possible use in big-time television," and that he was the first candidate. Hoolie told him he'd need to change his "schlock name" and asked if he had any show-biz contacts because "it's not really what you know; it's who you know." Andy said he knew Tennessee Ernie Ford, Don Knotts, and, oh yeah, Jack Schneider, the president of CBS—"Does that help?"

Pat Paulsen was another early guest. He was staying nearby at Swingos, and he stayed for the whole live show. He asked what we did at the close, and we told him we did the "PJ Party" in night-shirts and pajamas. "All right," he said, "I'll think of something to do." He came out in his boxer shorts. That's a good guest.

I was writing and producing much of the live show's content and all of the skits. Hoolie was easy to write for, and that helped a lot. He could do any character I could think of, and any accent. He was a very talented comic actor, probably the most versatile talent in the history of our show. I started to think we could make it. I took care of everything for TV, and Hoolie took care of all the *Hoolihan & Big Chuck* business off the show, such as booking personal appearances—much the way Li'l John did later, for twenty-eight years.

Doing personal appearances is harder than playing ball in front of a crowd. Our first one was emceeing an amateur show in a sold-out theater. Hoolie was used to performing, but for me the anticipation was unbearable. It made the book reports I dreaded in high school seem like a walk in the park.

Maybe I shouldn't have worried. One of the acts was a juggler who had an assistant in a short dress and low-cut top. She fetched his props but kept looking backstage, flirting with me and Hoolie, looking more at us than at him. His big finish was twirling batons that she lighted on fire. He was standing on one leg doing this, spinning a hula hoop around his waist and another one on the leg he wasn't hopping on, and tossing the batons in the air. Then he dropped one. She wasn't watching. The baton rolled toward him and rested under his hopping foot. Flames went up his leg. You could smell hair burning. The guy finished and raced backstage, smoking in every way, swearing at the assistant and really chewing her ass out—all in a backstage whisper.

This was followed by our first parade, in Lorain County. We were supposed to ride on a float, but it was broken, so they told us to ride with Santa. He was on a long float, seated in a chair on a riser at the back of a flatbed trailer. Hoolie and I were up front. We started waving and got to where a bunch of kids were waiting. They ran up to the float, reached to shake our hands, and reached up to Santa. He was drunk. He started swearing, "Get the (bleep) out of here, you (bleeps)!" Good Jesus, this was Santa Claus dropping F-bombs, man! Hoolie and I jumped off the trailer and walked.

I wondered what I'd gotten into.

CHAPTER 9

ROWDY AND THE KID

POOP PATROL AND JUNK IN THE TRUNK

We were filling awfully big shoes. For years after we started, people would look at us and say, "Hey, there are those two guys from the Ghoulardi show." A lot of them called me Hoolihan.

You can tell when people recognize you. I'd stop on the way home almost every Friday night at a little pizza shop in North Royalton. The woman at the counter was really shy. She looked down and never said a word. She'd smile but never talked. This went on for about a year. Finally she was getting over me coming in and said, "Do you know who you look like?"

I said, "Well, that's who I am."

She gasped. "You're Kirk Douglas?"

But I really was starting to get recognized. Partly thanks to our family dog, I found that this was not always a good thing.

We got the dog in 1962, after I bought our first home. It was a typical six-room bungalow on a tiny lot in Parma, but it was home—and for me, no home is complete without a dog. I let it be known at TV8 that I was looking for a puppy. One that wouldn't get too large. In a few weeks, Ernie called me and said, "I have a puppy for you."

"Oh, great," I said. "What kind is it?"

"It's a Rhodesian ridgeback," he said.

I'd never heard of them.

"No one has," he said. "They're a very rare and beautiful breed of dog. They're reddish-brown hounds with very short hair, much like my Weimaraners."

"Whoa," I said. "Wait a minute. Your Weimaraners are big dogs. How big will this puppy get?"

My dog Rowdy won fame playing King the Wonder Dog, around the time we moved to Parma.

Ernie paused and said, "They're a very sound dog."

I had never heard the word "sound" used to describe anything before. Ernie was from the East Coast, and I thought perhaps this was some kind of nautical New England expression. But to me, "sound" sounded like it could mean "big." I reminded him my home was a small Parma bungalow on a tiny lot, and I asked him, "How big is a 'sound' dog?"

He got a little upset and said, "Don't worry about it—trust me!"

When our puppy was five months old, he weighed eighty-five pounds. His name was Rowdy. When Rowdy matured, about two years later, he was the most handsome 120-pound dog you ever saw, and we loved him dearly.

We lived near State Road Park in Parma, and at least once every day I walked him to the park and let him run through the woods to get his exercise and do his "business." When I wasn't home, June let Rowdy out in the backyard for "business." I assigned my sons Mike and Mark responsibility for this backyard business and gave it an exciting name: Poop Patrol. They would patrol the backyard for poop and put it in a bucket. When I took Rowdy to run in the park, I would bring the bucket to empty into the woods, where it would biodegrade. Life was good. It was possible to have a big dog and live in a small home in Parma. My family and I were in total harmony with nature.

Having a ridgeback was special. When John Morrow, the center with the Browns, heard I had one, he told me he bred them, and came over to the house to see the dog. June and I had dinner a few times with him and his wife from that connection, and I still have the recipe for Swedish stew his wife made with beer.

I was still a full-time engineer at TV8 after *Hoolihan & Big Chuck* started, and being relatively low on the seniority list, was still rotating all three work shifts. Early one winter night, I was working the four-to-midnight shift, "switching" the six and eleven o'clock news shows, and heard Dick Goddard predict we were in for a stretch of frequent snow. As usual, he was right. It snowed every day for a week.

I moved to the midnight to 8 a.m. shift, and my sons informed me at suppertime one evening that Poop Patrol had been postponed for several days because of the snow. I told them not to worry; it was just a temporary problem. But the snow kept falling.

Then Goddard gave us a new weather term to add to our vocabulary: *February Thaw.* He predicted unusually high temperatures for perhaps a week. But he also warned us not to think spring was here because we would return to our cold Cleveland winter after the thaw. That morning, as I drove home from the station at about 8:30 a.m., the air was noticeably warm, the sun was out, and birds were singing. Once again, Dick was right on target.

I ate breakfast and went to bed. When I got up about suppertime, my sons told me that the snow in the street had melted and asked if we could throw the football around, before it got dark. We did. It was a pleasant preview of things to come. My sons did their homework, watched a little TV, and went to bed. I took Rowdy for his walk, watched a little TV with my wife, made my lunch, and went to work. As I drove home from TV8 the next morning, it was even warmer, almost seventy degrees. The birds were really singing, the Parma streets were filled with the sounds of running water in the sewers, I thought, *more football in the street after school!* I went to sleep with a smile on my face.

My wife woke me up about 2:30 in the afternoon. I knew something was wrong. She said, "We have a big problem. You won't believe our backyard!" I looked out the back window, and what to my wondering eyes should appear? At least one big pile of poop in every square foot of our backyard. The snow had just about all melted, and it was still getting warmer. My wife was in a panic. "You'd better get that cleaned up before the neighbors see it," she said. "Hurry! Before it starts to smell!"

I hurried to get dressed. In minutes I was in the backyard, shovel in hand. I got a big, sturdy cardboard box from the garage and began filling it with poop. When my kids came home from school, I told them to change clothes and help me—"No one eats supper until we're done." We finished the gruesome job about two hours later, and the big cardboard box was filled to the top.

My sons went in to clean up for supper. I stood there, looking at the box and wondering, *What the hell am I going to do with this?* I couldn't leave it for the rubbish men. They'd kill me. I thought of flushing it down the sewer with a hose, but there was too much for that. The box was so heavy I could barely lift it. So I decided to put the box, a shovel, and a flashlight in the trunk of my car. I would leave for work an hour early, take the box into the woods of State Road Park, scatter the poop over a large area, chop up the box with the shovel, go to work, and no one would be the wiser.

About 10 p.m., my family went to bed, and I set out on my mission. The sky was overcast and the park was unusually dark. It was perfect. Or so I thought. As I drove slowly through the park, I passed a squad car with two of Parma's finest eyeing me suspiciously. They turned around and began to follow me. *Damn,* I thought. *No way can I do it now.*

I left the park. The police car stayed at the park entrance. I decided not to risk another pass and went to work.

Late that night, it got very cold and started to snow. Goddard was right again. As I was leaving the station at 8 a.m., morning news bulletins were warning of hazardous driving conditions. It took me a while to get home. It snowed all day and all evening. I had to shovel the drive that night to get out to go to work. It snowed frequently for the next several weeks. I forgot about the box in my trunk.

Then the weather really warmed up, and the snow melted rapidly. It was a Saturday morning, I had the day off, and June asked me to do the grocery shopping. I drove to the Food Town at Snow and Broadview roads and bought four bags of groceries.

The bag boy recognized me. I never saw such a look of admiration on anyone's face in my life. He couldn't tell me enough about how much he enjoyed watching me on TV, and how he and his friends never missed the Friday night show. He helped me carry the bags to my car and asked for my autograph. I said, "OK, but let me put the bags in my trunk first." I fumbled with the two bags I was carrying and got my car keys out of my pocket. Stooping and hunched over, I opened the trunk.

As the trunk lid opened fully, a piercing odor stung my nose. I jerked back, my head hit the trunk lid, and my eyes began to water. Confronting me was the Mother of all Poop Piles. The cardboard box had disintegrated, every square inch of the bottom of the trunk was covered with dog poop, and there, in the middle, was a shovel handle sticking out.

The bag boy tried to muffle a gagging cough. His look of admiration for his hero, Big Chuck, turned to the frightened stare of someone looking at Hannibal Lecter! He put the bags on the ground and quickly stepped backward.

"Wait!" I shouted. "I can explain."

"Ugh—that's . . . that's all right," he said, still walking backward.

I started walking toward him. "Wait," I said again. "Uh, here's your tip."

"No, that's OK," he said, breaking into a sideways run.

At first I wanted to run after him, but I thought that would really freak him out. As I stood there watching him run back into the store, I knew that somehow I must explain this incident to him or it would always trouble me, as I wondered what he must think of his hero, Big Chuck, who has a poop fetish.

I went back to the store a few times over the next couple weeks hoping to run into him, but I never did. To this day I sometimes think of this incident. And I wonder if, when he sees me on TV, he thinks of it, too.

I've been living in Hinckley for almost forty years now. I have an acre of lawn, and I still have a big ridgeback—Buddy, my fifth one. I still pick up dog poop, but I don't throw it into the woods anymore. I have a "Doggie Septic System." I figure the bag boy must be at least fifty years old now. I sure hope that somehow he reads this, or hears about it, and will no longer wonder if Big Chuck is riding around Parma with a trunk full.

THE COMING OF THE KIELBASY KID

The woods of State Road Park were good for more things than Poop Patrol. We often used them as a shooting location for skits after starting "The Kielbasy Kid."

I thought of doing it because my hero, Ernie Kovacs, had a segment called the Kapusta Kid in Outer Space. *Kapusta* means cabbage in Polish, and that knocked me out because you never heard ethnic things on a network show in those days. The Kielbasy Kid was an homage to that, and I decided to make him a Western hero. Hoolie said I looked the part. Instead of a gun, I carried a kielbasy in a holster. Using it instead of a gun must have been the gag in the first twenty episodes.

I thought the Kid should have a sidekick, like the Lone Ranger, so I came up with the faithful Indian companion Kishka. That was originally going to be Joe Dannery, the booth announcer and radio newsman who became my good friend and next-door neighbor in Hinckley. But the night before we were going to do the first skit, when I was at

I broke my ankle playing basketball after being pushed by a priest. Needing a good reason for the Kielbasy Kid to have a cast, I had him shot with an arrow.

The Kielbasy Kid, in my stable in Hinckley. The horse, White Lightning, was given to me live on-air at midnight by Soul Man and Bill Turner. We used the horse in many sketches.

home writing it, the news came on. One of the stories said a TV8 personality had been in a big car crash. It was Joe, and he was seriously hurt. He'd be hospitalized for weeks.

We were set up to shoot the next day. This was one of the times when the show had to go on. I'd gotten to know a musician, Tony Carmen, and knew he was pretty funny. I asked if he wanted to do it. He did. With a headband and a feather, we had our Kishka, and Tony became one of the show's pioneers.

Hoolie played Marshal Dullen and other characters, and the episodes were set up like minishows. The opening, shot at Joe Dannery's place in Hinckley, showed the Kid riding a horse backward. The close showed him struggling to climb onto the horse, but tumbling all the way over it onto the ground.

The Kielbasy Kid's archenemy was Big Stash. That was Russ

Tony Carmen became one of the first characters on *Hoolihan & Big Chuck* when he played Kishka, the Kielbasy Kid's faithful companion, in 1967.

Cormier. He had called one day and said, "I'm six-foot-seven, I saw your All-Star footage, and I'd like to play on your team." Just like that, he joined the basketball All-Stars. Russ is a Canadian Indian, a real character, and we're close friends to this day. He'd come to games wearing his big Indian hat and a long-haired wig, so I thought to use him in a skit.

We introduced him with the Kielbasy Kid and Kishka in a saloon. Kishka says, "We gotta get out of town! I hear Big Stash is coming!" The Kid says, "So what? I'm pretty big myself." Kishka says, "No, Big Stash is so big he uses manhole covers for tiddlywinks! He's big and he's tough!" Hoolie is the bartender, and he says, "I hear Big Stash coming, man." Kishka runs out, and Stash walks in. He was wearing boots, adding to his height, and we shot the scene so he looked even bigger. He busts the table and says, "Gimme some whiskey!" I start pouring him drinks, giving him whatever he wants. He breaks more stuff, and I ask him if he wants to have another drink. He says, "I would if I could, Kid, but I heard Big Stash is coming."

KING THE WONDER DOG

The best Kielbasy Kid skit I ever did, and by far the best skit we did to that point, was one we shot with Rowdy at State Road Park: King the Wonder Dog. I got the name from Yukon King, the husky on *Sergeant Preston of the Yukon,* a radio show when I was a kid.

In the skit, the Kielbasy Kid is trapped under a fallen tree in the snow, and King races to the rescue. Or so it appears. King—Rowdy—tears off through the snow while the Kid struggles in pain. Finally, King comes into view. The Kid sits up, smiling in pride and relief. But King doesn't even break stride. He bounds onto, over, and past the Kid, and keeps going. The Kid sits up with a paw print on his face.

It was an immediate hit with viewers and became one of our most requested skits. The Kielbasy Kid became a staple of the show. Chill Wills guest-starred in one skit, and Buddy Ebsen was in another as the Kid's Uncle Jed.

We were starting to make a mark, and it looked like *Hoolihan & Big Chuck* might make a run of it.

Buddy Ebsen was starring on *The Beverly Hillbillies* when he played Uncle Jed in a Kielbasy Kid sketch. Hoolie played a lumber salesman, and Jed said he wanted some some two-by-fours. Hoolie asked, "How long?" Jed said, "A lo-o-ong time."

THE SHORT GOODBYE

Then we hit trouble. Station manager Chuck Bergeson did not like us, and he especially did not like Hoolihan. Even though we were beating Johnny Carson in the ratings—and program director Ted Baze thought we were the only local show in the country doing that—Bergeson would slam us around the station. In the fall of 1968, Baze told Hoolie and me that he had good news and bad news.

The bad news: "You're going to have to be off the night show." The good news? "We're going to put you on Saturday afternoons."

We wondered if CBS had come up with its own late-night show. No, Ted said—it was Bergeson. The show was working. Bergeson couldn't get rid of us, but he would move us and we'd die. What could I do? I figured the show would end someday anyway. I'd be an engineer. That was my real job.

We decided to go out in style by having an awards show. We set up tables in the studio for an audience and nominees. Ralph Gertz, a station projectionist who was a master of makeup and a big contributor to the show, played a waiter who kept running

I'm holding the first local Emmy ever presented in Cleveland, for the sketch "King the Wonder Dog" in 1969, while director of photography Cook Goodwin shows his award.

through, carrying a tray. Hoolie and I announced that the award for best editing went to Bob Soinski, for "King the Wonder Dog." Bob came up to accept and collided with Ralph. Next came the award for cinematography, which went to Cook Goodwin. He wasn't there, so Bob accepted for him—and collided again with Gertz and his tray. They were hilarious. Every time Bob went to accept an award, Ralph got knocked over. At the end of the show, we ran the credits on a roll of toilet paper.

We were inundated with mail after that, and Bergeson was blasted in the paper for moving us. He came in and accused us of orchestrating a campaign.

"You can tell them to stop writing now," he said. "You're going back to Friday nights."

"King the Wonder Dog" still had legs, too. My coworkers at the station said I should enter it when the Cleveland chapter of the National Academy of Television Arts & Sciences presented its first local Emmy awards in 1969. I thought a skit from a movie show could never win because there was no category for it, and most awards were for news. I had to enter for "outstanding achievement in entertainment," the biggest and toughest category—and was elated when I was notified the skit was nominated as a finalist.

We made a big to-do out of it. As they say, just being nominated is an honor. My wife and I got dressed up for the event, and I got really nervous. What if we *did* win? I'd never seen an Emmy show. Would I have to go up to the stage? Make a speech? I figured I'd watch what other people did, just in case, but never got the chance.

"Entertainment" was the first category as well as the first Emmy ever presented in Cleveland. "King" won. I just shook hands with everyone and said thanks. It was quite a night.

WHY YOU CAN'T REST ON YOUR LAURELS

I didn't get many phone calls, but I got one from a guy who wanted to talk to Chuck. He was really nice.

"Chuck, man, I watch you every week, never miss your show."

I said, "Thanks a lot!"

He said, "You're pretty tall, aren't you? You know what I like is when you run and jump on your horse." I figured he meant the Kielbasy Kid, where I jump and miss. He kept talking. "Is Mark really your son?" I didn't recall that I mentioned him on the air, but I said yeah, I have a son named Mark. I was really enjoying the call.

"I really like when you beat up the bad guys," he said. "Or when you walk down the street and shoot the hell out of the outlaws."

I said I really don't shoot anybody; I use the kielbasy. No, he said, "You shoot the hell out of them!" I said no, I use my kielbasy.

He paused and said, "Is this Chuck Connors?"

Big Stash, Russ Cormier, started playing on the All-Stars in the early 1970s. After United Airlines transferred him to Chicago, he flew back weekly for games.

CHAPTER 10

BUILDING THE LAUGHS

OUTRAGEOUS SKITS BECOME THE STAPLE

People finally stopped referring to Hoolie and me as two guys from the Ghoulardi show. Starting with our filmed opening— "From the heart of Playhouse Square in downtown Cleveland, from high atop the Television 8 building, it's the *Hoolihan & Big Chuck Show*"—we had our own identity. The opening, by the way, was something I took from old radio shows, where announcers always seemed to be saying that some orchestra was playing in a "beautiful" ballroom from "high atop" some hotel, something few people remember now. I always liked that.

I really knew we made it when we were doing a skit where I needed to shoot into a building being torn down. I asked permission to shoot at the Sterling Lindner Davis department store. We had shot one of our early skits there in Santa's Crystal Palace, in what turned out to be the store's final holiday season. This time the construction workers told me to come around back and ride up the freight elevator. Spray-painted in the elevator were the words *Hoolihan is a fag.*

"Man, we're in graffiti now," I said. "That's the biggest compliment." I'd hear about people talking about us at parties. You know you're starting to make it when people are making up stories using your name–"Chuck's gay" or "He's a Jew, you know."

We were getting famous for doing outrageous skits of all kinds. Tim Conway would still come back to town when he couldn't stand another smoggy, sunny day in California, and he'd do walk-ons. He'd put on a headset, walk behind us on camera, and just walk off.

Conway, still returning frequently to Cleveland, would just walk on the set of the live *Hoolihan & Big Chuck Show*. He sometimes donned a headset. This time he has the mic on his nose.

Gene Hickerson, the Hall of Fame guard from the Browns, loved our show. When we were still live, he would come to the station every so often and do a walk-on. Everybody knew him. Sometimes he was on and we didn't even know it. Once he showed up in a three-piece suit, carrying a map, and cut in to ask us where Cleveland Stadium was.

Our first animation was a skit with Hoolie reading the newspaper and being annoyed by a fly. After he sprays it with insecticide, the fly sounds like a plane crashing, and it looks like it's going down in flames. The capper is that a small parachute opens, as if the fly had a pilot escaping.

I didn't know anything about animation, and we didn't have computer-generated effects. We did it the same way we superimposed names on news stories or put Ghoulardi into movies. I cut

King the Wonder Dog in front of the news desk. I created Hoolie's "Readings by Robert" in homage to TV legend Ernie Kovacs.

the fly out of white paper, moved it on a black background, and photographer Bob Begani shot it, frame-by-frame, with a hand-held Bell & Howell news camera. For the chute to open, I made a hole in the card and stuck in a Kleenex tissue with strings attached. When I pulled the tissue through the hole, it looked like it was popping open. I used powdered sugar for the smoke and flames.

I was inspired especially by Ernie Kovacs, who was very inventive in his use of television. So Hoolie's "Readings by Robert," like the Kielbasy Kid, were an homage to one of Ernie's characters, Percy Dovetonsils. I like viewer participation, so we'd have them send in stories or poems for the readings. We never got any flak about the limp-wristed, lisping Robert. I think that was because no harm was intended, the character was off-the-wall, and because I made fun of everybody, especially myself.

BUT ALL SERIOUSNESS ASIDE . . .

From day one, we were making music videos. I was really into that. One of the first was also the first serious thing we did on the show, a video with Dion's "Abraham, Martin and John." It was something I personally wanted to do.

I was nervous as hell about running it because I'd have to introduce it. We were live, which didn't bother Hoolie at all, and normally I could just shut up and let him talk. For this, I wrote a little intro. It said that while I was always thinking of comedy skits, I really wanted to do this serious thing because it was important to me. I asked viewers to please bear with me. We didn't have a good teleprompter, so I memorized it.

The song has a twenty-second lead-in before Dion's vocal, and the first few seconds of the video have an American flag waving. I told Bill Turner, the director, that he should just dissolve to the video if I started to stammer. I told everybody. I didn't want anything to go wrong.

The eleven p.m. news ended, we went into the opening of the show, and Bill came out of the control room into the studio. I had asked him to open with a two-shot of Hoolie and me. I looked at the monitor, heard the music start, and began my intro. Bill, standing next to the camera, dropped his pants and started waving around. I couldn't believe it. He's a real prankster.

I put my head down, put my hand to my face, and swallowed a laugh. Hoolie pressed his lips together, hard, and made a whimpering sound in the back of his throat, trying to cover his laugh. *Boom*, the control room went to the video.

As it turned out, people thought I got choked up and couldn't finish. They wrote letters: "What a beautiful piece. We felt like you did. It's nice to see someone that emotional!"

FLYING HIGH WITH MUSIC VIDEOS

I loved a lot of sixties music. It was a romantic period. I wanted to make a video for the song "Up, Up and Away." The only visual I could think of was a guy who used to sell balloons on the street downtown. What if a kid was pointing at the balloons, and then got a bunch to hold?

We used Bill Turner's kid and got a dummy to match him in silhouette. We showed the kid taking the balloons, showed the balloons going up, cut back to the kid, and then pulled him up out of the shot with a rope. When you saw the bunch of balloons again, the dummy was hanging onto it, looking just like him.

We had a big bunch of balloons, but I thought: *Let's make it bigger*. We had no idea where they were going to go, so we attached a note asking whoever found them to come to Channel 8. They'd win something just for telling us where the balloons landed.

As soon as we let the bunch go, Hoolie said, "You know, you've got to be careful. You don't want it to go around the airport." I said not to worry, the wind wasn't blowing that way. The balloons went straight up, next to the Hanna Building, and really looked good—so good that people were running to the windows in shock. Instead of laughing, they were terrified for this kid they thought was being carried away. We did get flak for that because some people called the station to complain we were scaring the hell out of them. Then, scaring us, the balloons headed straight for Hopkins Airport—with the note saying who was responsible. But they ended up way out east, past Chardon, but still in our viewing area.

We did a video for "Gitarzan," a Ray Stevens novelty song. Hoolie beat a conga drum, and I portrayed Gitarzan by swinging from a rope wearing an animal skin. Tony Carmen followed, in an animal skin and longer wig, as Jane. He swung into me with his legs wide open and got nailed right in the crotch. I don't know if he laughed or groaned louder, but it was amazing he could finish the skit.

When the movie *Deliverance* came out, I did two take-offs of "Dueling Banjos"—"Dueling Accordions," which won an Emmy, and "Dueling Tubas." And from the earliest days we used film of famous people, editing ourselves in to make it look like they were doing skits with us. We had some old black-and-white news footage of Richard Nixon campaigning in a pea coat, pumping gas at a gas station, and looking into the camera. With Bob Soinski's help, and me in a pea coat, we did a thing where Hoolie drove up, and Nixon gassed him up.

When *Dead Men Don't Wear Plaid* came out in 1982, Hollywood promoted how clever it was to have Steve Martin interacting with stars of famous movies through editing. People in Cleveland said, "Hell, I remember you and Hoolihan did that in the '60s."

YOU THAT MAN THAT PLAY ON TV?

When we first started the show, I was really under stress and inhibited. I didn't speak well, especially next to a pro like Hoolie, and I tried to be what I wasn't. To this day, I'd rather not do something in front of a live audience. I'm not good at it. Ernie said, "Just lay back, let Hoolie go, get your zinger in once in a while." As time went by, I started becoming popular as the local blue-collar kid who made good. It struck me that people liked me for what I was, which was a huge relief. I didn't have to talk like Hoolie did. I didn't have to change. After I realized this, things were a lot easier for me.

When I first started with Hoolie, we did a lot of family things with kids' jokes. Kids will laugh at anything. Then we were at a dinner of all adults, which intimidated the hell out of me. I thought I had to change and be more adult. I tried to do something that I'm not and be a wise guy. It was in Orrville, the home of Smucker's, and I said, "Everybody's proud of that. But I was talking to a guy who said, as popular as Smucker's is, they still wanted a more homey name. They might call it Mother Smucker's." The audience didn't laugh, didn't boo, didn't respond. They froze. I never forgot that and never tried anything like it again. It was a good lesson. I didn't like being a wise guy and I wasn't after that. It could be right for other guys, but not for me.

I was nervous the first few years about being recognized. Now I expected it and would be paranoid if no one recognized me. It was a 180-degree turnaround from when I started. I'd walk with my head down. I remembered how Ernie was. He sure wasn't shy, but he didn't want to be recognized. Maybe that's why he'd walk with me.

It seemed to happen at once. I was pumping gas one day and noticed a woman at the next pump looking at me. I said, "How you doing?"

She said, "You that man that play on TV? You be Big Chuck?"

Yeah, I am, I said.

"No you isn't," she said.

"OK, I'm not," I told her, laughing.

She said, "Yes you is!"

For forty-seven years I took Interstate 77 to work, passing through my old Fleet Avenue neighborhood. I had just passed it one day when a cop pulled me over. I wasn't speeding, and I watched him walking up in the rearview mirror. When he got to the car, he stood right against it and didn't bend down. I was talking to his chest. It felt like a scene in *Magnum Force,* the Clint Eastwood movie.

"I just came back from a call in your old neighborhood," he said. He either recognized me going by or knew the car. "Somebody found a body under a bed. We had to run a check on the body."

Oh no, I thought. *What if it's someone I know?*

"We found out it was the hide-and-seek champion from Poland," the officer said.

There was a two-second pause before I got it. I busted out laughing.

"Take it easy, Kielbasy," he said, and he walked back to his cruiser. Never bent down. Perfect delivery.

I was waved over at a police roadblock another time where they were doing spot checks on cars. I rolled the window down as the cop walked up. He looked and said, "Get out of here, Kielbasy."

Maybe a dozen times I pulled up behind somebody at a light, and they recognized me in the rearview mirror, turned around, and waved. I can't even make people out in my rearview.

One guy pulled up beside me at a stoplight, looking straight ahead. He was picking his nose, really had his finger jammed up there, and then looked at me. I got embarrassed that he was going to be embarrassed. We pulled away, got to the next light, and he looked at me. I looked at him. He popped his finger in his mouth, like he was eating what he snagged, and imitated our laugh. "Ha-haaaah!"

YOU'D KNOW THE LAUGH ANYWHERE

The laugh at the end of skits—that high-pitched "Ha-haaaah!"—was as much a part of our show as anything. It was unique to us, and it became a real Cleveland thing.

Ninety percent of it is Jay Lawrence's laugh. Jay was a friend of Ernie Anderson's who was a disc jockey on KYW and WKYC and later WBBG. His engineer worked as a replacement at Channel 8, and he had a tape of Jay cracking himself up on the air.

The original recording had a gap in it, a long pause while he caught his breath. I tried editing it out, but it didn't sound right; it sounded edited. So I found another laugh, short and goofy, from an old commercial and tried inserting it in the gap. I guess you could say it's in the same key because it sounded like one continuous laugh. I told everyone I would use this laugh "stinger" until I found something better. Never did.

Our very early skits didn't have the laugh. One time I showed some of them to an audience and discovered that if the laugh wasn't there, they didn't laugh. With the laugh added, they did. It's like they were groomed or conditioned by us over the years: Wait for the laugh, and you know the skit's over. If you didn't hear the laugh, there might be more coming.

God bless Jay Lawrence, now retired in California.

CHAPTER 11

TRIBE FEVER

THE HAWK AND MCDOWELL

I was getting to be buddies with some of the Cleveland Indians about this time because I was still doing the games—even though it was getting awkward because people would recognize me as Big Chuck.

Sam McDowell and Ken Harrelson ("The Hawk") were big fans, and I really liked those two guys. They were real characters, and there'd be a big buzz whenever I used them on the show. Both of them did "New Talent Time." Hawk did a chicken imitation, the best I'd even seen. He'd stick his neck out, put his nose in profile, and go walking and picking with his arms flapping behind him. Mc-Dowell played an old-time pitcher like you'd see on a newsreel—winding up and throwing with a real jerky motion, like on a piece of old film, except he did it in real time.

They also teamed up to do Abbott & Costello's "Who's on First?" routine as a skit for the show. It was before a game at the stadium. I was directing, and McDowell was pitching that night. They came in a little early, and I had everything on cue cards for them to read. It took forever, one mistake after another. They would start laughing and swearing. I was trying desperately to get it done.

McDowell said to Cy Buynak, the clubhouse manager, "Get us some beer."

"You're pitching tonight," said Cy.

McDowell said, "Get your ass out of here. Get us some beer." He and Hawk were both chugging, and they were smoking like crazy. It got to be almost batting practice time, and we were still trying to finish the thing. We made it. McDowell had eight or nine beers,

Hawk had four or five, and McDowell won that night, 2-1. He was awesome, a sure Hall of Famer, but alcohol got in the way.

I got to know Harrelson by directing a show he did on Channel 8, *Hawk's Nest*. We looked a lot alike, except for my chin and his nose, and we were exactly the same size, which set up several skits. In the first thing we ever did, Hoolie plays a plastic surgeon with a German accent, and Hawk comes in with his uniform on to get his beak nose fixed. Then he's wrapped up in bandages, and when they unwrap him it's me in the Hawk's uniform.

"How do you like that?" Hoolie asks.

"The nose is fine," I answer, "but what did you do to the chin?"

ALVIN DARK LOOKS THE OTHER WAY

Second baseman Vern Fuller played on our All-Stars basketball team for a few years. He loved it, and he played real hard. I never saw anybody dive for a ball in a meaningless game the way he would. He wasn't clumsy at all, but it looked like he was killing himself, diving into the metal chairs.

He called up once during baseball season, when the Indians had a day off, and said he'd play softball for us. I was leery because I knew ballplayers couldn't do that during the season. "Don't worry about it," he said. I couldn't talk him out of it. He and manager Alvin Dark were battling because Vern wasn't getting enough playing time. We introduced him at our game, the crowd loved him, and I said, "You've got to forgive Vern; he's a little nervous. He's not used to playing to such large crowds." He played a few games, and we decided not to say anything or show him playing in our highlights. We'd just say he was at the game and show him on the sidelines.

Now, every big-league team puts a squad together at some point to play their farm clubs. Usually they use guys who aren't playing. Fuller played on the Tribe's team, and we asked about it when he came back. He was terrific. He made great catches, hit for extra bases, hit a home run. Alvin went up to him afterward and said, "I heard you had a great couple days there. You know what? You must be playing ball somewhere I don't know about."

That's all Vern heard about it. Dark was on to it. He was a great

Vern Fuller of the Indians was a regular on the 1970-vintage Hoolihan & Big Chuck All-Stars basketball team. Back row, from left: Hoolie, "Kishka" Tony Carmen, Vern Fuller, Andy Hale, Herb "Soul Man" Thomas, "Big Stash" Russ Cormier, me. Front row, from left: Casey Kassarda, the Browns' "Man in the Brown Suit" Abe Abraham, my brother Paul Schodowski, Bill Russett.

guy. I made one of the funniest videos you've never seen with him.

When I wasn't doing the games because I was on the air, I worked the tape room pulling highlights. I'd make a package for the news, and I saved tapes because I was looking for stuff with Hawk and McDowell that I could use on the show. One tape showed Dark coming out of the dugout during a rain delay. You could see it was raining, and he looked out at the field, staring a long time. I took the Fortunes' song "You've Got Your Troubles (I've Got Mine)" and made a music video with his face "supered" over a series of errors. It took me forever. I was a little hesitant to show it on the air.

I remembered Ernie once advised me, "Don't ask—just do it and say 'I'm sorry, I'll never do it again' afterward." But because Channel 8 was carrying the Indians, I showed it to Bill Turner. He ran and showed it to Chuck Bergeson, the station manager. Bergeson snatched it up and never gave it back. I heard later he showed it to anybody who came through the station to see him.

JUST LIKE *MAJOR LEAGUE*

I think the movie *Major League* came directly from the 1960s Indians. Hawk and McDowell told me Chico Salmon was afraid of the dark and horror movies, and slept with the lights on, but he used to watch our show religiously. He didn't go out and party with those guys, and if they were playing on a Friday night and the game went longer than normal, he wouldn't even shower. He'd change clothes and go home so he didn't miss the opening of the show. He'd watch us but not the movie. It was too scary. He loved the "PJ Party" at the end. I was sorry I never met him and had a chance to put him on the show, but when he was leaving the Indians I sent him a nightshirt like we wore during "PJ Party."

Dark used to let me hang around the dugout, and the view there could be like watching a movie. Once, the Indians were ahead by one or two runs in one game, trying to hold in the top of the ninth inning with the bases loaded and two out. Somebody hit a blooper to right. Hawk came flying in for the catch, dived, slid on the wet grass, and caught the ball. While he was still sliding, he raised his hand up quickly to show the ump. The ball flew out and went behind him. He lay on his stomach smiling, showing the empty glove, then saw the batter running like hell for second. Hawk looked in his glove and started scrambling around on his knees for the ball.

McDowell tried to develop a curve when he started losing velocity. It made his fastball look faster. He never got more than two runs out of the Indians, and they were leading a game 2-to-1 in the ninth. There were two outs, a runner or two on base, and the batter up had been razzing McDowell the whole game: "You're a one pitch player; you can't throw anything but heat"—trying to get him mad and throw the curve.

Duke Sims, the catcher, went out and said, "Blow this guy away. Forget him. Let's get to Swingos. No extra innings."

"No, man, I got a curve. He ain't gonna hit it."

Sims said, OK, throw it, but break it off in the dirt so he can't hit it. He went back and gave the curve signal. The batter started razzing McDowell that his fastball wasn't as good as it used to be.

Sam started his windup. Sims knelt on his knees with both hands waiting to block the ball in the dirt, and Sam threw a 105-mile-an-hour fastball right down the pipe. It caught Sims right in the kisser, knocking him backward. It was shown on "Bloopers" for weeks. Yet Sam and Duke remained buddies.

McDowell was pitching another game when a batter came up who hit him all the time. There were two outs. Dark wanted a pitching change, but he wanted McDowell in the game. He took out the second baseman, put McDowell at second, and put in a new pitcher so he could change back. Sure as hell, you knew they were going to hit it to McDowell. It was a screaming line drive. He knocked it down because he didn't want it to get past him. The ball dribbled away. He was on his hands and knees scrambling for it. The hitter was running from first to second, and McDowell did a spastic-looking lunging move, still on his hands and knees, to tag the bag. He was a couple inches shy, so he did some weird wiggling move to reach the bag just in time for the out.

As the Hawk came running in from the outfield, McDowell asked him, "How'd you like that play?"

Hawk said, "It looked like a monkey trying to (bleep) a football."

BIG CHUCK'S BIG SHOT

When I was setting up cameras for games, the grounds crew would be cutting the grass and setting up the batting cage. One of them used to see me play with the All-Stars and knew I hit a lot of home runs. "Get in there," he said, nodding to the cage.

I grabbed a bat, and he pitched. I was used to hitting a softball, so even at batting-practice speed I was hitting everything to right field. I finally got the timing down, and he said, "Two more." I hit one and could tell I hit it really good. I pulled it to left and figured it was way in the stands. There was a Pesta pickles sign on the facing of the deck, and I hit it right over that into the upper deck. I thanked him and said I had to get back to work.

A guy in suit was standing in the dugout, watching. He came out and introduced himself. "You play ball?" he said.

I said, "I play softball. That was just batting practice." We talked for a minute, and he was sizing me up.

He said, "How old are you?" I looked younger than I was for many years, and I told him I was about thirty-five. He smiled.

"Forget it," he said.

I was in a celebrity home-run hitting contest after that. Mike Garcia and Bob Feller were pitching. Herb Score had started announcing, so he was in the contest. The guy from the grounds crew told Hawk, "Chuck's going to hit it out of the stadium."

Hawk right away started betting, big money, for real—betting on me. I was nervous enough without that added pressure.

Garcia, the Big Bear, was pitching to me. He was a great guy who had a chain of cleaners, loved the show, and had his Big Bear softball team play us a couple times. He was just lobbing pitches in. I went up, and Hawk said, "Come back here and take this bat." He gave me the biggest bat I ever saw. He said it was a regulation bat, but maximum weight and maximum length, and it belonged to pitcher Dean Chance. He couldn't hit, but he was strong. "If he ever hits it, it's going to be gone," Hawk said. I went up to bat, and there was the Big Bear, smiling his ass off.

I had three pitches. "Don't overswing, just hit it hard," I told myself. Garcia threw, and the ball looked right there, fat. I swung and almost broke my back. I don't know if it was a spitball or what that he threw. Hawk had a look like, *What the hell?* and I could see him arguing with the guy from the grounds crew. Garcia did the same thing on the next pitch but threw really fast. I swung so late the ball was already in the catcher's mitt. Garcia was laughing and said, "Where do you want it?" I showed him. I hit the third one hard, right on the button. It was a line drive that nearly carried to the outfield, but it was an out.

Herb came up right after that, and right away hit a home run. That was my big chance and I blew it.

CHAPTER 12

MOVING UP BUT NOT OUT

BECOMING A DIRECTOR

I was still working as an engineer in 1969, when a couple of the directors at TV8 asked that I be put on a shift where I could help with specials they routinely had to do. I was helping on my own and making suggestions because I was good at finding music for certain situations, and I got really interested in special effects and camera uses. It was hard because I had to work a full engineering schedule, and the union frowned on me helping management outside my job classification. If someone asked for something really complicated, I'd do it on lunch break or after my shift.

Then program director Bob Huber made an offer I couldn't refuse. He wanted me to become a director. That was unusual, because directors in Storer Broadcasting normally came from the production department and had college degrees. I had no college. I had zero experience directing newscasts and other things they did every day. I'd also have to leave the union and lose some job security. With three kids, that really worried me. But Daddy Bags, station manager Ken Bagwell, told me he liked my energy and some of the creative things I was doing on the show and while helping to direct. He talked me into it and promptly gave me my first assignment: to write and produce an Easter special. At first I was overwhelmed, but I realized after getting into it that I could handle it, and I was really into it.

I wanted it to be totally different from the Easter specials you'd see every year on TV, as different as our skits were. Making it a redemption story, I built it around a hippie-type young man played by Andrew Russett, a good-looking kid who studied acting in col-

Moving from engineer to director in 1969, I sit at master control with master storyteller Clyde Freeman.

lege and was a brother of a guy on our all-star team. I used artwork from Salvador Dali, music from the Beatles, Simon & Garfunkel, *Jesus Christ Superstar* and a guitar Mass, and I shot most of it in the Flats and at St. Malachi Church.

Because it was shot on film, I also worked with Bob Soinski to try out movie techniques I'd been studying, like the use of subliminal scenes. Russett's character would be walking in the Flats, remembering when he was a kid, or walk into the empty church and get flashes of the Vietnam War or Kennedy assassination as he looked at the Stations of the Cross. The film was shot at sixteen frames a second, and we studied how many frames we needed to put in before a viewer would actually recognize it and not just notice an interruption. We tried it on people in the control room. They wouldn't notice a scene lasting four frames unless they were told in advance it was coming, but they would register a scene of six frames. Four frames was not long enough for the brain to react.

Near the end of production, I got worried I overdid it, and that the show was too different. But it was too late to change; it had to air. Two or three minutes after it did, on Easter morning, Ken Bagwell called me at home. I was really nervous. I wanted to show it to him in advance, but the station trusted me; it would be OK. No one prescreened it. I expected the worst, but he said he saw "much more than an Easter special," and that I made the right decision to become a director.

NOW YOU SEE IT, NOW THEY DON'T

That gave me a little swagger. I started getting all kinds assignments for specials and station promotions, as I wasn't directing news as much. Because I was doing more and had a crew, I was really inspired to put more production into *Hoolihan & Big Chuck* skits, getting more and more into using film and away from studio skits. I did a really involved piece using the song "Snoopy vs. The Red Baron," with Hoolie actually flying a biplane. We'd get compliments on Monday morning.

I used subliminal techniques again, too. Joe Dannery used to have barn dances in his barn in Hinckley. It was a huge party, with a lot of friends and people from the station, and everybody getting loaded. One year we had a photographer shoot it for the show.

My brother, Paul, was there. He graduated from South High in 1956, and you have to know that it really was exactly like *American Graffiti* in those days. Everybody was shooting moons. You'd see at least one a day. After a South High football or basketball game, you'd go to Manners drive-in, sit in your car to eat, and see a car cruise by slowly, with somebody mooning everybody from a window. Paul was the unofficial champion of Cleveland because he would find unique ways to shoot a moon and not get caught. You could sit talking with your wife, he'd shoot a moon, and you'd see it but she wouldn't. He was once on an elevator in a downtown hotel with some guys, going to a South High football banquet, and it stopped at the wrong floor. Another party was going on, taking up the whole floor, and a table with name tags was set up across from the elevator. The elevator went up. Paul punched the floor again. The door opened, you heard a big scream, and the door closed.

At the barn dance, with the photographer shooting, I called, "Hey, Paul, you're going to be on TV!" He turned around and shot

Hoolie hams it up for a publicity photo with the plane he flew in the "Snoopy and the Red Baron" music video. Hoolie flew the plane wearing a Snoopy head that I constructed between station breaks.

a moon at the camera. He never lost his touch. I said, "I'm gonna use that." He said yeah, sure.

We put it in the highlight film, at four or five frames, and tested it in the control room. I'd see his ass, but the crew wouldn't. I called Paul before the show and said, "We're showing the film of the barn dance, and I put your moon in." He said, "Get out." I told him to watch and see. He called a minute after the film ran. All he said was, "You're gonna get in trouble, man."

I didn't. Nothing happened, because nobody saw it.

But Paul did.

GOING HOLLYWOOD

I was still in touch with Ernie Anderson, who was doing very well in Hollywood. He became the voice of ABC-TV, a top commercial talent, and one of the highest-paid people out there, making something like $2 million a year. He and Tim Conway called one day and told me to get some tapes together. They wanted me to come out to Hollywood to spend a week with them, and they were going to show the tapes to some people at CBS.

It was my first-ever big airplane trip. I was nervous as hell because people were hijacking planes in 1970. I started to worry because the plane wasn't moving. Then Russ Cormier, Big Stash, who worked for United Airlines, came in from the back of the plane. "I just wanted to tell you Jim Brown's up in first class," he said, and left. We'd just played a basketball game at the arena with Brown for his Black Economic Union.

A stewardess came by and asked what that was all about. I told her a friend who works for the airline said Jim Brown was in first class. She said, "Really!" She got all excited and told another stewardess. They were really buzzing. Then she came back, looking disappointed. "I thought you meant James Brown," she said.

Jim had two seats. I went up, spent a long time talking with him, and asked if he remembered knocking me over on the field during a Browns game, when he was being ridden out of a play by two linebackers. He was amazing. He could run full force to the sideline and then, without slowing, plant one leg and turn like a rabbit. On this play, I was running the parab mic at the line of scrimmage, right on the sideline, and waited too long to get out of the way. Jim stepped on my foot, looked me right in the eye, and twisted his body to avoid running into the big metal parab as I fell back. He remembered the incident, "but I didn't know it was you."

One of the regulars on the Ghoulardi All-Stars was videographer Ralph Tarsitano, known as Tarts. His father, whom we called Pappa Tarts, acted as the team's coach. He used to make wine, "dago red," and we'd drink a gallon of it before, after, and during games. We had paper cups, and it looked like we were drinking water. Knowing Ernie would love some, Tarts had brought me a big Dan-Dee potato chip box with a huge gallon wine bottle in it. The top was sticking out, so they had it duct-taped. You couldn't check it as luggage, so I carried this thing on the plane.

I didn't want to look like a hick who'd never flown before. I wanted to have nice luggage and be cool. I got all dressed up. And I walked off the plane in Los Angeles carrying this box. Ernie greeted me.

"You really are Polish, man," he said.

We went directly from the airport to a rehearsal for *Pat Paulsen's Half a Comedy Hour*. Edwina, who by then was Ernie's wife, was in a scene with Pat. Henry Fonda was in it, too. They were onstage rehearsing with three cameras in the otherwise empty theater. Paulsen was on an operating table, Fonda was playing a doctor, and Edwina was a nurse. She saw me, waved, and said she'd see me backstage.

Oh man, I thought—*Henry Fonda.* He was huge at the time, a superstar, and drew more attention because of his daughter and son, Jane and Peter.

I could see something go wrong in the rehearsal. Fonda thought it was something he did, but the cameraman was moving to get the shot, which meant the director should have started it sooner. The director called to stop for a break, to go over the problem. Everyone left except Ernie and Fonda, who walked down the steps to me.

Ernie said, "Chuck, Henry Fonda. Henry, Chuck Schodowski," and left. Fonda and I shook hands. Here I was in a huge empty theater in Hollywood, holding Henry Fonda's hand. This icon was looking right at me for what seemed like an eternity. *The Grapes of Wrath* was all I could think of, but that was thirty years earlier, and I wasn't going to bring up his daughter's controversies.

He said, "So you're a TV director."

"Yeah," I said, "for a couple years now—and by the way, that wasn't your fault. The director should have moved that camera sooner."

He said, "This is so much harder than doing film. Shooting a film, you do one thing, one little bit at a time, and do it over and over. With this, you've got to do the whole sequence. It's like live theater."

He started repeating how hard it was and said making mistakes made him nervous. It reminded me of Imogene Coca doing the skit in Cleveland. I said no, it's actually pretty easy—"just pretend the camera isn't there."

"So I should make sure . . ."

"No, that's not your responsibility," I said, explaining that the cameraman couldn't get the shot in time. "Just do your lines like no one's there."

He seemed satisfied and said to come backstage. "Ernie said he'd see you there." Backstage, I heard a big argument going on—Edwina's voice and a guy's voice. It was Tom Smothers. She was screaming, arguing about some charity, and they were both swearing. I was nervous and excited from talking to Henry Fonda, and now this.

So this is Hollywood, I thought. I'd been there about ten minutes.

ERNIE'S WORLD

Ernie lived in Studio City right next to a storm sewer where they filmed the horror movie *Them!*. I saw binoculars on a table inside the house and jokingly asked Edwina if she was spying on somebody. Oh yeah, she said—Lee Marvin. He was building a house near them. "He's living here now," she said. "See that upstairs balcony? That's his bedroom. He came out one time, and the railing wasn't finished, and he fell off into a bush in his jockey shorts."

Besides the wine, I'd brought Ernie some football film of the Ghoulardi All-Stars. He rented a 16mm movie projector and a screen and introduced me to a neighbor he invited who'd been a silent film actress. I said, "Ernie, she's not going to be interested in this shit." He said, "What do you know?" He started the film, and it was boring as hell. The neighbor was being polite, and I felt sorry for her. Then I was surprised to hear a voice doing comic narration for the film that I didn't remember. It turned out to be Tim Conway, who'd come over and was standing behind the screen.

Ernie announced we were going to have lobster for dinner. He scoffed when I asked if he meant lobster tails. "No, no, we're gonna have lobster," he said. "Where I come from, you eat everything." We went to get them at a carpeted supermarket that looked like a hotel lobby. A sign on the tank said "Do not touch the lobsters." Ernie climbed the ladder beside it, reached in, and grabbed a lobster. "This is a three-pounder; you don't want this," he said. A manager came running over, upset and shouting, "Can't you read the sign?" Then he stopped and said, "Oh! I'm sorry, Ernie!"

Everyone knew him. As we drove down the street, we saw a big tractor trailer with red, white, and blue flags all over it. Ernie waved and got a greeting back. It was Evel Knievel.

We ate the lobsters the way Ernie insisted—until all that was left was shells that looked like plastic. We finished a whole bottle of Boodles gin, drinking martinis and talking until three in the morning. At 7:30 he was waking me up, telling me we had to get going. My ears were ringing. We were going to a recording studio where he was recording the Mercury Cougar spot—"the man's car"—they used for years. On a big divided highway, he suddenly stopped the car, put the blinkers on, ran down the inside lane, and jumped over the guardrail to get to a little shopping center. He took some stuff from a cooler next to a store, and a guy came out waving and yelling, "What are you doing?" Ernie held up two cans, and the guy shouted, "Oh, Ernie! OK!" It was a liquor store, and Ernie had a couple of hair-of-the-dog canned martinis for us.

At the studio I knew Ernie was losing patience with the producer, a guy from Florida who called him "Ernie baby" and kept asking for retakes on a read I thought was perfect. Ernie said, "Look, you got the best read in the world, but I'm gonna do it one more time for you." He did that and said, "Now you have not only the best read, you have two of the best reads in the world." We started to leave. The guy's voice came over the intercom. "Ernie, if you could just . . ." Boom! Ernie slammed the door behind us.

I asked how much he got for a spot like that. He said it could be as little as $500 or as much as $50,000. He didn't know. He never wanted to know.

GOOD ENOUGH TO STEAL

Ernie took me to CBS for a meeting. I heard years later that Conway paid for it. They racked up the tapes I brought—some Kielbasy Kid skits, "King the Wonder Dog," some music videos—and watched. They weren't really laughing. As the screening went on, I got really discouraged. They were politely saying, "That's pretty good" and "That's nice," but I thought at least they would laugh. I was nervous anyway, and I started feeling sorry for Ernie and Tim for bringing me out there.

That set one thing in my mind: "I don't want to come out here. This is not a good idea."

Funny thing, though. There were a lot of variety shows on TV at that time. Over the next six months, on three different shows, I saw three of the skits I took out there. One of them had Hoolie playing a villain and putting a girl, played by Tony Carmen, on a railroad track. We filmed it outside, at track level, with one shot looking through the handle of a pump. The variety show not only copied the skit, it used almost exactly the shots I did.

We went to Conway's house in Malibu and set up at the round bar he had in the middle of the living room. It was the only time I saw him serious. He was starting to do things and write with Joe Flynn from *McHale's Navy,* and he thought they could do a movie every year. "That'd be enough for me. TV is too tough," he said. He was serious. TV was tough.

The phone rang. He answered it and was on for a long time. Ernie and I sat drinking and talking for an hour and a half. We were getting ready to leave when Tim returned and said CBS had offered him $2 million to do another TV show. We asked if he was going to do it, and he said he was. Ernie was surprised and asked why, after he'd just told us how he'd had it with TV.

"Because they're giving me $2 million," he said.

DOING WHAT'S RIGHT FOR THE FAMILY

Tim and Ernie had set up a job for me as assistant director on *The Della Reese Show.* They really wanted me to go out there. But I was turned off by the whole Hollywood thing and said I probably was not going to do it. The money right away would have been more than I'd make in Cleveland, but the cost of living was higher. Our show was booming, and I was enjoying being a big fish in a small pond. That's all I ever wanted to be. I was finally comfortable with it. I didn't think Hollywood was a place to raise a family. My oldest son had a girlfriend whom he later married, and they had five kids. I didn't want to disrupt that or break up my family. So I didn't take the offer. Ernie was upset for years afterward, and he kept trying to get me out there.

June and I added two more daughters, Melissa and Michelle, giving us five kids. When we did move, we moved from Parma to

Hinckley. It wouldn't have happened if it weren't for my friend Joe Dannery, our booth announcer, who had a great, Ernie-type voice and was the narrator on my Easter special and many skits including the Kielbasy Kid and Soul Man. Joe lived in Hinckley, knew I really liked it there, and let me know when the house next door to his was for sale. It's quiet, and we're sort of isolated up on a ridge. It takes no longer to get to Channel 8 than when I lived in Parma. It's the best of both worlds. I live in the country and work in the city.

I'm born and died in Cleveland. I love Cleveland.

I became a director and got a new photo, with WJW's familiar "8" logo of stacked TV screens.

CHAPTER 13

JOHN, ART, AND SO-O-O-ULMAN

LI'L JOHN GETS DISCOVERED

Early in 1971, I wanted to do a skit with "Bridget the Midget," a new Ray Stevens record. The song was called "Bridget the Queen of the Blues," and the lyrics went, "She can sing, she can dance, she can really do it all."

I needed a Bridget who could dance. I called Dick Blake, who was and still is a dance instructor, and asked if he had any girls in his classes—or, even better, any short women, because I didn't want it to look like we were making fun of kids.

"I don't have any real little women," he said, "but I got a real little guy."

I said, "Really!" I thought it would be great, an even funnier skit, if it had a guy dressed like a woman. I asked his name. It was John Rinaldi. I called, we talked, and the first thing I asked was if

he was related to Dr. Rinaldi. "That's my uncle," he said.

We shot the skit at a place called Bonnie's on the West Side. John didn't really believe we were serious, so he brought a couple of guys with him, like bodyguards. But we were serious, and that was his first appearance on the show. I started using him in more skits, and the payoff was always something to do with

John in costume for his first skit, "Bridget the Midget," at Bonnie's Lounge on the West Side.

Certain Ethnic guy. In the skit on the right, the balloon gets big, but it's my head that explodes. I designed the special effects using small pieces of paper to make it appear that my head was blowing up.

his four-foot, three-inch height. He got so good I started using him in skits where size didn't matter, and he became a regular.

THAT CERTAIN ETHNIC GUY

I was creating new characters and adding more and more people to our stable of actors. One character I started to do more myself was the Certain Ethnic guy, with a big mustache, porkpie hat, and gaudy striped sweater.

Polish jokes were making the rounds in the '60s and '70s. They were funny, and I wanted to make skits out of them, but I didn't want to use the word *Polack,* or even *Polish,* or limit us to a single ethnic group. So I coined the term "Certain Ethnic." I could be a Certain Ethnic, and Lil' John could be one, too. The character was so popular and versatile that we started to use him in skits that weren't even based on ethnic jokes. The character was broader and funnier than if there was a specific group identification. I was asked if I was going to do anything on it when a Polish pope, John Paul II, was elected in 1978. I said absolutely not; we'd leave that for *Saturday Night Live.*

We started "Certain Ethnic" in the early years of *Hoolihan & Big Chuck*, and within a few years it was all over the country. As far as I know, I did it first.

THE ART OF FRIDAY NIGHTS

Art Lofredo was taking night classes in television production at Normandy High School, and he started sending me tapes of comedy skits. In 1974, he sent me a tape I really liked. I asked him to come down to the station and redo it, and we'd use it on the show.

Art became a tremendous addition. He was a real good mime, could play a great Certain Ethnic, and played old guys really well, even though he was just twenty-five. He said he got that from his father, who was old when Art was growing up. I used him in more and more skits, and my goal was to get him a job at Channel 8. It took a year or two, but he made it. He was a housepainter in those days, but I knew he'd be a huge help because he was very creative and really interested.

He was game for anything, too. Streaking got big around 1974, especially on college campuses and after a guy streaked the Academy Awards while David Niven was onstage. When "The Streak" came out, another Ray Stevens record, I wanted to do a skit using Art. I didn't know how to make him look naked, so I took three or four pairs of my white jockey shorts and dyed them different shades of pink—I still have one pair left—and it was perfect. He really looked naked. I got Cook Goodwin to shoot it, and we went downtown to get some outdoor shots on Public Square. It took a lot of nerve to do it. Art put on a topcoat, Cook set up the camera, I'd take the coat, and Art would run toward Cook. I'd follow him, Cook got the reaction shots of people waiting at a bus stop, and we'd jump in the car to go someplace else.

We went to Halle's on Euclid Avenue at East 14th Street. Art was standing on the sidewalk waiting, I took the coat off him, and Cook shouted, "Wait, wait, wait!" An old lady came out of the store, looked at Art, screamed, and started beating the crap out of him with her purse. Art took off running, with her beating the hell out of him. We didn't get any footage of that, but to the final year we were

Art Lofredo, in dyed underwear, dashes past an old gas station in Hinckley for "The Streak." The bystanders reacting to him are me and a singer with the Tony Carmen Trio who did not want to be identified. I gave her a fake nose so she wouldn't be recognized.

on the air, people would request "The Streak" for oldies night.

Art was with us to the end and has more skits than anyone except John and me.

SOUL MAN JOINS THE FAMILY

In 1969, Channel 8 hired Herb Thomas, a nineteen-year-old black kid fresh out of high school, as a janitor and print shop trainee. He was really interested in what I was doing, and he started helping me make props and asking how different things worked. I really liked him and took him under my wing. I talked to him like I did to my kids.

Here's how to get ahead, I told him: Do everything they ask you to do, then do something on your own. Don't even tell them; just do it. That's what I did, and that's what I told my kids to do. Just do it. If they don't find out, that's OK, just keep doing it. If you meet someone people don't like, take it as a challenge, and try to make them like you. You don't have to like them, just try real hard to make them like you. I've done that to so many people—crabby people who still are crabby but not to me. I'm like their dearest friend.

Like Art, Herb and I became very good friends. I used to bring him home for meals, and he'd come to the games when my kids were playing Pee-Wee football. I'd have the kids call good friends or older people in authority "uncle" because they became like part of the family, and that included Herb. To this day, my son Mark, a grown man who looks like my clone, will see him at the West Side Market and yell "Uncle Herb!" It raises some eyebrows. But Herb really is part of our family.

I wanted to use him on the show, partly because I desperately wanted to have some blacks on the show, beyond my friends from the foundry. I put them in skits when I first went on the air because I didn't know anybody else, and because they could do it. Just like I took off on Polish jokes with myself, we'd do takeoffs on black jokes, the way *Laugh-In* and other shows did later. People at the station were leery about it, but my experience with the guys was that it would be OK.

One of the guys was my good friend Phil May, who was in a Christmas skit in our first or second year. You see Santa coming down a chimney with his back to the camera. He turns around and it's Phil, who says, "What'd you expect after coming down four thousand chimneys?"

Another was Frank Morris, a real tall, good-looking guy. We used to imitate the way he walked because it was like a statue, nothing but his legs moving. I did a skit with him where we were digging in a ditch with hard hats on. He says, "I'm getting hungry," and I say, "Me, too—why don't you go to the deli and get us something?" He walks up to the counter and asks for a kielbasy sandwich and a big piece of watermelon. In the next scene we're eating, and one of us says, "I don't know how you can eat that stuff." The camera pulls back, and I'm eating the watermelon while he's eating the sand-wich.

We'd do stuff like that, where there's a play on a stereotype. We never got flak for it. I think it was because I did it in all honesty, and we were laughing at ourselves and the stereotypes.

I used Herb for a few things before trying what became his biggest role and one of our most popular skits. I was a little leery myself but kept remembering my buddies and how well what I did with them went over. I knew it would be OK.

"Soul Man," starring Herb Thomas, was born.

The skits opened with a shot of an old-fashioned radio, evoking the classic serials, and a narrator announcing that crime does not pay because of the "champion of justice" and the city's most feared crime fighter. I was mild-mannered TV producer Ed Tarboosh. I think I used "Everett Strongheart" originally, but Joe Dannery used to make up names—and when I gave him the script for the voiceover, he changed it to Ed Tarboosh without me knowing.

In one favorite skit, I see a crime and look for a phone booth to change in. I can't see one and desperately look around. I'm in a parking lot, find the door is unlocked on a Volkswagen, and jump in there. I take the Soul Pill; smoke pours out, and Herb jumps out in his superhero costume. Not only has Ed Tarboosh changed into Soul Man, but the car has changed into a big Cadillac.

I got the car from Central Cadillac, which lent it for free because it would be in a Soul Man skit. Here's what things were like back then: I asked them when they had to have the car back, and they told me they'd be there until six o'clock. We shot in the afternoon. I took the car back, and the gates were closed. So I left my car at the station, took the Cadillac, and went to visit everybody I knew. "Hey, Big Chuck's got a Cadillac!" I brought the car back the next day. They weren't even worried about it.

We did quite a few Soul Man skits through the '70s. They were enormously popular, constantly requested, rerun over and over, and are on our "Best of" DVD collections. When I'd rerun the skits in more recent years, young people would ask in amazement where we got the skyline shot of Cleveland that only had the Terminal Tower. They'd ask if we had a car club supply all the vintage cars we used. I'd tell them we shot the skyline ourselves in 1970, and the cars were what we drove then.

Herb became our most-used photographer. Soul Man died out when he got busy as a news photographer and was hard to get for skits. In later years, he became our exclusive cameraman on the show, which was really nice. He went to Vegas for all our shows, and there he was, shooting again, at my retirement party in 2007. He went on to become a producer and a music producer, has a gospel group called the Soul Warriors, and has won many Emmys. He's had his own success. I knew early on that he would do that. He tells people I raised him. Like I said, he's part of the family.

He's so much bigger now that he couldn't get one leg into that superhero costume, but everywhere for years he'd be recognized as Soul Man.

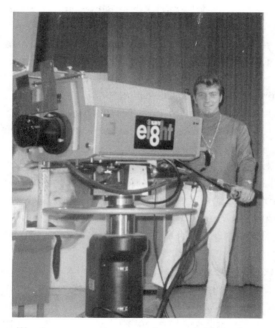

Wearing a peace sign around my neck, I operate a news camera with WJW's 1970s color logo, spelling out "ei8ht."

CHAPTER 14

NEW TALENT, PLUS PIZZA

THE COMING OF "NEW TALENT TIME"

I remembered an old show, *The Original Amateur Hour,* which was hosted by Major Bowes on radio and Ted Mack on TV. I wanted to do something using that format, and that's where I came up with "New Talent Time." But I added a twist. The talent we'd use would be offbeat, crazy things you'd normally never see—guys playing songs by hitting the top of their heads. Jell-O slurping. Dancing dogs. Tricks that didn't work.

One day our station manager told me Lawrence Welk was coming on a tour of stations to plug his show, and he wanted us to use him as much as we could, including on *Hoolihan & Big Chuck.* I said that was fine, but the station manager wanted to add that "I gotta warn you—the talk is, he's a little temperamental." I still wasn't used to working with celebrities, though I was almost never awed by them, and was a little worried. I had in mind Welk would be crabby.

When he arrived, he talked like he did on TV, with that North Dakota German accent we once parodied on "Parma Place." I told him my name, and that might have helped. He said a few words in Polish, and luckily I knew what he meant. I told him what I wanted to do. As soon as I said "Ted Mack," he said he knew Ted, and that seemed to win him over.

I wanted him to play an accordion and to say "Just call me Larry" when Hoolie asked his name. I got him a small twelve-bass accordion. No problem, he was going to do it. Then, very politely, he asked, "Can I dance, too?" I knew then it was going to be good, and it was. He played the accordion, stopped to do a little dance, and we hooked him off. He loved it.

This was near the beginning of "New Talent Time," and we got so many letters that we had to stack them up. The talent floodgates opened. We would prerecord segments—"New Talent Time" was never live, even when the rest of the show was—the night before the show between the six and eleven p.m. news. It lasted from the early days of *Hoolihan & Big Chuck* through the entire twenty-eight-year *Big Chuck & Lil' John* run. The segment was so popular for so many years that we exhausted every stupid thing people could think of. Somebody would suggest something, and we'd say we did it five years ago, or twelve years ago. We kept doing the segment until there was almost nothing we hadn't done.

HOMAGE IS ONE THING, RIPPING OFF IS ANOTHER

After we'd been doing it a few years, a guy saw me on the street in front of the station. He said he was a writer from Cleveland who was now out in Hollywood, knew Ernie Anderson, and was working for Chuck Barris. "You know where he got the idea for *The Gong Show*, don't you?" he said. I said, "'New Talent Time?'" He said yeah.

I'd been ripped off before. But after talking to him a few minutes, I mentioned we once did a bank-robbery skit in the alley behind the station. Art Lofredo and I are the robbers, and I go to buy stockings to put over our heads. Hoolie, playing a limp-wristed store clerk, says, "We don't sell stockings anymore, only pantyhose." So I buy a pair of pantyhose. When Art and I come running out of the bank, we're tied together. We can't run, we're going around in circles, I start to fall, and money is flying all over. It's a funny skit. To the day I retired, we got requests for it. I said I'd seen the exact skit—even the alley looked similar, and the store clerk was effeminate—on *The Benny Hill Show*. It was a direct steal. I told the guy that, and he put his head down and said, "Yeah, I wrote for Benny Hill for a while. In fact, he's got a couple more of your skits."

Everybody steals, and it's no big deal. I did it, too. But at least, when I stole something, it was only the joke. I tried to add something and change the format. It was never an exact duplicate. Ernie

Kovacs and Steve Allen were two of my heroes. I got ideas from them, and they influenced David Letterman, too. When he started his version of "New Talent Time" in the 1980s, at least he changed it to "Stupid Human Tricks."

MEET MUSH AND THE PIZZA FIGHT OF THE CENTURY

It is nice to get credited. A book called *Horsemen of the Esophagus* by Jason Fagone credits me with being "the father of competitive eating."

I was always trying to invent new things, and that one happened almost by accident.

We were taping "New Talent Time" with a jug band called Smash. They were dressed up like hillbillies, and they were excellent musically. When we were done taping, one of them said he wanted to show me something we might be able to use on the show.

He took a Whopper out of a bag and ate it in something like five seconds.

He was a music major at Cleveland State named Mariano Pacetti. I told him I'd like to use his speed-eating on the show, but that we should have something that lasted longer than five seconds. That's when I came up with the "Pizza Fight of the Century." I wanted it to be more than a simple contest, so because I used to box, I made it like a fight, with a ring and a bell.

Setting it up like that would also prime the pump. It's easier to show the idea than to explain it and say, "We're going to have a pizza fight. Write in." We did the same thing when we started arm wrestling. For that, Mariano challenged a competitive arm wrestler, Jerry Brickey, who hung drywall for a living.

Mariano went against one of the guys in his band for the first pizza fight. It was no contest. Mariano's style was to just jam stuff into his mouth. He'd get it mushy and push it down with his hands. Our champion was born, and so was his nickname: Mushmouth.

Mush is a very likeable guy, and he became a big star on our show. He was eating champion for a long time, at least three years. He lost only once, to a German shepherd—Chris, the Fairview Fireball— until a fifteen-year-old kid from Cuyahoga Falls, David "Coondog"

Hoolie and me with Mushmouth and one of his
managers. Mush was the heavyweight pizza-eat-
ing champion of the world for almost a decade.

O'Karma, knocked him off. But Mush remained champ by winning
the rematch.

Besides being eating champion, Mush joined the Hoolihan &
Big Chuck All-Stars almost immediately, where he was a valuable
addition as an entertainer.

I wanted the All-Stars to be more of a family show that people
would talk about later, and I spent a lot of time thinking of things
to do. With the Ghoulardi All-Stars, we'd just show up, play a game,
and have parties afterward. I added dancing cheerleaders, most of
whom came from Channel 8, who were very well choreographed by
two of the cheerleaders and Lil' John. Thinking back on it, we had
dancing cheerleaders years before the NBA thought of it.

We also entertained at bars near the games instead of having just
a private party afterward. People would get on the phone and tell
their friends to come down. The place would fill up in an hour, so

the bars loved it. I played banjo, John played cymbals and danced. We had two accordion players, Dave Stacy—a bank manager who wrote "I Lost My Kielbasy Down the Sewer"—and Whoopie John.

Mush played sax, but he could play ten instruments. He was taking singing lessons, too. I used to make him sing "O Sole Mio," and he'd sing it in Italian.

I became very close friends with him and his family, who came from Italy. His mother made my daughter Michelle's First Communion dress and attended both Michelle's and my daughter Missy's weddings. Mush's brother Augie played at Missy's wedding.

His parents were very proper. Every time Mush came down to tape a pizza fight, his mother would get mad. She'd say, "You're going to hurt your throat. You're going to scratch it!" She'd really get on him and give him the silent treatment when he came home. He purposely wouldn't say anything. She'd finally come around and say, "Did you win?" She sort of liked it, too.

Mush is the only person I know who did exactly what he said he was going to do. We'd be on the bus for a game, and he'd say he wanted to finish CSU, go to Vegas to play in a show band, arrange music, get married, teach music, and have his own jazz band. This is what happened: He finished CSU, went to Las Vegas, played in a show band, arranged for performers *including* Tony Bennett, got married, moved to Georgia, teaches music at the University of West Georgia, and has a very successful jazz band called Razzamajazz. He writes songs, and he records for several labels.

COONDOG GOES NATIONAL

Meanwhile, Dave O'Karma, the Coondog, went on to become a nationally known competitive eating champion and one of the main characters in Horsemen of the Esophagus and a TV docu-movie on competitive eating. He also writes for *Cleveland Magazine*. He had a whole stable of competitive eaters. At age fifty, he continued to be our champ, and in 2005 he actually made arrangements for Kobayashi, the legendary champion from Japan, to come to Cleveland for our show.

I think what really drew Kobayashi was that Kevin Salyer, the vice president of programming at Channel 8 and a big backer of our show, talked to Bob DiBiasio of the Indians. Kobayashi is a baseball nut, and he wanted to go to a Tribe game. I assured Bobby that the guy is world famous, and people would know who he was. They brought him out, sat him in the first row, and the players came out and asked for his autograph. They also asked him to sit in the dugout, but Kobayashi said he was "not worth." He said he'd come back anytime he could go to a game.

He had just won his fifth Nathan's Famous hot dog–eating contest at Coney Island by eating forty-nine hot dogs, with buns, in twelve minutes. A few months after that he ate fifty-four in ten minutes. These are kosher dinner franks, and the buns are big, too. Try breaking it down. That's 5.4 hot dogs every minute, or one every ten seconds for ten minutes. These guys drink gallons of water in preparation, forcing it down to stretch their stomachs. Coondog says it's no longer a sport; they're screwing up their bodies to win.

That's a long way from the Pizza Fight of the Century. We were just having fun.

MAGICALLY UNLUCKY CHARMS

Some ideas didn't work out. A guy called me and suggested investing some money to make Kielbasy Kid charms—little kielbasys, like the Italian malocchio charms. We'd sell them. I thought it was pretty funny. He'd make them, and I'd plug them on the air. I was barely getting by, but I went in on it. I made appearances at drugstores to plug them and even put an ad in the paper. I wanted to make a commercial, but Chuck Bergeson was going to make me pay for the airtime, even for plugging the charms on the show.

I called it the best investment I ever made because I got all my money back. I broke even.

CHAPTER 15

ALI AND OTHERS

WORKING WITH THE CHAMP

In 1975 I got a chance to meet and do something with the world's biggest celebrity at the time: Muhammad Ali.

Richie Giachetti, the boxing trainer from Cleveland, knew Ali's trainer, Angelo Dundee, and was a friend of Lil' John's. I think all Italians know each other. Giachetti told John that when Ali came to town to fight Chuck Wepner at the Richfield Coliseum, he could probably set something up for us to do with Ali. *If* we were interested.

Was he kidding? Muhammad Ali? He was the most recognized person in the world.

We arranged to shoot a skit on the Friday before the Monday fight. I planned to use it on that night's show. I couldn't contact Dundee or Giachetti that day, but they had said to go to the Coliseum; we'd be expected. Tarts—photographer Ralph Tarsitano—and I went out. It was a hell of a big empty place, with no one around. Ali was supposed to be there until four o'clock but someone told us he left. I was counting on the skit so much I said, "I know where's he staying. Let's try there."

We went to the Marriott on West 150th Street off Interstate 71, where Ali was staying. He used to travel with Fruit of Islam bodyguards, a crisply dressed and intimidating group that would pick up local help. They said there was no way we were going to see Ali, but a couple of the local guys recognized me. They started laughing and vouched for me, saying, "This guy's OK. He does some funny shit, man. He's OK." They all went into a little huddle to confer, came back in about twenty minutes, and said OK.

Tarts had to wait downstairs while I went alone with one of the bodyguards on the elevator to the eighth floor. We got off, went to the stairwell, and walked down two floors. It was like a spy movie. Nobody else was there. Ali must have rented the whole floor. We walked down the hall. The bodyguard knocked on the door, went inside, came back, and said, "OK, you can go in and talk to him." I went in alone. The room was a suite, and I didn't see anybody. It was quiet as a tomb. I said, "Hello-o-o," looked around, and went into a huge bedroom.

Ali was lying on the bed on his stomach. He looked up, turned over onto his side, and waved me to come in and sit on the bed. I put my hand out, and he gave me his left hand. We shook hands, and he pointed to his right hand and said, "I think I broke my knuckle. Don't tell anybody." And he winked. At the fight, three days later, he fought with one hand. People were booing because there was no action. I knew why.

For us, he was fantastic. He was so quiet and soft-spoken, you could hardly hear him. But the minute the camera came into the room, he was Muhammad Ali, bigger than life, just the opposite.

Tarts came up, and we shot a Ben Crazy skit in Ali's room. I was a psychiatrist, and you couldn't see who the patient lying on the couch was because, by sitting next to him, I was blocking his face. He was snorting and waving his arms, punching the air. I said, "I've concluded that you have what we call a hostile psychosis, that you're prone to violence with the slightest provocation. With this kind of problem, you'll never make any money. Who'll hire you?" I suggested we start therapy right away, said a few months of my care would make everything all right, and slapped him on the shoulder as he jumped up his face now in front of the camera. He said, "What do you mean hitting me and calling me hostile? Don't no man hit me! George Foreman, Joe Frazier—all of you are crazy!" He slapped me on the shoulder, I went down, and he huffed away. Boom, that was the joke.

I needed the skit for our opening and had to hustle back to the station to edit it. When we left, there was a whole line of people waiting outside to hit up Ali for money. You could see why he needed a barrier of people around him.

Muhammad Ali reminds me to keep his little secret for the Chuck Wepner fight, after shooting a skit in Ali's room at the Marriott.

They told me I could come back to the Coliseum the next day for the weigh-in, which would be a five-minute cut-in on *Wide World of Sports*. My family had moved to Hinckley by then, only a short drive away, so I took my son Mark, knowing he'd love it. I don't know what I expected, but it was different. Nobody was in the Coliseum parking lot, and when the guard let us inside, it looked deserted. Then we saw there was a big riser set up in a room with a group that included Howard Cosell, Don King, James Brown, and Redd Foxx. There were photographers and the camera crew but very few other people—maybe ten in the whole room. Don King, who used to watch our show and come to the station once in awhile, saw me and shouted, "Big Chuck, my man, come on up here! Come on up!" So I went up on the riser with this group of celebrities, imagining people watching around the country, saying, "Who the hell is that guy?"

When we left, there were only two cars in the parking lot, mine and Cosell's. Cosell was there climbing into his car. Mark rolled down the window and shouted, "Mr. Cosell!" Cosell looked up and gave him the goofiest wave in the world, nothing like you'd see on TV.

BUMPING INTO CELEBRITIES, WITHOUT POSSES

You could literally run into celebrities at Channel 8.

We were going to shoot a skit one afternoon when I realized I left something on my desk. It was Ernie's old desk, which I inherited, against the wall in a corner at the end of a hallway downstairs. The cameraman was waiting, so I raced down the hall, jumped on the elevator, and stood close to the door. As soon as the door opened, I'd fly out. But I was looking down at something, not paying attention. When the door opened, I jumped, and—*bam!*—hit my head against somebody else, exactly nose to nose.

It was George Hamilton. He said, "Whoa, you're in a hurry!" He laughed it off, and I was impressed he wasn't mad. But there wasn't time to do more than apologize. I had a skit to shoot.

I had finished working the sign-off shift one night and left through the back door of the station for my car. Brownwell Court, the back alley, was deserted. Or almost deserted. There was Yul Brynner, in a full-length white fur coat with a big collar. He was in *The King and I* at the Hanna, coming from a post-performance "afterglow" party, and staying at Swingos. He was all alone and fearless. I greeted him, and he talked to me at length as we walked. I can't imagine something like that happening today.

I was impressed he didn't have an entourage—as much as I was on another day, when I went to the lobby with a question for Marge, the receptionist. A strikingly handsome man, older than me, was sitting in jeans and a sweatshirt on the visitors' couch. It looked like Paul Newman. It *was* Paul Newman. He just walked up, said, "My name is Paul Newman, and I'm waiting to see so-and-so," and sat down. Newman never worked at TV8, although people think he did. He worked as an actor for an ad agency that did commercials at Channel 8 during the late news in the mid-1950s. He was there a lot.

Bob Hope didn't have that posse hang-up, either. I was just sorry he didn't have better timing. He was in town when Hoolie and I were doing a dunk tank–event for charity in front of the station, and he said he would come by. I loved all the "Road" movies, so I'd be meeting one of my real heroes.

The dunk tank was probably the most brutal thing I ever agreed to do. It was late afternoon, because they wanted to get everybody leaving work downtown, and we drew a big crowd. I never left that tank. Hoolie and I got dunked so many times that I'd cringe every time someone threw a ball. You get punchy and irritable, and then it gets cold. It was summer, but there was a cool breeze, the sun was gone, and I was wet. After hours of this, I said I had to go to the john. It felt so nice that I toweled dry and stayed inside around fifteen minutes.

Naturally, that was when Hope came and talked to Hoolie, who got a nice picture. Hope came with one person, otherwise walking around freely downtown by himself with no entourage. Cleveland seems to be like that. The stars who came from here, as I met more of them, never had an entourage or posse, especially the athletes. They were comfortable without one. Paul Newman was a megastar, the biggest movie star going, when he walked up to the reception desk at TV8 and modestly introduced himself.

Tim Conway had become a big star on *The Carol Burnett Show* and was doing a show with Harvey Korman in Pittsburgh when he called and said he wanted to do a skit. He drove up for that himself, dropped off his wife, and, after we were done shooting, asked me how to get to the Football Hall of Fame. I gave him the standard answer: Get on Interstate 77 and go south until you're bored—when it occurred to me that this was a guy as big as anybody. He'd be driving around, getting gas, doing a tour, and doing it alone without some escort didn't bother him.

Debra Winger came to the station by herself and asked if I was there. So did Tom Hanks.

Drew Carey is the same way. When Lil' John and I were working with him in the '90s, he was really big, the star of two primetime shows, and he was happy to see us because he was a Cleveland guy who grew up watching us.

"I GUESS I BETTER PUT MY TITS ON"

Janice Pennington, one of the original "Barker's Beauties" hostesses on *The Price Is Right,* made a promotional stop at the station. We were getting her to do some "stay-tuned-for" spots. I never saw her "Playmate of the Month" spread in *Playboy* magazine, which was fairly recent, but I assumed she'd be buxom. I wrote a thing for her that went something like: Just sit there and stay tuned, and you're going to see two of the biggest, nicest, best formed—all the way down the line double-entendres that would lead up to "Hoolihan & Big Chuck," but which obviously referred to her boobs.

When she arrived, I handed her the script. We started talking, and all of a sudden I realized that although she had a very nice figure, she wasn't that buxom. I tried to think of a way to get the script back, but she was reading it. I kept quiet. She stopped reading, looked at me, and said, "Well, I guess I better go put my tits on."

I was sort of shocked. I'd never heard a woman talk like that. But she must have been used to expectations because she left and came back in a black *Playboy* sweater, definitely looking buxom. I was a little embarrassed about it, but she was great and later did a skit with us. Very professional and very talented.

ANN-MARGRET, WAYNE NEWTON, AND THE KIELBASY KID

Ann-Margret came to the station one Friday to cut promos for a CBS special she was on. Everyone was excited. I had to go to the control room while she was there, and everybody was watching her on the monitors. I said to the crew, "She's right there in the studio. Why don't you go out and look?" No, no, they had to do it that way. It was really funny.

I was busy working with Bob Soinksi on a Kielbasy Kid skit. I had to get it done for the opening that night. We were still using 16-mm film. The editing booth was off a hallway, with a doorway but no door. I'd stand over Bob's shoulder while he edited—splicing film, scraping it clean, putting on cement, putting it together. The whole process takes a minute. While he did that, I'd go out and get a drink from the water fountain. I read that drinking a lot of water was good for you, and while editing a skit I'd drink a gallon.

Ann-Margret went to the fountain while I was in the control room, saw Bob editing, and started watching. I came out, and she was really into it. She thought the skit was funny, and she'd never seen film being edited. I explained it was the exact same process as the 35-mm film used in her movies, and she asked more questions, which I answered. We were talking easily, and I wasn't nervous at all. Then I turned around and there was Roger Smith, her husband, giving me the dirtiest look you ever saw. Just looking daggers. I thought he was going to punch me.

It was one of the most flattering things that ever happened to me. Roger Smith was mad. *I* made him jealous.

I wanted one Kielbasy Kid skit every week in those days. I didn't know how many things you could do with kielbasy, but we were going to find out. I came in to work a four-to-twelve shift one day, and Marge at the desk said, "Where were you? Wayne Newton is here! He's watching Bob Soinksi edit Kielbasy Kid." Newton, a big star at the time, grew up in Virginia and Ohio, in Polish coal-mining areas, so the kielbasy thing really struck his fancy. At around 2:30 p.m., he asked if I was there and actually waited until I came in just to say how much he liked the skit.

He's really a nice guy. Years later, when we went to Las Vegas and saw him perform, he was told we were in the audience. He had a spotlight put on us and said, "Ladies and gentlemen, the Kielbasy Kid!" The Clevelanders went crazy, and nobody else knew what he was talking about.

POLES APART

I won an Emmy for directing Ed Asner and Ted Knight in a Channel 8 news campaign when they doing *The Mary Tyler Moore Show*. We were to tape between news shows one evening and then do an early morning session the next day. After the first session, we had some drinks with them at Swingos, where they were staying. I had to drive home to Hinckley and back afterward. They only had to go upstairs, and they took advantage of it. They were normally funny and bubbly, but they showed up all hung over and quiet in the morning. They brought doughnuts with them, and when Ted took a bite and swallowed, Ed said, "I think I heard something splash."

Something was bugging me the whole time, and I couldn't think what it was. Then Ted looked at me and said, "I think we're related." The second he said it, I knew what was gnawing at me. It was like I was talking to my father. Ted looked just like him. Ted's real name was Tadeus Wladyslaw Konopka. He was from Pennsylvania, and I vaguely remembered my father's family had relatives there with that name.

Bobby Vinton, "the Polish Prince," was also from Pennsylvania. He was enjoying resurgence in his career with "My Melody of Love" when Dom Ortuso, one of the biggest pranksters at TV8, said he was coming to the station. "Do you want to do something with him?" he asked. I did.

Vinton was in the studio waiting. I walked in and introduced myself, and he started speaking in Polish. I understand a little bit but can't speak it. We were speaking in English when Ortuso came in smoking a cigar. I introduced them, and Dom gave a little wave. It was awkward, and I thought it was rude that he wasn't talking. Then Dom said, "I don't think he can sing for shit." Vinton looked startled and gave him a shot back, something about being screwed up at the station. They started getting really hot and began swearing. I was shocked and worried. There was nobody but me to break it up, and it looked like things would come to that.

Then they started laughing. They set me up. They'd grown up together in Pennsylvania. I relaxed and said, "You're really having resurgence." Vinton smiled and said, "Only this time. I know it's not going to last. I'm making so much money, I'm just socking it away." What a great career he's had.

CHAPTER 16

REAL SPECIALS

ADMIRAL SCHODOWSKI ROCKS THE BOAT

Being TV's Big Chuck was still a sideline, and Channel 8 assigned me a full schedule of other programs and projects to produce and direct. One was a safe-boating special in the early 1970s that the U.S. Coast Guard wanted the station to write and produce. I didn't want to do the usual public service thing. I wanted it to be funny. So I asked Jim Doney to star in it, doing a Buster Keaton–type character with no lines, all pantomime. It was unheard of for someone like that, a respected newsman and the star of his own show, to play a bumbling comic character, but Jim liked the idea, and Bagwell thought it was great.

I called it "Don't Rock the Boat." We met at Hinckley Lake, and went to Kelleys Island, located across from a Coast Guard station to shoot the rest. We got there early in the morning, on a special ferryboat for us, and four or five cutters were standing by for the shoot. A chief warrant officer named Wolf greeted me, shook my hand, and asked if there was anything I needed. I said, "I want you to chase all the boats off the lake," and had to add, "No, no, I'm kidding," because they'd jump right to it, like I was an admiral. Really! It was great.

Doney would haplessly demonstrate the wrong way to do things on the water. Then chief warrant officer Wolf would explain the correct procedure. Jim did some fairly difficult stunts, which I wrote thinking I could do them as his double if necessary, but he never hesitated and never complained. We both won Emmys for it, and I knew my real talent was writing for real talent like Doney and Hoolie. They could do difficult things and do them well. They had to do things well to make them funny.

The Coast Guard loved the special. The next year my son Mark came back from swimming at the beach on Kelleys and said the Coast Guard was there, showing the film in a tent. That's what they wanted it for, boater education, and they used it for years. Years later, when Doney retired to Hawaii, he called and said, "You'll never guess what I just saw here."

BROCK PETERS AND *HEARTSONG, U.S.A.*

In 1975 I got an assignment to direct a show that would air on all the Storer stations across the country. It was the biggest thing I'd ever done by far: a one-hour Thanksgiving special titled *Heartsong, U.S.A.,* sponsored by the Cleveland Musical Arts Association and featuring the two-hundred-member Cleveland Orchestra Chorus, directed by Robert Page. It was going to star Gregory Peck as narrator, but he had to drop out at the last minute when his oldest son, a TV reporter, committed suicide. Brock Peters, who starred with him in *To Kill A Mockingbird,* took his place. It was to be shot on film. I would be directing a made-for-TV movie.

I met Peters at a big meeting with Page and other people from the orchestra and chorus. The first thing he said was, "What is my motivation for this?" It was the last thing I expected him to say. He was a star. I thought: *I have to motivate him?* I said, "You do this real quick and you can get out of here." He laughed, everybody laughed, and we went on.

We shot a lot of it in and around Severance Hall, but most of it was shot at Hale Farm. Peters had a great, beautiful voice, and there's a part in *Heartsong* where he says you can still feel the ghost of Old Man Hale. There was something spooky in the way he read it that really created an atmosphere and gave us a chill. He said he had to tell me a story it reminded him of. He was in a show on Broadway around Christmas one year when friends invited him to their weekend house in the mountains. It was dark and snowing pretty hard, and he got lost on a back road and pulled into a gas station for help. A guy in a truck told him exactly the way to go. On the way back, he said, he stopped again at the station to say thanks. "What do you mean?" the station attendant said. Peters described the man who helped him, and the attendant asked him to describe the truck. Peters did, and the attendant gasped and said he'd exactly described someone who was killed nearby in a truck accident three years earlier.

Obviously, Brock didn't need to ask me for his motivation. He brought his own experience.

The special opens with a jogger running through University Circle at Severance Hall. I used Art Lofredo for everything on that show, so when I needed the sound of footsteps for the jogger, I had Art run in step in the studio. I was listening and watching on a monitor, and it matched perfectly. We recorded the sequence, and I went on laying the show down on tape, totally forgetting about what Art was doing. I went out to the studio and, sure enough, Art was still running. He wouldn't stop until I told him to. It was one of the things that made me more determined than ever to get him hired at Channel 8. We did a Hoolihan & Big Chuck skit around then where he was a fisherman who gets the tables turned: Art takes a bite of a sandwich attached to a line and gets pulled underwater by a fish. In real life he's deathly afraid of water, but he wouldn't admit to it because he did not want to do anything to make me stop using him. For two days at home he filled his bathtub with water and practiced putting his head under in preparation for the skit. That's how dedicated he was.

Heartsong won an Emmy, and it got good reviews. William Hickey, the TV critic in the *Plain Dealer*, called it a "special treat," and said the fact that it was a local production was "especially gratifying about the program's excellence."

BURGESS MEREDITH AND THE BIGGEST SHOW OF ALL

My biggest project came about two years later. The Musical Arts Association liked the job I did on *Heartsong* and wanted me to do another movie. This was one was really huge.

Titled *The Wandering Muse of Artemus Flagg,* and written by Everett Dodrill of Cleveland Heights, it traced the American spirit of pioneering and inventiveness from colonial times to the modern day. It took the same character, Artemus Flagg, through all those eras.

Burgess Meredith would star, and the Cleveland Orchestra and Chorus, directed by Robert Page, would again be featured. Because of the success of *Heartsong,* they went out and got some bucks for a big budget. The sponsorship was entirely by Cleveland-based companies, including Stouffers, Sherwin Williams, Midland Ross, Reliance Electric, and Diamond Shamrock.

Everything would be shot on tape, and it would be the first time we used a minicam, our newest piece of equipment. It was to be shot on location at Greenfield Village, west of Detroit in Deerfield, which meant we took a big crew with a remote unit and generator. We utilized just about everything they had. We built elaborate sets and used costumes made by seamstresses who had their own truck. I hand-picked my crew from TV8. Every person was the very best at what he or she did. I felt like Cecil B. DeMille with all this under my control. Although overwhelmed and nervous, I gained confidence as we started shooting.

Peter Miller was the photographer, and I called Art Lofredo to be my assistant director. He could do anything down to building props, and this was my chance to get him a job at TV8. I used chorus members as extras, projectionist Ralph Gertz from our show, my daughter Melissa, and our nephew Rick Kole. There were things I could direct them to do, and because I knew their capabilities, I would save time and trouble. Bob Huber, the program director and a friend, came up to the shoot, and Herb Thomas would drive up from Cleveland just to watch and lend his support. Everett Dodrill came, too, and I'd recognize other faces in the big crowds that turned out.

On the set everyone looked for me to make contact with Burgess Meredith. When I found out he was from Cleveland—in fact, he gave the orchestra a hometown discount for his work—we were fine. He was crabby as hell when we were shooting, especially to Art and everyone else. I assigned Art to wake him up every morning, and Art would get so mad and frustrated he threatened to leave. That's saying something. I told him he'd have to thumb a ride home if he did.

With top-hatted star Burgess Meredith during shooting of *The Wandering Muse of Artemus Flagg*. Many of the extras who appeared in the movie were Cleveland Orchestra Chorus members.

Hollywood people think a director is god. They're trained that way, but Burgess didn't know what to make of me. He was a star who'd just won a Tony on Broadway, had leading roles in some of the best-known episodes of *The Twilight Zone*, and played the Penguin on *Batman*. He'd be signing autographs for people watching the shoot, and then he'd have a perplexed look on his face when they asked for my autograph. He never asked me about it, but I knew he wanted to, and I think that was why he never bugged me. He figured I was somebody he ought to know but didn't.

His nickname was Buzz, but I never called him that. He read everything from cue cards, and he insisted on his own personal cue card handler, a little old guy like him named Barney. Whatever Burgess wanted, Barney would do, and Barney would do it well.

One morning when I woke up, Art said, "Barney's gone. He's not here. There's some other guy here."

I couldn't believe it. How could Barney just vanish in the middle of the night? But it was true. He disappeared without a word and had been replaced by another cue card man—a nasty, mouthy guy who was just the opposite of Barney. When Burgess asked him to change something, he said, "Oh for chrissakes, whaddya want? This is good enough." I finally had to take him aside and tell him not to talk to Burgess like that. "Just shut your mouth," I said, "or Art's going to be the cue card guy, and I don't care where you go."

The next morning, as if by magic, Barney was back. Bob Hope was taping a special and wanted him, so they took Barney in the middle of the night and returned him the next day. It was like the CIA. I found out later that Barney McNulty was famous as the Cue Card King. He traveled the world with Hope, who called him his "right-hand man," and he said that Hope, Frank Sinatra, and Milton Berle were his most important clients. All I knew was that we were glad to have him back.

After several days of shooting, I realized a scene coming up would be hard and dangerous for Burgess to do. He had to get on a cowcatcher on a moving train. There was a little platform he could put his feet on, but he was no agile young man. If he slipped, he might get pushed along, because a cowcatcher goes almost to the track, but there was no way the train could stop. I knew screenwriter Everett Dodrill would be there, and I thought of asking him to change the scene, even though I'd told him I would do everything I could to avoid changes. I was almost sure Burgess would not want to do this. I couldn't blame him.

The shooting days were long, twelve to fourteen hours. At dinner each night, Burgess would turn into the nicest, warmest, and most interesting guy. One night he asked why I always ran away the moment we finished a scene. I told him I was running to the truck. He said, "Why run?"

I said, "I do this 150 times a day. If I walk, I'd add at least an hour to our shooting day. I trot."

Then he asked when we'd see the rushes—the quick prints that they rush for the director to see, first thing in the morning, after a day of shooting on a film. I explained that there weren't rushes because the movie was being shot with a minicam on videotape. He stared, not knowing what I meant. I said it was like audiotape—you rewind it and look at it. "There are no rushes. When you see me running, I run to the truck to make sure the scene was OK."

As we neared the day of the train shoot, he asked me again when we'd see rushes. After explaining the whole thing again, I had an idea: I'd let him preview the shot of the train when it comes steaming around the bend. This was just before Burgess was to run alongside the train, talking to the engineer; just before he gets on the cowcatcher. Maybe if he saw the scene of something we'd just shot, he'd be impressed and be more likely to do it.

We shot it the next day, and it looked like anything you'd see in Hollywood. It was beautiful. I called, "Burgess! Come on over here and look at this!" He came into the truck, stared at the monitor shot of the train coming around the bend, and yelled, "Barney! Barney! Come in here! Look at this! We just did this! We just shot this!" Barney was a little hip. He knew video, and he said, "Oh, that's nice."

I said, "You know, Burgess, I just thought of something. Wouldn't it look great if you were on that cowcatcher when it came around the bend?"

Burgess said, "Yes!" Yes indeed! Art and I winked at each other.

So we shot with him on the cowcatcher. We ran over our cable at one point, setting up, and had to run another line. I was worried that was a bad omen, but the scene went off with no problems—although Burgess started running back to the truck with me every time after that to preview his scenes. He actually slowed us up. But I expected that would happen, which is why I saved it to almost the last day of shooting.

Most days we had just enough energy left to shower, eat, and go to bed. But one evening, when we were dead tired after an extra-long day, we had to shoot another scene, without Burgess, for a voiceover.

It was an outdoor scene at night with a merry-go-round that we were supposed to find down a dirt road through the woods. Art Lofredo, Dick Lorius, Pete Miller, and I were driving and driving when we finally saw it. It was like something out of a dream. There was a lea surrounded by woods, five or six acres of nothing but grass, with an enormous carousel in the middle, lit up and playing music. A rich guy had built it for his kids. I couldn't believe it.

Pete started setting up his camera. I got on the carousel. I was so tired, but I enjoyed the moment so much—a little piece of magic.

The carousel went around, and I saw only Pete and Dick in the grass. Art was on the carousel, too. Then Pete and Dick followed. No one said a word. It was a magic moment of music and gentle motion, the right thing at the right time. It calmed us down. We were pushing every day.

"Let's do this now," I said.

Everyone was quiet on the way home, tired and mesmerized by the moment. It was ten or eleven, and we'd have to get up at 5:30.

I said to Art, "Let's go get those Big Boys."

Art was a big Big Boy fan like me. From age sixteen, when I became really independent, until I got married at twenty-two, I lived entirely on Manners' Big Boys. They were all I ate. I loved them and never tired of them. We had seen a Big Boy restaurant on the way to Greenfield Village before the movie started and agreed to go there to eat.

It was way farther than we thought, a half-hour each way, and we each ordered two or three Big Boys to bring back. By then it was after midnight, and we could hardly keep our eyes open. I made a big Manhattan and ate the first Big Boy. I don't remember Art leaving. I don't remember going to bed. I only remember that I woke up to find I had three-quarters of a Big Boy left. I ate it for breakfast and went back to work.

One night during supper I asked Burgess if he'd done any movies lately. He said, "Yeah, I'm shooting a movie right now. As soon as we finish this shoot, I'm going to return to it." He said it was about boxing, and he played a fight trainer.

"Who's in it?" I asked.

"Bunch of nobodies," he said—and they were. He didn't know the names, and I didn't know the names, which were Sylvester Stallone and Talia Shire. The movie, of course, was *Rocky*. I realized later I was working with the guy who was in the film inspired by the Ali-Werner fight, which led to one of my skits.

We finished shooting almost on schedule, which was one of the things I became known for. Dominic Ortuso, the program manager and a good friend, set up an event complete with togas to welcome me back to Channel 8. I felt like a conquering hero in Rome.

The whole shoot took three weeks. *Hoolihan & Big Chuck* went on without a break because I left pretaped shows in the can. I had fifteen-hour work days, seven days a week, and went from that to twelve-hour days of editing—and then had to touch up some scenes. I also started lobbying to get Art Lofredo a job, which finally paid off when he was hired as a camera operator and studio technician.

Artemus Flagg won an Emmy. Herb Thomas said he heard comments that no one else could have handled directing it, which really made me feel good. It was the biggest thing I'd ever done.

Burgess was on the set about two weeks. Before he left, he told me we did more in one day than they would have done in a week or two in Hollywood. I had enough experience to know it was true. I really worked him, and he said he never worked so hard for so little money.

I said, "Is that a compliment?"

He said, "I think so."

What a great guy. I really liked him.

CHAPTER 17

FLYING WITH HOOLIE

Being Big Chuck was far from my full-time job at Channel 8. I wasn't doing remotes anymore because people would recognize me, and that would get in the way, but I was a full-time engineer and director.

For Bob Wells, being Hoolihan was even more of a sideline. He did it as a freelancer after resigning as a staff announcer in 1971. His commercial voiceover business was doing well, especially in Chicago. He had an apartment there, and he flew his own plane, so he'd be gone two or three days a week. He kept doing weekend weather and our show, but he really wasn't into it, and he could be hard to get hold of. Rather than work around his schedule, I started using Lil' John and Art Lofredo more and more in skits because they were available.

I often directed weekend news, so I saw a lot of him doing the weather. Hoolie said things you can't imagine. On Pearl Harbor day one year he said, "I used to know a guy who was half black and half Japanese. His name was Spade Coolie. Every December 7 he would attack Pearl Bailey." When we first got satellite photos, we'd get images of the region, with dots superimposed to show the shape of Ohio. Hoolie showed it and said, "Here we have the new satellite picture, and by the way, I want to thank Governor Rhodes for getting all the Boy Scouts in Ohio to form the outline and spell out Ohio in the middle. I thought it was a great idea!" He did it with a straight face, so the phone rang off the hook with people wondering why their Boy Scout wasn't invited and why they didn't hear about it. When radar images first came out, he pointed to the anomalous propagation, or false echoes, stopped on Lake Erie and said, "And this one right here, we've just confirmed, is a Russian submarine

"Lil' John" Rinaldi joined *Hoolihan & Big Chuck* in 1971, quickly becoming a mainstay.

about ten miles off Sandusky." The phone started ringing again.

He actually knew a lot about radar, as a pilot who flew fighter jets in the air force. But because he was an F-80 pilot, getting into the plane he had was like getting off a Harley onto a tricycle. That can make you careless. It could make me crazy.

I was with him once flying near the Lahm Air Guard Station in Mansfield. He liked to get on the phone talking to airports, so he wasn't paying attention to where he was. A guy cut in and told him to get the hell out of the area, he was too low and close. He said, "Ohmigod!" and started doing all these things at the controls. They were scrambling a squadron of jets right under us, and they were so close I thought the wings were coming off from the turbulence. I can't tell you how scared I was. Hoolie said, "Ooh, that was close."

He'd pick me up and fly me back to Kelleys Island. He picked me up one time to go to southern Ohio, and a huge thunderstorm was coming. He said, "If we go around, we'll never be there in time. Want to fly through it?" I said, "I don't know, can you do that?" He could, and it was the scariest thing I've done in my life, with thunder and lightning in pitch blackness all around us. Hoolie's gutsy, and maybe you've got to be a little goofy to be a fighter pilot. Sometimes, flying to Chicago, he'd have to pee from drinking coffee all day. He'd take the plane as high as he could, pull the canopy back, go into a sideways dive and lean out. He's nuts. I love him!

It was pitch black and foggy one summer night when we were coming back to Kelleys. I said maybe we should just land at Wadsworth—I could go home to Hinckley from there. He told me to look for the airfield, and I wondered how low we were. He said, "Well, we're too low. We're over the lake." Which we couldn't see. We were flying in total blackness. He was really good with instruments, and he was staring hard at them. "I don't understand this," he said. I asked how he knew the thing was accurate, and he said, "Just keep looking." We were going lower and lower. The darkness was consuming me, and I could hear my heart beating. He said, "I don't understand it, we should be right over"—and when he said those words, the runway lights appeared right below us. It was unbelievable. He pulled up a little, circled, and put us down right on the button.

Kelleys has a real short runway. It runs up to a road and becomes a field on the other side. A sign on the road says "Beware of low-flying planes." I go by in a golf cart and stop, but for all the years I've been going there, I've never seen a low-flying plane. When Hoolie once picked me up from Kelleys, however, the wind was blowing from one direction, and it changed while we were gone. Hoolie didn't check the wind sock when we returned. We were landing with the wind. Hoolie couldn't get the plane down because of it. So he slammed it down, and we hit and went flying across the road into the field. I thought we crashed. It was rougher than hell, trees were coming closer and closer, and he was hitting the brakes and spinning the plane. It was only a few feet to the trees when we stopped. He turned us around and taxied back. An old guy smoking a pipe, real calm, watched us get out of the plane, with Hoolie all embarrassed. The guy took out the pipe and said, "Looks the opening of *The Hoolihan & Big Chuck Show*."

He was always teaching me how to fly. Coming to Kelleys, he would circle around the water tower right across from my house, which I think was illegal. I'd come out and wave, and he'd go land at the airport. We'd do the same thing coming back, and June would know to go to the airport to pick me up. One time he had me take over and said, "Go ahead, circle the water tower." I did and said, "Geez, I can see my dogs on the ground and everything." I marveled about how well I could see, never thinking that when you make a turn in a plane you lose altitude. I was circling, seeing clearer and clearer, and started waving to June, not noticing I was corkscrewing down. Hoolie finally noticed and yelled, "Oh shit, you're going to corkscrew us into the ground!" He grabbed the controls and took over. That was a close one.

He taught me when you get in trouble and lose power, you have a four-to-one glide ratio, your forward speed divided by the sinking speed. You use it to pick out a spot somewhere you might have to crash-land.

Once he was going to pick me up at Burke Lakefront Airport. I was having a cup of coffee, waiting, and saw a little plane come in. It bounced on the runway, screeched around, and stopped. It was Hoolie, all embarrassed about the landing. He said it was more like a controlled crash. He was in some arrangement where his plane could be rented out, and he'd be given another if he needed it. They'd given him a high-performance plane they used for acrobatics, and he got carried away.

"This is neat," he said. "You can do loops and all sorts of things."

It was getting dark as we flew back one night, and he said, "This is neat, because instead of having a gas gauge, you actually see the gas in the tube," pointing to a vertical tube to my right on the side of the cockpit. "You see the gas level?" I said no—I saw the plastic tube, but I didn't see gas. "No," he said. "You'll see the level, the top of the gas." He started to lean over to look, and I heard the plane putt-putt-putter. The engine stopped, and all I could hear was wind. I said, "This is it, man," and started looking for the four-to-one ratio spot to land. I was going crazy.

He was calmly turning dials and gauges, turning over to the other tank, in the other wing, which he never told me the plane had.

"Why didn't you change earlier?" I asked.

He said he always liked to run the tank out to empty.

"Please," I said, "don't ever do that again when I'm with you." I almost crapped my pants.

It was always an adventure. He was going to teach me landing as we approached Freedom Field in Medina off Route 18. You have to cut back on the throttle but maintain your lift. It's a balancing act at the controls. I was begging him to take over, but he waved me off. "You're doing fine!" he said. Then the stall warning went on. He calmly said to put the nose down a bit. Don't stall the engine. I was still begging him to take over. I was right over the runway and sure I was going to stall. Hoolie chuckled, took over the controls, turned the plane hard to the right—I was about to land on Route 18—and slammed it down hard on the runway. They call it a pancake landing. I think he enjoyed it.

He didn't have to be flying to make trouble, either. When we took one of our tours to Las Vegas, he stood at the cockpit door talking to the pilot while I greeted the group boarding. The pilot excused himself for a few minutes and left his uniform coat and hat. Hoolie put them on. As the other people boarded, he backed out the door, pretending to be talking to someone in the cockpit. "I don't care what you say," he said, "I'm not flying this hunk of junk anymore" and stomped off.

The people boarding were in shock. Hoolie came back, taking off the coat and hat, and said to them, "Just kidding."

Try that today!

CHAPTER 18

THAT WAS A CLOSE ONE

PERSONAL APPEARANCE, AERIAL ADVENTURE

Hoolie kept booking our personal appearances, and in the early 1970s we became real popular. We didn't refuse anything. And being a pilot with his own plane, he was especially happy to book us for a pilots' convention and air show at Summit Mall in Akron and at the Akron airport.

I was nervous as hell about it. Hoolie couldn't care if the whole world was watching. I said, "You do all the emcee things, I'll do whatever else we're supposed to do." It was a Sunday, a really windy day, and I left early. At the airport, they asked if one of us would ride in a hot-air balloon. I said I'd do it.

The balloon came in from Kings Island. It looked like it was tied to the bumper of a truck. As I went around the truck to it, I heard some guys arguing. They weren't just disagreeing.

"I'm a pilot, not a daredevil!" one of them said. "You can't go up in this wind!" Uh-oh. He said, "It's getting worse! There's a storm coming!" It was, too. The sky was getting black. I heard the pilot repeat that he wasn't a daredevil, and the guy from the air show reply that they were in a bind, telling him they'd advertised that Hoolie and I would take part in some things. I was about to step in and tell him not to go up on my account. As I approached, the pilot said, "OK, if we're going up, we have to go up right now. Right now! This second!" They saw me and shouted to get in.

The crew was already untying the balloon as I climbed into the basket. I didn't even have both legs in when it jerked up. I pulled my leg in, and up we flew.

There was an immediate problem. We weren't supposed to go up yet because they were dropping skydivers into the mall parking lot. They were falling past us as we went up, inches away, yelling at us, really upset. "Goddammit, you (bleepers)! What the (bleep) are you (bleepers) doing? You trying to kill us? You a-holes!"

The other problem was that we were headed right toward the storm. I really could have enjoyed the ride under other circumstances. Under these circumstances, I asked the pilot what we were going to do. He said, "I'm going to look for the first open spot to put this thing down!"

I said, "Can you steer it?"

"Absolutely not!" he shouted. "You can't steer a balloon, only make it go up and down!"

Don't worry, he added—we'll find something. "Look over there," he said. "Beyond those buildings there's a neighborhood. We get lucky, we'll get an open field."

It was windy and dark. He had the balloon so low, at rooftop level, that people could recognize me. They were out in driveways, running down the street. I could hear them yelling, "Chuck!"

We came across a highway. I thought maybe the pilot could set us down, but he couldn't. Cars swerved off the road. We went up a little bit. We were going over chimneys so close I could touch them. Finally, the pilot said, "Oh, great! Hang on!"

There was a field in front of us, with a horse in it and a fence. The pilot put the balloon down, and we hit the ground so hard I thought we crashed. I fell backward and started to get back on my feet. He grabbed me and said, "Get down!" When the weight comes off a balloon, the top of the bag comes down and then goes back up. When that happened, we were jerked up with tremendous force, then slammed down again. This time, the basket tipped over. It was still moving because the balloon was blowing. I could see the horse running around, houses coming closer, and the fence. Then I saw hands coming in all around to grab and stop us, never knowing that a ground crew follows a balloon. They got us just in time.

At home later, I told my son Michael about it. He had been out with Claudia, the girl he was dating who's now his wife, and her parents. He said, "Yeah, we almost got run off the road. Claudia's parents were saying, 'Look at that stupid jerk in the balloon!' I said, 'I think that's my father.'"

Three men in a tub—Hoolie, Tony Carmen, and me—for a skit shot in Garfield Heights. When the cops asked what we were doing, we pointed to the sign in the background: "Help keep our city clean." While we were shooting it, my uncle rode by on a bus.

GETTING BUGGED AT A DEMOLITION DERBY

We did everything from parades to demolition derbies. Sandusky Speedway booked us for one of those. They asked us to be in a "squash-the-bug" thing and emcee other track events. It sounded fine. Demolition derbies are always on muddy tracks where you can't get good traction, so I didn't worry.

We got there and saw they had real races, on an asphalt track. That's where "squash the bug" was going to be—with a Volkswagen Bug. Hoolie and I were on one team, and three or four guys were on another. They paid to get in because there was a prize. We all were in cars, the Bug was in the middle, and each team would try to push it across the other's line, like a football. I said, "Hey, this is asphalt. Are we going to do this on asphalt?" The guy setting it up said, "Yup!"

He gave me a tip. In a demolition derby, they try to smash your radiator so you'll overheat, and that'll put you out right away. "Keep the front of your car away from that," he said.

The crowd was getting into it, and I saw my kids right next to where we were squashing the bug. We each got our own cars, with all the glass taken out. There was no buckle on the seatbelt, and I knew it was going to be violent, so at the last second I tied a big knot into it. We got going. I maneuvered around so they couldn't hit me, and a guy passed me and stopped. He put his car into reverse and flew back at me to hit the radiator full speed. Steam came inside the car, and I couldn't breathe or see. I was against the wall where my kids were, trying to untie the damn seatbelt. I got cracked again, then finally untied the damn thing, crawled out the window, grabbed the railing, and climbed into the stands.

Hoolie was still out there. He demolished two cars, and all that was left of the Bug was the rear end. He slammed into it. But another guy, whose car was steaming and stopped, got out near the goal line, grabbed the VW bumper, and tried to drag it across the line.

Hoolie was steaming, too. He didn't see the guy, backed up over his leg, and broke it. He screamed in pain. The other guys, his buddies, scoffed and said, "Don't worry about that a-hole, he shouldn'ta been doing that anyway."

There were more events, and they asked if we would ride in the pace car. I asked what we'd have to do. "Just go around a lap and then turn off." It sounded simple. Then I looked behind me, where guys were driving lying down in asbestos suits, looking like mummies. They were burning alcohol, and the whole place reeked of it. We took off for our lap, got to 120 miles an hour, and these cars were just idling keeping up. I saw the guy with the flag to start the race. He couldn't hear, but the pace car driver was shouting, "No, no! Don't wave!" We had to cross to the infield! He waved the flag, and it sounded like an explosion behind us as all those cars hit it. They passed like we were standing still, and we skidded onto the grass crossing in front of them. I was scared as hell.

Hoolie and I emceed other events between races. We were standing on the back of the rescue truck for one when a car flipped. The truck took off with us hanging on. We got to the car, which was dripping alcohol, and here came a guy with a fire extinguisher, smoking a cigar. Hoolie yelled, "Not there, not there! Put that cigar out!"

I went up to sit with my kids in the grandstand. A car lost a tire, and it went flying by. It could have killed us all.

I said I'd never do it again. The next week, we were getting ready to do our show and somebody told us that the guy Hoolie injured was coming to the station to talk to us. Right away we figured we were going to get sued or worse. But all he wanted us to do was sign his cast. There was plenty of room. It went from ankle to hip.

JUST LIKE KING THE WONDER DOG

I went on my own to a dogsled race in Brecksville. Doug Adair, the news anchor, went every year because he'd win. Now I was asked to be in it, and they told me I could pick any dog team I wanted. I looked them over and said, "Give me the biggest dogs. What's that?" The guy in charge said it was malamute—"They're usually the lead dog." I asked if he could put all malamutes on my team, and he said sure.

Doug had a regular team of little dogs with a malamute as lead. My dogs took off and almost jerked me off the sled. We went down a hill and flew way ahead of Doug. I saw we were coming to a snow fence and tried pulling and shouting to turn. The dogs were growling and snapping while they were running, but they weren't turning. They ran right up and over the fence, and I went flying. The crowd behind the fence went flying.

The guy in charge ran up laughing. "All these dogs are lead dogs," he said. "The ones that aren't in the lead are upset; they're trying to get up there. That's why they didn't listen."

I wished I had listened to him earlier.

SO WHY IS YOUR HAIR GREEN?

Hoolie and I were supposed to do a promotional thing at Chippewa Lake, where they had a souped-up speedboat called Dynamite. A big crowd was gathered around the lake, and the event people asked if we could water ski. We both said yes.

We got in the water. I didn't want to look really stupid, so I told the guy in the boat, "Don't open this thing up all the way. We're not Sea World skiers."

The boat had two exhausts, and it was a good distance away. He fired it up, and two jets of hot water blew straight out and hit us each in the kisser. Hoolie couldn't get up on his skis. He tried again, couldn't do it, got mad, and left the water. I said I'd do it myself, don't worry.

They dropped Hoolie's line, and I repeated: *Don't go fast.* The boat took off, and I was skiing and waving. He started going faster. I gestured to keep it down, but he sped up. I had told him I'd let go if he went too fast, but he was going way too fast to let go. He crossed over our own wake, and I went airborne for what seemed like ten seconds, frantically trying to think how I'd land. I hit the water and rolled on top of it, tumbling over and over. The crowd cheered.

I pulled myself out of the water. Jerry Jaswa from Channel 8 came over and told me there was a line of people who wanted my autograph. He lined them up. I put on a towel, tried to dry off, and started signing. People were looking at me really funny. I must have signed a hundred pictures for a half-hour or forty-five minutes. When I finished, Jerry leaned over and said, "Chuck, you got a big snot hanging out of your nose." Water snot—a big chartreuse thing hanging up over my ear.

I said, "You let these people look at me with this? Why didn't you tell me?"

He said, "I didn't want to embarrass you."

YOU GET WHAT YOU PAY FOR

I missed out on a lot of family things because of personal appearances, so I tried to take family with me whenever I could. But anybody who has a media deadline misses out on all kinds of things. It comes with the job.

We only took enough money from the All-Stars to cover the cost of uniforms and a bus, but I used to tell Ernie Anderson I felt guilty about taking money for personal appearances because I was not a performer. I didn't deserve to be treated as an entertainer. He said the time alone was worth something, and he said, "You ever notice that the more people pay you, the better they treat you?"

I never forgot that because it's so true. I once went to my old neighborhood to do something at a carnival. Hoolie wasn't around, and I didn't like doing things by myself, but I agreed to make an appearance because it was my neighborhood. I had to park far from the field and the stage. When the woman who booked me saw me walking up, she stopped me and said, "Here comes Big Chuck, kids! Go get him!" They were

With June at a New Year's Eve party. I missed a lot of family events because of personal appearances. It came with the job.

grabbing and pulling me like an attack. She encouraged it. When you get paid nothing, sometimes you get treated like nothing. Ernie was right.

CHAPTER 19

PLAYING FOR LAUGHS

THEY SAY PART OF THE GAME IS MENTAL

The All-Stars were riding high in the 1970s, and Hoolie did the booking for the games. He told us he'd booked one at a mental institution. He thought we'd play the staff.

Truthfully, I can't remember the name of the place. But we drove through a huge gate when we got there, and no one was in sight on the grounds. There were several old buildings and an enormous old Gothic mansion that looked like something from a horror movie. It was dark. I said, "Are you sure this is it?" There was no sign of life, nobody there to greet us, and the front door was locked.

We found a side door that was unlocked. We opened it, and a tremendously old guy was standing alone in the dark. It scared the hell out of me. But the team was behind me, and after we walked into a dark hallway, the guy pointed us down another dark, deserted hallway. We could see light at the end of it. As it turned out, the old guy was the security guard.

Usually you could hear the crowd and smell the popcorn before our games. There was a feeling of energy and anticipation. This was really creepy. We got to the end of the hallway, entered the gym, and there was no reaction. People in the stands were talking to each other and making out with each other. A huge guy sitting in the front row stared at me. I said hi. No reaction. Then he stood up, and in a real loud voice, said, "Hey, Big Chuck, you big (F-bomb)." Not smiling, real serious.

We got to the locker room and started dressing for the game. A guy who seemed to be in charge was real nice, but we learned there was no referee. It was getting worse and worse. I told my brother

On and off the court, the All-Stars were an entertaining troupe in the 1970s. Back row: Casey Kassarda, Soulman, Hoolie, Chuck, Ralph Gertz. Front row: Whoopie John, Bill Turner, John, Dave Stacy.

to keep an eye on the big guy in the front row because he didn't like me. I glanced over at him later, during the game, and he was staring at me the whole time, not looking at the game at all.

We did our regular stunts, Globetrotter-type stuff, and nobody laughed. Twenty minutes or so into the game, a guy ran out from the stands, grabbed the ball, and started dribbling. The crowd went crazy because it was one of them. It was the first real crowd reaction all night. Before we knew it, there must have been fifty guys on the court, going for the ball. Hoolie said to one of the other players, "Hey, you better stop this," assuming he was on staff. But it turned out he had the other players were patients, too. We finally got the ball, and they started fighting with us.

We formed a sort of circle and moved to the locker room. "Forget it," I said, "let's get out of here. We'll put our clothes on in the cars." The place was going crazy. We grabbed our clothes. The guy in the locker room we assumed was in charge said, "I get to go home every other weekend. I get drunk." He was a patient, too.

We left the way we came, only faster and carrying our clothes and wondering what the hell just happened. It was unbelievable that this place existed, where no one seemed to be in charge.

Hoolie also booked us against a motorcycle gang on the West Side. They were really nice but warned us that a rival gang was ticked off at them—telling us what we should do if a fight started.

BUILDING THE ALL-STAR SPIRIT

The All-Stars were much more than a celebrity team playing school faculties and other groups for charitable causes. We were an entertainment troupe with different skits for different sports, on and off the field. One of the favorite bits for softball was to take a grapefruit and paint it white. Our pitcher would just groove it to the batter, who'd be a mayor or police chief or school principal. They couldn't resist the pitch, couldn't miss it, and the grapefruit would splatter all over.

We put balls on cords, and we threw pies and buckets of water. I created a physical prowess act for me and Lil' John at basketball games. John would do a handstand on my back, and the crowd would love it. Then I'd do a handstand on John's back. For that, the crowd would go wild. There was no trick to it. John wrestled at Ohio State, and pound for pound he is the strongest man I know.

Abe Abraham, "the man in the brown suit" who retrieved balls on extra points and field goals at Browns games, was with us for a few years as basketball coach. We'd take out a football and throw it to him. The crowd would cheer, and he loved it.

We settled into more of a routine than we had in the Ghoulardi days when Ernie had us taking on all comers. We played a game a week, on Thursday nights, and Hoolie's wife, Barbara, did the announc-

John doing a handstand on my back was a regular act for the Hoolihan & Big Chuck All-Stars. The announcer would say, "That was great! Why don't you reverse it?" and I would do a handstand on John. The crowds loved it.

ing. My sons joined the team, which was a thrill for me. My daughters played, too, and were cheerleaders. Russ Cormier—Big Stash—transferred to Chicago for his airline job, but it enabled him to fly back for games every week.

Storer Broadcasting had the feeling of a family in the 1960s, which sounds corny but is true. It was something that other stations never really duplicated. With the All-Stars in the '70s, we kept a family feeling going.

The pranks never stopped. One time we took a bus trip to a small town for a softball game at night. The diamond was a converted football field. When we got there, I had to go and asked if they had a john. I looked in and saw there were no stall doors or screens; it was wide open. I told John and Dave Stacey, "Don't let anybody in." Big mistake. I sat down to go. Thirty seconds later, kids started streaming in with pictures for me to sign. I couldn't stand up, so I had to sit there on the pot, all embarrassed, but it didn't seem to bother the kids at all. John and Stacey had a line of about one hundred kids outside, telling them to go get my autograph. I signed every damn one. I could hear them laughing outside.

PART OF THE GAME IS PHYSICAL

I said we stopped playing football when we got older than the refs, but it also got too rough playing teams out for blood. Bill Russett got his leg broken.

Hoolie broke his foot playing football, broke his finger playing basketball, and got a big gash in his chin playing hockey. He finished the game and then got stitches. He was bleeding all over the ice. John had split lips, and there were lots of sprains and bruises.

I got pushed—by a priest—and broke a foot playing basketball, had several broken fingers, and have an artificial joint from a badly broken wrist. That happened in a softball game with Hoolie in the late 1970s, the night before I was supposed to go on two weeks' vacation on Kelleys Island.

I always played left field or shortstop, but for whatever reason was on first base for this game. It was on a football field, so the lights weren't right. The batter hit a nubber, and George Mondock, our

John joined the Hoolihan & Big Chuck All-Stars softball team and learned that he needed to open his own store.

catcher, threw the ball to me. I couldn't see it in the lights. The runner was right next to me, going around to touch the base, and I reached back to swipe-tag him with my glove hand. But he ran dead into it with his chest. It sounded like a stick cracking, and it burned. I sat down and slowly started to take my glove off. My hand looked pretty good, but my thumb was all the way back. I stood up and grabbed it. We were playing a team of firemen, and they told me to leave it alone. One whispered, "I think you better sit down," and he was right. I was pale and feeling sick.

They put my hand in a plastic thing, put me in a pickup truck, and we went flying through intersections. We were near Canton. When we got to the hospital, we found there had been a big car accident. Victims were lying on carts around us. They put me in a wheelchair, next to a woman on a gurney who was crying and bloody.

She looked over and said, "Big Chuck!" She was crying, but she found a piece of paper and said, "Sign this!" I got a pen, she held the paper with a bloody arm, crying all the time, and blood from her face dropped onto my hand while I signed.

A nurse said, "If you sign one for me, I'm going to give you something to take all that pain away." I don't know what she gave me, but within fifteen seconds I took a deep breath and said, "You know, I don't really think this is broken." And I meant it.

SO FUNNY I FORGOT TO LAUGH

We had injuries doing the show, too. It happens with physical comedy. I had one concussion when Tony Carmen cracked me on the head with a breakaway bottle that didn't break. I had another in a skit with the Brecksville High School football team that was a takeoff on a New York Life commercial. The announcer in that spot says, "They're always there for you," while an average guy in street clothes runs down a football field with players blocking for him.

We did ours with the Certain Ethnic character. The players block, I run and slam the football down in the end zone, and they pick me up on their shoulders. Hoolie is the announcer. They zoom in on him and he says, "Once again the New York Life team blocks out your money worries ... but ... miss one payment"—and then it's me getting the ball, and the line just lets all the tacklers in.

The guys wouldn't hit me in the run-through, and they were holding back. It's not funny that way, so I told them to just cream me, "and as soon as I see you coming, I'll go with you." But I purposely didn't. When the first guy hit me, he sort of picked me up and slammed me down. I didn't even feel the other twelve guys that piled on me after that. I don't know if I was out for a few seconds or what. It was painless.

John played a karate expert in another skit. He knocked me down, started kicking me—after I told him not to hold back—and actually broke my ribs. I didn't realize it until the morning.

John always does exactly what I tell him.

CALL FOR DR. BEN CRAZY

I'm not really a doctor, but I played one on TV. Maybe getting banged-up so much was part of the reason I was doing a Ben Crazy skit just about every week. Hoolie and I did those from day one and never stopped. We had more of them than anything else, including the Kielbasy Kid. It went on for so long after 1966, when *Ben Casey* went off the air, that some kids probably didn't realize that our opening was a take-off on the show's real opening. Our skit showed me chalking symbols on a board while the real *Ben Casey* announcer said, "Man, woman, birth, death, infinity." I added a dollar sign, with the sound of a cash register and our skit-closing laugh.

So many doctors sent me ideas because of Ben Crazy that we actually did skits based on what they sent in. A doctor at Parma Hospital thought of the skit where the Certain Ethnic guy is unconscious and a group of doctors can't bring him around. They call Dr. Whoopie, who pulls out an accordion and attaches a tube from the bellows to my nose. He starts to play a polka, and I immediately revive.

I'd meet doctors at events. They'd have a drink or two and slip into thinking I was a doctor or knew a lot about medicine, getting into technical things. I had no idea what they were talking about.

DON'T KNOCK THE ROCK

We were still adding new segments and people to the show, but I'd revert every so often to stuff I did on the Ghoulardi show, adding audio and visual drop-ins to the movies, which were mostly horror and sci-fi. But one time Hoolie and I got *Jailhouse Rock,* which for us was like a first-run movie. The station saved it for a promotion.

I previewed the movies ahead of time, timing segments to know where breaks were and how much time we had for other stuff, and thinking of things we could do. *Jailhouse Rock* built up to the big choreographed production number in the jail cells. Watching it, it occurred to me that the tempo was close to the same as "Who Stole the Kishka?" I checked it, and Bob Soinski said it fit perfectly. I told the director, Pete Berkobein, to cue the polka up with the scene during the show and stay on it for about ten seconds.

We were live. "Stay tuned," I said when the commercial break before the production number ended. "It's the big jailhouse scene coming up."

One, two, three, go. The scene changes, and "Who Stole the Kishka?" comes in. The dancers were right in step. Everything fit way better than I expected. It was perfect. I was only going to stay on it for about ten seconds and cut back to the soundtrack music, but "Who Stole the Kishka?" kept playing. I went to the control room. They were wiping their eyes laughing, figuring people at home were doing the same thing. I let it go all the way through.

The phones started ringing. The good ol' boys, the hardcore Elvis fans, were irate. They were really mad, and this was serious. They were going to kill us. I didn't think much about it until the phone calls came in the next week. They were telling me they knew where I parked, they had my license plate number, they knew where I lived, they followed me home. It scared the shit out of me. I started taking a big iron bar with me to work because I had to walk down a back alley to the station. But then one said they liked me and weren't going to kill me—they were going to kill Hoolihan and only castrate me. Oh, thank God!

It finally blew over, but it was no joke. All over a stupid thing like "Who Stole the Kishka?"

Ninety-eight percent of our calls were good, but there was some scary stuff. There are weirdoes out there. And also some pranksters.

I answered the phone at my desk one time, and a guy with a heavy accent said, "Why you always making fun of Polish peoples?" He sounded on the verge of tears. "You are bad man, you are making fun of people you are Polish." It sounded like he was crying. I felt awful and tried to explain.

Then he started laughing. It was Dennis Kucinich, at that time the "boy mayor." He held open forums for his ward as a councilman, and he'd hear four hours of that accent at a time. Dennis was a fan of the show, like the other mayors through our run. His brother Gary, who was in the marines and a bodybuilder, even went up against Mushmouth in a pizza fight. Dennis brought him but waited in the car. I don't think he wanted to be seen.

DO YOUR OWN THING, MAN

Sometimes the show and the outside world intersected in odd ways. We had a thing on the show where we said, "Do your own thing," and that was one of them.

A small circus was in town, and a wrangler brought snakes from it to the show. This was some fly-by-night circus, and the guy had a big suitcase with a boa constrictor and a whole bunch of other big snakes inside. They were crawling all over, and I wouldn't touch them. It didn't bother Hoolie, but I don't like snakes. The guy said he had to do something afterward and would stop back for the snakes. We said we'd meet him at Casey's, a basement bar next to Channel 8 that just reeked of drugs. We went over, and the waitress said, "Oh, Big Chuck," sounding high or a little spacey. "Whattya got in the suitcase, man?"

I said, "You really don't want to see." She said, "Come on, show me." Being a prankster, I figured I'd open it, she'd scream, and it'd get a laugh. I opened the case, expecting a big reaction, getting ready to slam it shut.

She stood staring into this giant tangle of big snakes, took a deep breath, and said, "Oh wow, man. Do your own thing."

WHEN THE TABLES WERE TURNED

There's a difference between a prank and a felony, but that doesn't mean a crime can't have a comic element.

One afternoon a guy in a tie and a sharp white uniform stuck his head around the corner by my desk and said, "You have something wrong your typewriter? What's wrong?" I did, actually—some of the keys were sticking—and I told him. He pulled out a pad, wrote something down, gave me a tag, and said he'd bring me a replacement.

He took the typewriter, and I noticed that other guys in clean white uniforms like exterminators were carrying all sorts of stuff down the hallway. They took everything and never came back. They were in the Hanna Building across the alley, too. I went outside and saw their truck driving away. They were so calm and professional that I was convinced they were legitimate. When we realized we'd been had, somebody called the police, who came down and questioned everybody.

It was bold, out in the open, and we had to give them credit for that. Hoolie and I mentioned it on the air and got chewed out for it.

It wasn't the first time. B&B Appliance used to sponsor John Fitzgerald's sports show, and every so often he'd have to do a commercial for them. They'd send a truck and unload console TV sets to make a display for him to show or describe in a voiceover. I usually answered the back door in the evening because I was working as switcher and could hear the doorbell. I answered one night, and a couple of guys with a raggedy truck said they were from B&B and were there for the TVs. I even helped them carry the stuff out and load their truck.

A half-hour later, the bell rang again. "We're here from B&B Appliance."

It had to be some kind of inside job, but we got our asses chewed out because I didn't check their IDs.

THE MASTER OF DISGUISE–AND PRANKS

The actual pranks could be really elaborate, such as one that Dom Ortuso set up with Jim Prunty at the downstairs bar next to the station.

A group of us sat drinking. A big guy with jet-black hair at the end of the bar ordered a drink, said to leave the bottle, and chugged right out of it. It was gin, the hardest thing in the world to drink. He hit it hard, got louder and louder, and came over to us. He said he wanted to "buy this guy a drink," pointing to everybody except me. "Yeah, except him," he said, making it clear he hadn't overlooked me. He was really loud and aggressive. Kidding around to lighten things up, I said, "Was it something I said?"

He got really mad. He said I was the guy who did something with his wife. "Hold on, wait a minute," I said. I didn't know what he was talking about, and he really meant trouble. He was screaming, and you could see people getting alarmed.

He pulled out a gun and shot in the air. It was the loudest thing I ever heard. Before the shot finished echoing, I was out the door to the parking lot. I don't even remember getting there.

It was Ralph Gertz—projectionist, editor, and, more important, man of a thousand faces. The gin bottle was filled with water, and he had a blank in the Magnum handgun. Everybody followed him into the parking lot, laughing. I'd bought all of it.

I said we had to do it again, this time with director Bill Turner. Neil Zurcher set it up.

We went to a place in Vermilion that had dancers and a bar overlooking the floor with tables. We sat at a table. Gertz was at the bar in makeup, wearing a white Panama hat and suit. I worked with him every day, and I didn't recognize him. He was that good. He arranged with the bartender for the gin bottle to be filled with just water.

A dancer named Rusty Belle came out, did her act, walked up next to Turner and, looking at me, said, "Oh, Big Chuck!" I introduced Turner as our director, and she stage-whispered to Ortuso, "You know what? I'm more impressed with people behind the scenes," really laying it on. Turner pounded down drinks, and she got really chummy.

Gertz was staring. Turner said, "Who's that guy?" "My ex-boyfriend," she replied. Turner asked if he was dangerous. Gertz glared. Turner said he was worried, and we'd better get going. I said, "OK, we'll wait until she dances again." When she was done, Rusty came back to the table, completely ignoring everybody but Turner. Gertz was fuming. Turner said, "We gotta get out of here." I stalled.

Gertz ran down, same as before, shouting and pulling the gun. Turner jumped up, and the dancer grabbed him and said, "Don't go!"

This time, Gertz pretended he was having a heart attack. He fell against the table, knocked it over, and fell to the floor. It was even more realistic than what he did to me. The dancer grabbed Turner and said, "You've got to help him!"

Turner leaned over. Gertz reached up and grabbed him.

Gertz was best known for playing Santa Claus. He had a real beard that he'd dye white, and the resemblance was uncanny. He did a lot of volunteer work for community groups, hospitals, churches, and schools, and he made countless visits to houses on Christmas Eve, taking Lil' John in an elf suit. They'd greet the kids and have a drink every place they went. Once, John said, Ralph announced at 3 a.m. they were supposed to make one more stop. "Forget it," John said, "It's way too late." But Ralph insisted and pounded on the door until a guy came out and shouted, "I'll kick your ass!" Ralph was offended.

"He really thinks he's Santa Claus," John said.

He played Santa in holiday promos for TV8 that a lot of viewers remember, had a part in *Artemus Flagg*, and did a lot on our show. He was especially popular as The Old Timer. In a favorite Kielbasy Kid skit, he and the Kid are sitting at a saloon table, and The Old

Timer tells the Kid to always shoot first and ask questions later. The Kid draws and fires, shooting him out of his chair to the floor, and says, "Why is that, Old Timer?"

Gertz died in 1997. I was directing the six and eleven o'clock news and figured I'd run out to the wake at seven. It was a short window but my only shot. He was going to be buried the next day. Nobody else was there when I arrived at the funeral home. It was quiet. The casket was in a huge room, and Ralph was in it, with a cowboy hat and boots on. I stood about ten feet away and started looking around for cameras. This would be the most elaborate prank yet. The obituary was even in the paper. I was frightened to go up there—really frightened.

The styles scream early 1970s in this publicity photo. Fans sent in handmade posters, which we proudly displayed in the background.

CHAPTER 20

IN LIKE FLYNNSKI

THE SHOW GETS A FAN AT THE TOP

Bill Flynn came to the station as general manager in 1977. He was really brash, devil-may-care, a good drinker, and very much like Ernie Anderson. He had that kind of impact. Station executives tend to be behind-the-scenes guys, but that wasn't Flynn. He got written up regularly in the papers for saying or doing something. An article in *Cleveland Magazine* had an illustration of him on top of the Channel 8 building, like the ape in our show's opening, saying he dominated Cleveland much like *The Hoolihan & Big Chuck Show*.

He came with a reputation that preceded him, but he said that if you were doing your job, you had absolutely nothing to worry about. I really liked him. He was gruff but really honest and knowledgeable. He used to call me Polack, which was his style, and he noticed how much work I was doing. He said, "Hey Polack, what the hell is this? You're always here." He gave me the biggest raise I ever had. I was directing news once and he said, "Do you guys realize that's the best goddamn director in Cleveland?" I said, "Don't start, everyone's going to hate me." We became pretty good buddies.

He loved our show, and he was one of the few guys who really made us feel important. When CBS came up with a Friday movie at 11:30 p.m., I said, "Uh-oh." But Flynn checked our options as an affiliate and told them no. He said we were making too much money on Friday night to change. It was a battle. He would not move us to Saturday night, like CBS suggested. So the *CBS Friday Night Movie* was shown on Saturday night on TV8. He would not preempt us for

I pulled the first winning number in the Ohio Lottery at Parmatown Mall on August 22, 1974.

sports either. CBS was going to air a West Coast Cavs basketball game on a Friday night, and he didn't carry it. He took flak in the papers, and we got a lot of calls, but he honestly told them he stayed with us "because they make more money." That was his job, he said, and more fans were going to watch us than basketball.

The show got lots of promotion. He put us on two prime time specials, and he made sure we were featured on *PM Magazine*.

I couldn't get over what a big change it he brought. In 1974, when the Ohio Lottery had its first drawing, I pulled the first winning ticket. Hoolie pulled the second. It was on a stage at Parmatown, with a crowd of a few thousand people. Hoolie told them, "Simple virtues like lust and greed have brought you here." The event was front-page news. It was historic. But Channel 8's news didn't even mention us.

Flynn would have a party every Friday in the conference room, with food and booze for whoever wanted to come. It'd start about 5:30 p.m., and he'd drink until the wee hours. We were taping the show by this time, so I'd usually hang with him to the end. Every St. Paddy's Day, he'd hire a couple of limos to shuttle people from

Channel 8 to the Flats, day and night. He'd have parties at the drop of a hat.

MARY HARTSKI, MARY HARTSKI

One time we were drinking at the bar on the top floor of the Howard Johnson's next to the station. It was late, midnight or one. Everybody was leaving, and he said, "So what can I do for you?" He suggested making me promotion director. I said no, I wasn't cut out for that. But our show had been moved to midnight from 11:30 on Friday because they wanted to air *Mary Hartman, Mary Hartman*, the soap opera parody. It was killing us. People were used to watching us after the news. I said, "Can you move *Mary Hartman* out of there? And let us go back to 11:30?" I was feeling no pain, so I had the courage to ask.

He said, "Write that out and have it on my desk in the morning." In the morning? I went home, wrote and rewrote, got about three hours of sleep, and got to the station about 8:30. Sure enough, Flynn was at his desk, drinking coffee. I gave him the note and, *boom*—we were moved.

Mary Hartman moved to 7:30 p.m., which brought all kinds of gripes in newspaper columns, in phone calls, and from religious groups. The show was controversial because of the risqué way it parodied the "adult" themes in soaps, and they didn't think it should run in "family viewing" hours. Flynn stood his ground.

We started a takeoff on *Mary Hartman*, a spoof on a spoof, called "Mary Hartski." It was a hit that reminded a lot of viewers of "Parma Place," and if I ever did anything to endear myself to Flynn, that was it. The minute I did that, he was in my corner, and I could do no wrong.

One time in the hallway, he came up behind me and said, "Hey, Polack, what the hell is this you did? You used a telephone number beginning with 888, and this guy is calling me bitching it's his number." I told him I'd asked for a dead number I could use when the phone guy was at the station. I wanted to use 888, for TV8. He said there was no exchange like that, so I used it. Was there a problem? No, Flynn said—it was a relief from the *Mary Hartman* calls.

He wanted to do *Bowling for Dollars*, and he got panned for that. He had a bowling alley built in the basement. Dick Goddard hosted the show, and it was pretty popular. I did a "Mary Hartski" episode where she goes on and wins. It was fun and current, and Flynn loved it.

"You know what? Nobody likes *Bowling for Dollars* except the people," he said. To boost our six p.m. news ratings, he put on cartoons at 5:30. "No one likes it but the people," he said. It worked. He did a show with live phone-ins called *Ask the Manager* that I directed. He'd done it successfully in Boston, and it was huge. He aired *Scared Straight,* the special where convicts tell kids about the horrors of prison. Other stations were afraid to touch it.

DON'T SAY THAT WORD

During a public appearance and a local mall we gave away little Frisbees. Come out and meet us, and get a Frisbee, we said. A guy from Wham-O happened to be in town watching.

Flynn called me. "Did you guys say *Frisbee?*" he asked. "This big blowhard asshole from Wham-O says he's going to sue the station. Don't worry about him. Just say 'flying disc.'"

I said we probably wouldn't do it again. No, Flynn said, "I want you to do it again. Why don't you do something?" He wanted us to jerk the guy around.

I said, "How about if we do a man-in-the-street bit, and stop people and say, 'Pardon me, what is this?'—showing them a flying disc? They'd all say it's a Frisbee."

"Do that, do that!" he said, laughing.

But I didn't really want to do it. It wasn't funny. Flynn said I chickened out. I said I'd do something else, and I wrote a monologue about how we could not say the word *Frisbee* anymore.

"See this?" I said, holding up a flying disc. "It looks like a Frisbee. But it's not a Frisbee—it's a flying disc. It smells like a Frisbee. But it's not a Frisbee. It flies like a Frisbee. But it's not a Frisbee. Don't call this a Frisbee." We must have said Frisbee a hundred times.

Flynn loved it.

PLENTY OF OTHER WORK

TV8 was doing a program called *Kids World,* which was part local and part syndicated. Tim Iacofano, our new operations manager who went on to be a major TV producer in Hollywood, gave it to me to do. He liked my directing, and he told people he liked the way "he just does it." He'd give me an assignment, and I'd research, write it, and do it. He didn't have time to sit and go over every detail, and neither did I.

My daughter Michelle did perhaps the best *Kids World* story. It was about our Hinckley neighbor, "Grandpa Eastwood". She (like me) was nervous, but did such an outstanding job. He story won an Emmy. I was so very proud of her.

Kids World won two gold medals from the International Film and TV Festival of New York City, in 1978 and 1981. *Hoolihan & Big Chuck* won another Emmy in 1978, too. The show was still going strong, though Hoolie was able to do less and less.

Iacofano liked using me, so I got more and more. I was working my ass off.

JERRY LEWIS, IN THE BAD DAYS

When I got a chance to work with one of my heroes, Jerry Lewis, it wasn't what I hoped. Storer had begun airing his annual Labor Day telethon for the Muscular Dystrophy Association. It was quite a commitment of airtime and commercial time. Hoolie and I did the first one or two years of the local fishbowl cut-ins, where people would throw contributions into a big bowl and we'd interview them. Then Hoolie dropped out, and Lil' John jumped right in. We did it for about twenty-five years, and Jerry Lewis sent a nice telegram complimenting us on our years of service, but it meant Labor Day was another occasion that we never celebrated with our families. My wife of fifty-two years and John's wife, Sherry, of thirty-three years, are destined to be saints. We were never home.

Jerry came to Channel 8 to promote the telethon in 1977. Hoolie and I were taping our show from about 3 p.m. to 5 p.m. on Friday afternoon, and Jerry was taping an hour earlier on the other side of the studio. Harveys Acks, who was a standout on the All-Stars who now works at Channel 3, had a lot to do with the telethon. He told us he'd ask Jerry to tape a promotion for our show. I said, man, please do, because I was a big fan. Jerry wouldn't do it because he said he'd be obligated for anyone else who asked. I told him immediately that I understood. But Jerry continued to play to the crowd, listening to himself talk, saying that with his busy schedule he'd never have enough time.

He was now fifteen minutes into our tape time, and I was getting antsy. We only had a certain window of time to get our show done. As he and the crowd were finally leaving the studio, I told him again that I understood completely. I was disappointed but still happy to meet him. I was a huge fan of his films and shows, and as a big Al Jolson fan ran out to buy "Rockabye Your Baby With a Dixie Melody" when Jerry recorded it on Decca in 1956. It was outstanding. He can really sing.

We saw him in the hallway leaving the building. He said he was going to WHK to see Gary Dee, the shock jock, because Dee was saying on the air that a lot of the telethon money went to Lewis—an untrue claim that Dee retracted and the station apologized for. He said he was going to straighten Dee out, put an end to it, and shut the station down.

A year or two later, when Lil' John was co-host, TV8 asked us to host a different telethon at Parmatown Mall. One of our guests was to be Dee, who was kooky but sometimes brutally honest. We were waiting to go on, and I said, "Jerry Lewis told us he was going to straighten you out. What happened?" Dee looked around, like he was checking who might overhear, and said, "You know, that sonofabitch pulled a gun on me and scared the crap out of me. He was shaking and nervous and ranting out of control. That's what scared me." I don't know what actually happened, but I did learn later that Lewis was having a rough time in his life because he was hooked on pain pills, which can really mess with your emotions.

Dee was a story himself, a guy who was really popular but flamed out. A local country singer and club owner at that time, Roger Martin, did a couple events John and I were at, and he's on one of our

CDs. He was a Vietnam veteran who was pretty talented, but he battled a drug habit that kept him from doing bigger things. He'd call Gary, sometimes while he was high, and told us he used to crash at Dee's house. John asked what it was like. He said it was an ordinary large house but had no rugs and almost no furniture. You'd sleep on a mattress with a blanket on the floor. You wondered why a guys with his income he would live like that.

MEL TORMÉ, A NICER GUY

Dom Ortuso talked about starting a weekly show with a local singer, Scott Reed. We had dinner with him and Flynn and set up a taping. Mel Tormé, "the Velvet Fog," happened to be at the station doing a promotional appearance. I introduced myself and asked if he could say something to use on the show. We were taping that night, and the set was already up and lit.

"How long is that gonna take?" he asked. "I'm really close to time for this plane, and I don't want to miss it."

"Ten minutes," I said.

He looked at his watch and said, "Is this ten minutes for real, or 'ten minutes'?" I said it was for real. He said, "Promise?"

He did the spot, and he did it in seven minutes.

Almost nobody would do that for an unknown singer even he didn't know.

LUCKING OUT IN LAS VEGAS

I always wanted to play blackjack in Las Vegas but was too intimidated by the speed at which they did it. If you don't do something, the dealer starts tapping impatiently. I tried it anyway when Hoolie and I led our second tour to Vegas. A guy came up behind me with one-hundred-dollar chips, a wealthy guy from Cleveland, and said, "Aw Chuck, can I sit and play with you?" I told him I'd like to, but I had to go. I didn't want him to see I was playing dollar chips.

John was on the trip, too, and he played roulette. A group of high-rolling, oil-rich Texans were playing, betting big chips, and a guy in a big cowboy hat said, "Come on over here and give me some luck." He rubbed John's head, and he won. So he pulled up a stool for "my buddy," bear-hugged him, took two piles of chips, and handed them to John. "That's for you," he said. "Bet whatever you want."

John hadn't prayed like that since he was a little kid. "I know I've been a bad guy, but please, please let me win . . ." John said he did a whole rosary, didn't win, and went through all the money the guy gave him.

At two or three in the morning, when hardly anybody was in the casino, I decided to go back and try my luck. The dealer started educating me, telling me everything about blackjack, then stopped and put his hand to his ear, listening. "Can you be here for the next ten minutes or so?" he asked me. "Someone wants to see you."

Up above the floor, the house watches you. One of these security guys grew up watching me in Cleveland. I can't remember his name, but we used to show posters he'd send, and I recognized him, grown up, from the pictures. He came down and asked me, "You want to meet Martin Sheen?" I said, yeah, that'd be nice.

Sheen was by himself at a roped-off table with a drink in front of him. His head was propped up. He could hardly keep his eyes open. The guy introduced me and said I was a director in Cleveland who had his own show. Sheen invited me to sit down. He seemed drunk and tired as hell. I said, "Can't sleep?" Yeah, he said. He was shooting something in L.A. and got on a plane for Vegas at eleven p.m. He ordered me a drink. Looking for conversation, I mentioned him playing a Polish guy in *The Execution of Private Slovik,* for which he won an Emmy, and said I especially liked that he made potato pancakes, which is something I do. He's from Dayton, and his given name is Ramon Estevez. He took the stage name Sheen in honor of Bishop Fulton J. Sheen, whom he loved, and he mentioned his wife, Janet, is from Cleveland. I found out later that she also went to South High School, my alma mater.

He was a really nice guy, but he was exhausted. I left him alone.

CHAPTER 21

BIG CHUCK & LIL' JOHN

THE END OF THE HOOLIHAN ERA

Hoolie quit in 1979. It happened on short notice, but I figured something was coming. It had been for a long time. He'd been busier and busier with outside work and little theater after quitting his Channel 8 announcing job in 1971, and in 1976 he left the weekend weather, too. He had become a born-again Christian, and he got a job at WSUM, a daytime radio station in Parma that was switching to a religious format with new owners. He did that while doing our show on a freelance basis. Then he was offered a job running a religious TV station in Florida.

I had been adding more characters to the show for years, but Hoolie was the most talented actor of what became a very large cast. He was one of the mainstays that I call the Big Four—me, Hoolie, Art, and John. There are only a few skits with all four of us, and they're all good. I treasure those because it was so hard to get us all in at the same time.

In one favorite, Hoolie plays a Nazi officer with a big flag behind him. He says, "All right, send in the prisoners now." Art, John, and I are the prisoners. We get pushed in, all dirty in raggedy clothes, and stand at attention. Hoolie slaps a riding crop and says, "Someone has been stealing kielbasy from ze officers' commissary. Vee are going to find out who vas doing zis. Vee are going to put you through ze tick-tock punishment."

His accent is incredible. He's waving a cigarette holder, and the scene looks like something out of a movie. "Ven I count to three," he says, "you vill begin to tick-tock like zis. Tick—lean vun vay.

Big Chuck & Lil' John make an early personal
appearance.

Tock—lean ze other vay. You vill continue zis tick-tocking around
ze clock until one of you confesses. All right, begin."

We all lean the same way—*tick*. Art and John lean the other
way—*tock*. I'm on the end, and I stand up straight. Hoolie's watching. We all go one way again—*tick*. Art and John lean the other way.
I stand up straight. Art and John say, "Tock."

He walks up and blows smoke in my face. It's a tight shot. He
says, "Don't you realize, Schodowski, vee haf ways to make you
tock."

DECIDING TO MAKE THE SHOW GO ON

Flynn asked what I wanted to do. I was tempted to quit the show
and take him up on his offer to do something else. I told him I'd

keep doing it, but I didn't want to do it alone. He offered to interview potential co-hosts and asked if I wanted to audition candidates. It was up to me. There wasn't much time.

I figured a current cast member should become the new co-host because we already had skits in the can that we could use immediately. The two most prominent were Art and John. Art was a lot like me, laid back and soft-spoken—maybe too much like me. John was an energetic fireball. I had to tone him down. Neither one had hosting experience.

I decided to go with John. In September 1979, *The Big Chuck & Lil' John Show* was born, a show that would last twenty-eight more years—forty-four years in all of Ghoulardi, Hoolihan & Big Chuck, and Big Chuck & Lil' John.

OFF AND RACING WITH JOHN

John stepped right in and did our outside bookings like Hoolie did. He booked us at Cloverleaf Speedway. I immediately remembered the demolition derbies and the wild time we had with those. I said, "John, I'm getting tired of this crazy stuff, man." He said, "No, no, all we have to do is emcee between races."

We got there, and the guy told us we were doing the announcing. They were getting ready to start a race. Cars were lined up by a low wall. They had roll bars, no windows, and the doors were welded shut. The guy looked at me and said, "Wanna ride in the race?" I didn't, but I didn't want to say no. He asked again, and another guy yelled, "Big Chuck's gonna ride with you!"

The driver said, "GOL-L-L-EE!" Good ol' boy. "Goddammit, come sit with me!"

I crawled in, climbing over the door. "Wait'll I tell everybody!" he said.

We took off. This guy started doing things I think he never did before to win. We almost rolled over, riding on two wheels for what seemed like an eternity. "Don't do it for me," I said, but it was so loud he couldn't hear me. We were skidding, we got hit one time, and then we hit the wall. I was sure we were going to crash, and I was scared—and this wasn't a demolition derby. It was a race.

When we got out of there, I said, "That's it. I'm never going to do this again."

So in 2006, John booked us again—this time at Norwalk Raceway. It's a beautiful complex where they have nationally televised races. This time a guy talked John and me into getting into dragsters. They fire up and explode, and they go so fast they flip up doing wheelies. The noise is unbelievable. That was a thrill, especially when you're over seventy, man.

But that's it. No more.

JOHN HOLDS NOTHING BACK

We did our own stunt work. We used to do skits we easily could have been killed in.

For "Looney Legends," we were doing a take-off of *Gulliver's Travels*—only because I liked doing stuff with multiple shots like Ernie Kovacs figured out how to do. I had Lil' John duplicated eight times running around my body while I was stretched out and tied up like Gulliver.

The scene called for him to jump from my chest to my arm to the floor. So we set up boxes in the studio against the chroma-key background. Tony Lolli was to be the director. I told him I wanted to direct it myself, and he left the control room. John was practicing the moves and finally said, "The hell with it. I'll do it once. If I fall, I fall."

It was a pretty dangerous falling sequence that had to be done just right. John started out perfectly. But then he stumbled and came down almost head over heels, cutting his lip really badly. But he went on with it, figuring we had the good take.

Just before it was over, Tony walked into the studio and right through the shot. Couldn't use it.

JOHN TRIES ANYTHING, HO, HO, HO

Jolly Green Giant commercials were really popular around 1980. It was great, I said, that they always showed him in silhouette. I got John to do the Green Giant thing in similar silhouette, in a shot where you get no real perspective of size. Joe Dannery does the Giant's "Ho, ho, ho" voice, John lip-synchs, and I say, "Cut! That's really good"—like we're making a commercial. Then the lights come on, I walk in, and you see John's size.

Back then, however, we didn't have the fancy electronics and computer effects they have now. We had to paint John green.

We needed something that would wash off. I knew that Dick Goddard had water-soluble paint because he actually used to paint the numbers, temperatures and all, on a board for his forecast every night.

We painted John all over. He did the skit, it was really good, and he went downstairs to take a shower. But when he came back, he was still green. He was sore from scrubbing, and the paint still wouldn't come off. We were playing basketball somewhere that night, and we played the game with John as green as could be. Two days later, we had a personal appearance, and he was still light green.

It reminded me of the skit we did in the alley behind the station about 1971. We painted hearts on the side of the building. One said "Chuck loves June," another said, "Hoolie loves Barb," and the third said, "Lil' John loves miniskirts." We played girl-watching music while girls walked past, and John stood looking up their dresses, smoking a cigar. You couldn't see "loves miniskirts" on the wall behind him until he walked away.

I said I had to use something that would wash off, or that the rain would wash off, because it wasn't our building and I didn't want to get in any trouble. I scrubbed, it rained, but the paint didn't wash off.

The station moved from Playhouse Square to South Marginal Road in 1975, but I went back to the old building about ten years later because I wanted to tell the story on the air during a "Dick Goddard Night" on our show. Sure as hell, the hearts were still on the wall. I called for a photographer to shoot it—and showed it to Dick on the air and said, "Water-soluble paint, eh?"

CHAPTER 22

POLICE ACTION

ESCORTING THE ALL-STARS

The Big Chuck & Lil' John All-Stars entered the '80s hitting a peak as a big entertainment group. It was a great show. We had dancing cheerleaders, we had Cleveland pro athletes on our team, and we were competitive with other teams while still clowning around. We clowned around even more at the parties afterward. Most games were out of the city. We took buses, usually leaving about 5:30 p.m., so no one really had time for supper. We'd go to a bar and restaurant after the games, and the All-Stars became legendary as entertainers. Name the town and we'd know the bar where we were going.

Anytime we were near Sandusky, we went to the Cameo Lounge. They had the best pizza in the world. After midnight, they'd give the word we were there. Chuck Lacocca would close the door, and we played music. Whoopie John and Dave Stacy played the accordion, John played tambourine, Mush played sax, I played banjo. We had routines worked out. We'd come out with the banjo, playing "Waiting for the Robert E. Lee," and announce, "We can play anything you want! What do you want to hear?" Whatever they'd say, we'd play "Robert E. Lee" again. It was free entertainment. We had a ball doing it.

One night we had a huge bash, one of the best parties we ever had. On the bus trip home, to the theater in Brecksville where we used to meet and leave our cars, I told the guys to be cool, since the cops were probably watching us. I was tipped by Bernie Barabas, an All-Star we called Corky who performed on our "Dueling Accordions" skit. He also happened to be a cop who's now head of the

Cleveland Police SWAT unit. He told me he heard that the Brecksville cops sort of knew we'd be coming back late and watched us coming off the bus from the shadows. Like guardian angels.

We pulled in, and I saw two cop cars in the darkness. Everyone got off the bus a little tipsy, trying to be real cool. I put the banjo case on top of the car to get my car keys. I kept them there because I had no pockets in my baseball uniform and didn't want to lose them. Cars were pulling out, the cops were watching me, and it seemed like an eternity. I unsnapped the case. It was upside down. The banjo and the keys fell out. I just wanted to get out of there, so I opened the door, threw in the banjo, got in, and pulled out fast. I made a right turn, and the door swung wide open. I hadn't closed it.

No sooner had I pulled it shut and driven over the hill than two cops rolled up, one behind me and one alongside, lights flashing.

One pulled over next to me, rolled down his window, and said, "Chuck, have you been drinking?" I said, "Yes! No doubt about it."

Just as I said that, Lil' John and Dave Stacey came flying up over the hill, not knowing we were there. John hit his brakes, skidded sideways to avoid a cop car, and went up on a tree lawn. Stacey barely missed John and drove onto the lawn. He started backing out. It was three or four in the morning. The cop said, "We'd better get the hell out of here."

They decided to escort all of us to my house in Hinckley. Stacey and John really didn't want to do it, but they didn't want to argue with the cops. So off we went, one car in front of us, one behind, one alongside, about forty miles an hour all the way home. It was getting light when we got there. My sons Mike and Mark were getting ready to go to Highland High School. They saw me with all these guys, and one of them said, "Wow, you're up early, Dad." My mother-in-law was there, too, of all days, for a visit.

John had to leave right from there to his job at Cowell & Hubbard Jewelers in the same clothes he'd worn almost twenty-four hours. June took the shirt, rinsed it out, and put it in the dryer while he ate breakfast. Dave, a bank manager, also had to go to work in the same clothes he'd been wearing. I had to go to work, too.

The postgame party went across the street and expanded to a second bar when the All-Stars played the Cleveland Heights Police Department. From left: John, Dave Stacey, "Mr. Moats," me, Whoopie John.

John was sweating it because he was the manager at Cowell & Hubbard's Randall Park store. He had the only key, and he had to get there early to open before the mall did. He also had to get jewelry out of the safe and put it into display cases. After he got a tray from the safe, he put it down and rested his head on the counter. The glass felt so good and cool, he closed his eyes.

The next thing he knew, his boss was pounding on the door, and the mall was filled with people. That's when he started thinking seriously of getting his own store, so he couldn't get canned. He opened Rinaldi Jewelry, downtown on East 9th Street, in December 1980.

A NIGHT ON THE HEIGHTS

We played a lot of police departments at night. One of the best after-game parties we ever had was with the Cleveland Heights police. They took us to a bar, we started playing, and we formed a line marching across Mayfield Road to another bar, back and forth.

People left one bar, got in our line, and went to the other bar. The cops thought it was hilarious. We climbed on top of one bar, walking on it and playing instruments, all stepping in the same direction, with everyone singing and yelling, "Get in line!"

One time when we did this after a game in another town the bar partially collapsed. We scratched that stunt.

We went to the other bar, played there, and decided to make the trip back. The cops were all in baseball uniforms, and car horns were blowing. One guy in a car was screaming, throwing F-bombs at us. A couple of cops walked up and asked his problem. "I'm going to call the goddamn cops," he said.

"We are the cops," they said, flashing their badges.

We had a lot of cops in our skits, too, and played a lot of benefits for them. We always had a great rapport with the police, in the city and the suburbs, and they'd go out of their way to help us—especially the mounted police. I really miss them. Cleveland was one of the few cities in the country with them, and they were the first thing every new mayor wanted to cut. I did a piece on *PM Magazine* showing what they could do with crowd control. One guy could control a huge mob. They were a plus for the city.

When I did several take-offs on commercials for the Club, the anti-theft device, the police let us use squad cars. I went to get one, and the cop wasn't there to meet me as scheduled. He left the keys. John and I drove it back to Channel 8.

We played firefighters one night and went back to the firehouse for a party. It was close to Musicarnival, the old tent theater in Warrensville Heights. Engelbert Humperdinck was singing, and we could hear the music. A fireman said, "You want to hear him?" I said yeah, I like singers. So he took us over and said we had to crawl under the tent. It was like something from Norman Rockwell, crawling under a circus tent. I thought it was great. The fireman lifted it, and we crawled under and stood up. It was dark as hell. I expected we'd be in the back, but there was Engelbert—we were practically right next to him. My son Mark was with me, and the three of us stood in the shadows next to the stage.

A PICASSO WITH CRAYONS

Almost all the way through my career, people helped with skits—cops, lawyers, store clerks, steelworkers. In one "Soul Man" skit, Herb chases a pickpocket down an alley into a bakery. The pickpocket starts a pie fight with eight bakers like an old silent movie. I always wanted to do that. But a couple of the guys didn't show up for the skit. Three big-time lawyers, we found out later, were coming out of the Hanna Building from Pierre's, walking down the alley behind the station after work. I said, "You guys want to be in a skit?" Hell, yeah, they said. They recognized us. They kept their expensive suits on under their baker's jackets, and they had a ball getting hit with pies in the face, getting covered with whipped cream. One of them just asked us not to show the skit at a certain time because someone was going to be in town then and he didn't want that person to see it.

We couldn't do things like that now. We'd have to get permission. But in that thirty-year period from the '60s to the '90s, it was like I was given a magical key to Cleveland and could open any door. I could shoot skits wherever I wanted, just ask. Dave O'Karma wrote in *Cleveland Magazine* that I was like a Picasso with crayons who used the city as a backdrop and its people as extras. That's how I felt.

CHAPTER 23

SOME TIME WITH THE BROWNS

LIL' JOHN AND SOUL MAN GET MEAN

One of the top commercials of all time was the "Have a Coke and a smile" spot with Mean Joe Greene of the Steelers that came out late in 1979. I did a take-off with Lil' John playing the kid who gives his pop to "Mr. Mean," played by Herb Thomas. Herb guzzles the pop, busts the breakaway bottle on John's head, and says, "That's why they call me Mr. Mean." He walks off laughing. We shot it at the stadium, and even the Steelers loved it.

It got so much response that I wanted to do another one—this time using the very popular Cleveland Browns Doug Dieken and Greg Pruitt.

In that one, John gives Herb the Coke as he hobbles off the field. Herb drinks it, says, "Thanks, kid," tosses him his jersey, and walks around the corner. He coughs, grabs his throat, collapses, and does a death scene on the floor. John, Greg, and Doug peek around the corner and take his pulse. Doug says, "Pay him," and Greg counts out bills to John.

THE GAME YOU DON'T SEE ON TV

I met Greg and Doug in the locker room at the stadium because I needed them in full uniform. Diek was putting on his shoulder pads. I noticed long aluminum sheets bolted to them, going all the way down his back, obviously a homemade job. I said, "What the hell is this about?" Doug explained that defensive linemen tried to get their arms over his shoulders to grab under the pads, making it real easy to horse him around. With the metal sheets, they couldn't grab hold. I thought it was pretty innovative.

"It was the best thing I could think of," he said. "Most guys put razor blades there."

I realized that the NFL really is a brutal place. It brought back memories of running the parab mic, when I saw firsthand the punishment Jim Brown took. They'd tackle him whether or not he was carrying the ball. They'd kick him and step on his hands, which is why he got up so slowly—he would not put his hands on the ground for leverage. In one pile-up someone tried to rip his mouth open. It was nasty. Jim played for nine years with the Browns, a lot of time when he was hurt, and never missed a game. The only year he didn't lead the NFL in rushing, he played with a broken wrist. They cut the cast off in practice so no one would know. He wore shirts to cover it all season. Brown was really tough. The NFL has had many superstars, but only one superman. That was Jim Brown, and Cleveland had him.

I remembered Gary Collins playing with broken ribs one year and not telling anyone because they'd go after him. He dropped a few passes because he'd have pain you can hardly believe when he'd turn. It was very unlike him, and the crowd booed. Collins was a nice guy, talented and funny, and he appeared on Ernie Anderson's 1965 special. But he got so mad about the booing, after being a fan favorite, that he didn't come back for a team reunion until forty years after the 1964 championship.

Otto Graham had a long scar from a game in 1953 where one player was a goon assigned to knock him out of the game. Graham was elbowed so badly in the mouth that he was forced out to get stitched up. He came back in the second half with a bar attached to his helmet. It was when Paul Brown invented the facemask.

Center Tom DeLeone was a jokester who was buddies with Dieken and did some stuff with John and me. His wife died of cancer while he was away playing—she said on her deathbed that he had to go to the game. She insisted. Just think of it.

Tom told the story in a piece I wrote for *PM Magazine*. It still touches me. He also told about wanting to go away to college, while growing up in Kent, but had to work a couple of jobs because his dad died when he was twelve. Tom wasn't that big, but he was an overachiever, and coaches came with entourages to recruit him, offering scholarships and playing time. Woody Hayes drove up alone from Ohio State and asked to talk to his mother. Woody touted the team's graduation rate and said, "I guarantee you he will graduate." That was it.

Billy Reynolds was the last guy in the NFL not to have a facemask. He was a tough guy. I played goalie in charity hockey games and don't know how you could not wear a mask.

Reynolds would ref at basketball games the All-Stars played with the Browns. I used to make gin martinis in a mason jar the night before those games and put them in the freezer. I'd wrap it in a towel, and it would be slush after the game when I took it in the shower to drink. I could drink a lot, and I'd be dehydrated after games. Reynolds, who came from West Virginia, smelled it one time and said, "What the hell is that? Ever drink 'shine? You ought to try that. You won't need as much." He actually brought some moonshine to a game after that, and it was the strongest booze I ever had in my life. I was worried he'd get arrested carrying it around.

Marion Motley took tremendous punishment as a great fullback and one of the first two black players in the All-America Conference with the Browns. Like a lot of the Browns then, he played both offense and defense. There was a pile-up once after he went back to block a punt, and I thought the ball was getting away. It was his helmet. A guy kicked it off his head.

Motley was my boyhood hero, and I met him several times. The first was at a benefit game we played, and I brought a Browns lamp I wanted him to sign for my son. I didn't want to bug him, and I was trying to think of something original to say. He smiled as I walked toward him, and before I could say anything, he said, "Big Chuck!" He gave me a hug and said, "Here, sign this for my grandbaby!" He watched the show.

He showed me a championship ring. "Know how much I got for playing that game?" he asked. "Nine hundred bucks—and I was damned happy to have it." He was a mailman all his life.

PLAYING FOR LAUGHS

Doug Dieken was a fan of the show who used to do a lot of stuff with us, and he'd recruit other players for skits. One recruit was Dino Hall, a little guy who was tough as hell. I said, "Why don't you talk to Dino? You can do a 'Big Doug & Lil' Dino' night."

Not only did he do it, he brought along a whole bunch of well-known Browns. Doug did my part, and Dino did John's. John and I sat in the audience with the other players. It was hilarious. Doug is really a ham. It was around Halloween, and one of the guys was in a gorilla suit. Doug went into the audience to see who could answer trivia questions and said, "Hey, Dino, look at this—Mean Joe Greene is here!"

Bill Cowher, who was still a player then, was in the audience, purposely making a complete ass of himself, waving his arm and going, "Oooh! Ooh!" like he knew the trivia answers. Doug said, "Look at this jerk, Dino!" They were very, very funny.

Years later, when Mike Renda was general manager of TV8, he saw the skit on one of our oldies nights. He sent a copy to his counterpart at the Fox affiliate in Pittsburgh, where Cowher was head coach. They ran it on the news.

Doug is a jokester. He did a personal appearance with John and me in Akron, and he said he'd meet us at a bar in a seedy neighborhood. John and I were walking through the dark parking lot, and Doug and DeLeone ran from behind and grabbed us—choking me, swearing, shouting, "Give me your money!" We couldn't see who they were.

Dieken ordered a beer inside the bar and told the bartender not to open it. He crooked the bottle in his elbow, twisted it, and the cap came off. Very impressive. There's nothing to it, he said, and he showed me how to do it—the cap just catches your skin and twists. It's a good visual.

The next time we went to a bar, I said, "Let me show you something." People gathered around, I stuck the bottle in my elbow, and I couldn't do it. I cut myself and started to bleed.

"Come on, you can do it," John said.

The bartender said, "That's not a twist-off."

THE PLAN THAT COULDN'T MISS

John and I are huge Browns fans, and we never missed their games. Even at personal appearances we'd listen on the radio. (One reason Dick Goddard never schedules his Woollybear Festival when the Browns are in town is that he's also a big fan—in fact, he's an official team statistician—and knows he would lose a huge part of his audience. We appreciated that, because the Woollybear Festival is just a great time. It's a big slice of Americana that's also Ohio's biggest one-day festival.)

Then we both got VCRs at the same time, as payment instead of money for an appearance. VCRs were a new thing, and we thought they were great because we wouldn't have to miss games anymore.

It was a great idea, but it never worked. We wouldn't turn on the radio in the car so we could come home and enjoy the whole game after an appearance, but someone would always tell us the score or the outcome. We tried and tried so many times; it was amazing it never worked—until one time we made it all the way home without breaking the blackout. June was out doing something with the family, I set up beers and made sandwiches, and we started watching.

It was perfect. Five minutes into the game, the phone rang. It was my brother, Paul, who calls me once every five years.

Instead of saying hello, he said, "Chuck?" I said yeah. He said, "How about those asshole Browns?"

That time, for some reason, he had to call me. Foiled again. We still try it, but to this day our plan hasn't worked.

CHAPTER 24

OTHER SHOWS & GOOD GUYS

SOME PILOTS DON'T FLY

Ernie Anderson would sometimes call at three or four in the morning because he'd be drinking and forget the time difference. When the phone rang at that hour, June would say, "It's either something terrible or it's Ernie." He was still getting on me to come out to Hollywood, trying to get me a commercial part or directing job.

Then a friend of his and Dom Ortuso's in Hollywood came to Cleveland to produce a one-hour comedy for CBS. Ernie and Dom made him talk to me, saying I'd tell him what's funny in Cleveland. The show was the pilot for a potential series with the SCTV group, at that time Dave Thomas, Joe Flaherty, Andrea Martin, Eugene Levy, and Catherine O'Hara. Everybody but John Candy. I wrote a skit about a rock band arriving late to a concert. The curtain opens, and they are a polka band at a Polish wedding. They didn't use it, but it was stolen eventually.

The director was sort of flighty. I remember him wearing a white hat and capelike coat. He knew he'd better get me into something because Ernie and Dom recommended me, and he wanted me to do the Certain Ethnic character in a scene where he'd come in crying, begging for a drink. It was all wrong. I said, "The character wouldn't do that—he's dumb, but he has pride." Joe Flaherty did it instead. It was the only thing they were going to use me in. Ernie called me up, all mad that I refused to do the scene. He didn't understand the circumstances. He and Dom sort of chewed out the director, I guess, because I was invited to the wrap party at the Swamp.

The show was sort of a bomb. CBS didn't pick it up.

I wrote and produced my own pilot for a comedy series called *Sir Bentley*. I modeled it on the East Side Kids, who appeared in a series of 1940s movies. Some of them became the Bowery Boys. It was about a band trying to become successful so that one of the musicians would be eligible for a big inheritance. The name of the band was Sir Bentley, and its real-life leader, Pat Padula, was the one who first came up with the idea. Lil' John played the father of a girl who hung out with the group.

We shot it all in Cleveland, which is where I wanted to keep it. I believed that taking it to Hollywood would ruin it and make it like every other show. I wanted it to be different. But Ernie warned me that "different won't go" with a network, and he was right. *Sir Bentley* was a long shot anyway, and it didn't get picked up. But I think Proctor & Gamble owns it now and has it on the shelf.

SPECIAL SHOWS AND A SPECIAL MAN

The '80s were a very, very busy time. I was doing more than forty hours a week just directing, everything from news to commercials and specials.

Tim Iacofano assigned me to do a Cleveland Ballet special. The ballet was ten years old in 1982, and they had just staged their first production of *The Nutcracker*. I didn't know anything about dance, so I had to research it. The special was called *Of Dance and Dreams*.

That was a good year for me. The special won an Emmy. So did the *Kids World* shows I directed, which also won its second gold medal from the International Film & TV Festival in New York, the most prestigious award of my career to that point.

I was assigned a second ballet special in 1983. It was called *This Dance, Then Goodbye,* and it was mostly about Ian "Ernie" Horvath, who founded the Cleveland Ballet with Dennis Nahat. He was leaving to go to New York City.

Doing the writing and interviewing for the special, I began to think something must be wrong with him. Everybody I interviewed talked about him very sadly, as if it was about more than just leaving town. He seemed OK to me, but he grew a beard while we were shooting, which I thought was unusual. I said, "What's with the beard?" He said he got mugged in New York and wanted to cover the bruises. He shaved it off for the final shooting,

I figured something was wrong, and it was. The beard covered lesions. Partway through, I realized he was dying, not just leaving Cleveland, though no one told me that. He had AIDS, which was not well known at the time, and they were trying to keep it secret.

Imagine how courageous he was, carrying that knowledge and carrying on. He was a very talented guy with a beautiful family. When there was a party afterward, it was much too sad for just a going-away.

This Dance, Then Goodbye won a local Emmy. It received a sad but greater honor when it was shown at a memorial program for Ernie Horvath in New York in 1990. He was just forty-six when he died.

A VERY MEMORABLE GUEST

Channel 8 had a one-hour news and entertainment program called *Noontime*, whose hosts included Jan Jones, Dave Buckel, Anne Mulligan, and Mike Keen. I directed many of the shows, and I enjoyed it because they tried to get celebrities as guests. We had the very old Vincent Price, who I learned was an accomplished painter.

We also had a very old Gloria Swanson, who I found out later is Polish. Her mother's maiden name was Klonowski. I met her in the hallway after the show was over and started talking to her like you would anyone else. She interrupted right in the middle and said, "Brown rice." And walked away. It reminded me of Barney McNulty, the cue card guy. He would sign every note to me with "brown rice." It must be a Hollywood thing.

Another guest was Jerry Lucas, the basketball great from Middletown High School. He'd broken nearly every high school record in Ohio, led the team to back-to-back state championships, and set a tournament record as a sophomore by scoring fifty-three points in one game against East Tech.

After he went to the NBA from Ohio State, I started to hear stories about his superhuman memory skills. Some teammates were going to the movies one night, and he said he'd skip it. He was going to memorize the phone book—and he did. The story goes that he told them to pick out any page, say the name, and he'd give the phone number. I said it couldn't be true.

Then he came to *Noontime* selling a memory course. When I met him he asked, "Can I talk to your audience?" I said sure, they were in the cafeteria. He said, "It'll only take ten minutes, but I have to talk to them." There were maybe fifty people scattered at six or seven tables. He introduced himself and went to each table to talk. He asked me how they'd sit in the audience, and I said they'd be in rows of chairs.

"When I start naming names," he said, "take a wide shot from behind me, and don't cut away." On the show, he started talking about his book and gave me a cue. I took the wide shot. He said, "Would so-and-so please stand up." A guy on the end in the last row stood up, and Lucas said where he was from and what his wife's name was. He went down the row doing that, then the next one, until he went through the entire audience. I believed the phone book story after that. He was something.

He asked me later if I knew the capital of Arkansas. I said no. He told me to picture an ark coming down a waterway, and as it goes by you notice there's a rock—a little rock on the deck. Little rock on an ark. Little Rock, Arkansas. His premise was association. He said you could develop it into an incredible skill if you have the patience. I still use it. Nothing like he does, however.

SOME NICE GUYS JUST SHOW UP

I was so busy; I don't know how I did it when I think back now. My full-time directing duties came on top of the *Big Chuck & Lil' John Show* and its games and appearances, and I'd still come home and do stuff with the kids. I also did three or four years directing local Emmy award shows. In later years, when TV8 did it in rotation with other stations, they'd bring in people from outside and have a crew of seven assigned. I'd do it myself. I knew what I wanted.

But one year I got some help I didn't count on. The Emmy show was at the Crawford Auto-Aviation Museum in University Circle, and the public relations director told me singer Johnnie Ray was playing a club nearby. "Even if you could get him to stop in and say hello," he said. We couldn't pay him anything.

I left a message but never heard back. I figured Ray was probably doing two shows. But as we were doing the show, they wheeled out a piano. Not only was he coming, he'd made arrangements to do a few songs. People loved him. He was just a great guy. It's almost unheard of, what the old stars would do.

Another nice guy story. This one happened on Kelleys Island. There's a casino there—it's "downtown," half a block away from us—and my wife and I went one day. Our kids were young, and we said they could go downtown with us if they found something to do. Don't bother us for an hour, we said; let us talk, and we'll find you and go back home.

We were there for twenty minutes when Missy came running in. "This guy wants to meet you," she said. "He's playing a trumpet and people are listening to him. He wants to meet you." I told her not to bother us. No, she said, "he wants to meet you." I asked his name. She said it was Al Hirt. I laughed and told her to get out of here; someone is pulling your leg. She came back and I waved her off.

After an hour or so, we left and I looked for him. I heard a trumpet from a pier, but there were so many people you couldn't see who was playing. I got closer, and sure enough, it was Al Hirt. He had a friend he'd visit quite often on Kelleys Island, and he just didn't want to be recognized. Whenever he was taking a break there, he would watch our show on Friday nights.

One more nice guy. I finally bought a summer home on the island, and it was a lot of work. People don't go there to fix things, so you do it yourself. I'm an expert on fixing toilets. One day I was working under the house, sweating and dirty and crouched on my side in the crawlspace, really irritated. I never saw a snake there, but figured I would. Then I heard singing outside. I listened carefully and heard a really beautiful guitar, obviously live. Someone was singing about Big Chuck in a melody I'd never heard, under the house fixing pipes, and everything rhymed.

I crawled out, and there was Alex Bevan. He was going to stay there for inspiration to write songs. He mentions the Kielbasy Kid in one of them.

CHAPTER 25

MOTOR CITY BREAKDOWN

FLYNN PACKS HIS GIFT BAGS

It was a sad time for us when Bill Flynn was transferred in 1982 to another Storer Broadcasting station, WJBK, Channel 2 in Detroit. The Flynn years were special. He loved John and me, and the entire management and staff of TV8 loved him. We all chipped him to buy him a set of matching leather luggage. His replacement was Joe Dimino, who had also succeeded him in Boston, and who is remembered by a lot of people for marrying news anchor Tana Carli.

When they went to a meeting of Storer managers afterward, Dimino picked his bag out of the rack at the airport. Flynn said, "That's my bag."

"It looks just like mine," Dimino said, "only mine is real leather." Flynn said, "What the (bleep) do you think this is? Not only is it real leather, the people at Channel 8 bought it for me, which is a whole lot more than they're gonna do for you!" He was right. No manager before or after got a farewell gift like that, and we went through a lot of them.

Flynn called me after he settled in at Channel 2 and asked if John and I wanted to try our show in Detroit. I said, "Why not?" Wow! A market twice as big as Cleveland.

He told us to come up to Detroit and have lunch and talk about it. So John and I drove to Detroit, just to have lunch. That was Flynn.

He had just fired a popular weatherman at WJBK, Sonny Eliot. The whole town was in an uproar and wanted to hang Flynn. He also canceled Sir Graves Ghastly, the longtime horror movie host played by Lawson Deming—a great guy from Cleveland who then came back to be an announcer at Channel 8.

When we got to the restaurant, you could hear people mumbling, "That's the guy who fired Sonny." Flynn said he was on a diet, so he was only ordering a salad. Meanwhile, he had about four martinis. Then he got real loud, talking to us but really talking to the people around us because he heard the buzzing. "If these people knew what kind of an asshole that guy was, they'd be happy I got rid of him," he said. John and I were sinking into our chairs.

But we were going to do the show in Detroit. I wrote some promos, and we had to go back just to shoot them. It was a challenge. Detroit's a big city with beautiful buildings, but it's more deserted than Cleveland. I said, "We gotta go somewhere where there's people." They took us to Greektown, and we took a night to shoot the promos. They never aired, however, which might have warned us about the show's prospects.

PUTTING THE SHOW IN "A LOSE-LOSE SITUATION"

When I saw the Detroit show a few times it was loaded with bad commercials, and so many of them that the movie was constantly interrupted. Our skits were mixed in with commercials. It wasn't anything like our format, and it was pretty obvious they weren't going to do anything for us.

One time I said, "It's so dull in here. We have to have an audience." I wasn't there enough to book it, like I could in Cleveland, so they gave the job to an intern. We had a good show on the set; I'd written some funny stuff about Detroit and Cleveland, and the audience wasn't laughing. They were smiling and polite, but not laughing. We went through the whole show that way. Nobody laughed. After they left, I said, "What did we get into?" Then the intern told us they were from Greektown. They didn't understand English.

Flynn canned a lot of people, and he hired a woman as program manager who I guess didn't like the idea of us coming in. Maybe she just didn't care for us. But if Flynn hired someone and they didn't support a show, he wouldn't butt in. If you didn't do what he wanted, he just canned you. He apologized for putting us in a lose-lose situation. Those were his words.

I thought it was going to be like Cleveland. It wasn't. We got constant complaints. The Union of Poles got on my ass, threatening to come down to the station. The Italian Anti-Defamation League got on John, threatening to come down. Jews threatened to boycott, calling us anti-Semitic. The only people who liked us were the blacks. They liked "Soul Man." They'd recognize us on the street and say so. Cops liked us, too.

John and I would leave for Detroit at 5:30 p.m., after John closed his store. I would drive. We'd be starving, but we didn't have time to stop. We taped at about 8 p.m., and we had to fly to make it. We'd pack stuff and eat like crazy in the car. Then we'd get bored. So I got the idea to make very little sandwiches. John built a thing on the hump to put them on, and we could eat only one thing every five miles. You'd be surprised how that passes time. We played games. Once I made a tape that lasted as long as it took us to drive. The last song would be the *Rocky* theme, to get us pumped up as we drove in to the station. It worked perfectly.

We were coming back late one night, without a car in sight on I-75, and I was doing about 85 mph. I looked in the mirror and saw a car way behind us. He had to be doing 85 mph, too, keeping up and then gaining on us. It was the Michigan State Police. "We ain't gonna get any breaks here," I said. "They don't know who we are."

He pulled us over, came up with a flashlight, saw the table in the car, and looked at us like we were crazy. John and I have a few dozen police courtesy cards, and I put my license with them purposely. I fanned through them for the license, and the trooper asked if I was a police officer. I told him no; we were coming from taping a late-night show at Channel 2.

"We watch that," he said. "Some cops from Cleveland told us about that." He let us go and said, "Say something nice about the highway patrol."

The next week I said, "We had some car trouble, and the Michigan State Police are the nicest guys in the world."

We lasted for maybe fifteen weeks. Nobody really liked us in Detroit. They can't laugh at themselves the way Clevelanders can.

Even gay groups got on us. Back in Cleveland, we did gay spoofs for years and never had any problems.

Except for one time—the Wishing Well skit.

WHEN YOU WISH UPON A WELL

It was another skit where we took off on stereotypes, and it was very popular. I'm not in it—just John, Art, the wonderful Julie Ann Cashel, and a bodybuilder named Bob Klonk. John and Julie Ann are a couple strolling past a wishing well, and she wants a quarter to make a wish. John is too cheap to want to give it to her, but he eventually does. She makes a wish and—*poof!*—he is replaced by the good-looking Klonk. She's all fluttery because she got her wish. Then the bodybuilder asks Julie for a quarter, makes a wish, and—*poof!*—she is replaced by Art, who's wearing a flowered, blouselike shirt, false eyelashes, and waving a hanky, quite obviously a gay stereotype. The bodybuilder is delighted. The two guys walk off together, holding hands, with Art prancing.

It was drizzling when we shot it, in the park across the Shoreway from Channel 8. I told Art to sit in the car except for when we needed him. It was around 5:30, afternoon drive time, and some commuters recognized us and pulled off to watch us shoot. I could hear them talking, enjoying it. Art was made up so you wouldn't even recognize him. Unbeknownst to me, he got out of the car and slipped up behind me. He grabbed my arm and put his head on my shoulder. I said, "Get the hell out of here." I heard a guy say, "Oh no! Jesus Christ, not Big Chuck!" That's all Art needed. The more he heard that, the more he got me.

Some guys got in their cars and left.

Every time we ran that skit, one guy would call me. He identified himself as a gay man, and he said, "Why do you stereotype us like that?"

I said, "What do you mean?"

"You know what I mean," he said. "The way Art Lofredo is dressed."

"Why do you think it's stereotyping?" I asked.

He said, "We're just like anybody else."

"Well then," I said, "how do you know he's gay?"

He said, "Chu-u-uck."

OK, I told him, we're never going to run it again. Then we'd run it again. I'd tell him the same thing, and he'd say, "Chu-u-uck. That's what you said last time." He used to call Art at home. Art would groan whenever he saw us run the skit because he knew he'd get a call.

But the guy knew I'd always call him back. He liked me and our show. I really enjoyed talking with him, and we got to be good friends on the phone. Then all of a sudden he stopped calling. I hoped nothing happened. Maybe if he reads this, he'll let me know.

A SHORT NOTE ON COMPLAINTS

I won't say we never got complaints. One time John got a call in the dressing room at Channel 8 from the Little People of America. They were bugging him to stop making fun of little people. John said he didn't think he was making fun since he was in a lot of skits where size didn't matter. In fact, we exhausted every short joke there was. As time went on, John's height was irrelevant—and no help at all in coming up with skits.

They called again. "Stop calling me," John said. "I don't like little people. Everybody I know is six feet and over."

CHAPTER 26

BELIEVE IN GODDARD

TRYING TO TAME A FORCE OF NATURE

We used to have directors' meetings to talk about various issues. One problem we had was Goddard running over the time limit with his weather segment, sometimes two minutes too long.

I said, "Dom, this comes up every month. The only way you're going to stop him is somebody has to cut him. What else can we do? We're screaming 'Wrap it up, wrap it up' for two minutes."

"You know what," I said, "I'm the only one here who can get away with it. I can cut him, and he'll get mad, but he won't do anything about it." We're good friends.

I usually directed weekends, but once in awhile I'd do weekdays. The next time I did, I told Dick, "I'm not used to doing weekdays, and I'm really nervous, so don't run long. If you do, we have to cut things, and cram, and it gets really hectic."

So I warned him. He did the weather, I wrapped him up, and he went on. I started repeating in his earpiece, "Wrap it up, wrap it up, wrap it up." He kept talking. I said, "OK, stand by to roll commercial."

Everybody in the control room looked at me in surprise. "Five seconds to roll," I said. "And roll it."

Once you roll, you've got to take it on

Dick Goddard's high school photo. You can't knock Goddard. I got to be good friends with him, directing news. He was a big part of the Ghoulardi All-Stars.

the air. Everybody in the control room had bug-eyed looks. Dick was in the middle of something, and the commercial came on. I figured I'd hear "About time somebody did that," but the control room was silent and no one would look at me. I said, "Oh shit, what am I gonna do?" As soon as the news was over, everybody cleared out of the room as fast as they could.

Dick came over and looked in the door. I could see his reflection in the monitor; he was shaking his head. He'd call me Charlie when he was upset with me because he knew I don't like it. He just said one word.

"Charlie," he said, sounding real disappointed.

The next three times I did the news, he was off as much as ten seconds early—"or Big Chuck's gonna cut me again," he said.

In a month or so, he was back to running over.

PEOPLE WHO MEANT A LOT TO US

But you can't knock Goddard. I got to be good friends with him, directing a lot of news. He's a jock, too, and was a big part of the Ghoulardi All-Stars. He joined games whenever he could through the Hoolihan and Lil' John years.

When John and I first took over, Goddard offered his services in skits, and he did a lot of unannounced walk-ons to share his celebrity status because he felt we were struggling. He never said that, but I knew. He was helping us along. That was generous, and that's when I realized he's a pretty good comedic actor. He's always been a ham, but the skits showed how much more he can do. He was a wonderful addition to our show at a time when we needed it.

He also brought Julie Ann Cashel on board. She was the love of his life, and she was just wonderful. She was an animal lover like him, also a model and entertainer. She not only acted in skits, she'd set up skits, bringing models and extras we needed. Once I said we needed ten people for a party scene, and she got them. You could depend on her. She loved doing it, and she saved me so much work. She came to some of our All-Star games, too. She didn't drive, so Dick would have to drive her around, plus do the weather. They really went the distance for us.

THE GUARDIAN OF ANIMAL LIFE

Goddard really is Mr. Nice Guy. He's the kind of guy who gets out of the shower to take a pee. And he really is a freak about animals. He's not only the protector of stray cats and dogs, he's the guardian of all animal life at TV8.

During the news, they once started paging him—"Dick Goddard, get to the studio right away, Dick Goddard, twenty seconds." He went flying by, in the other direction, holding his arms out in front of him. He had a spider's web, with the spider in it, and was taking it to the back door to release it outside. He'd bring in birds and nurse them back to health.

His protection of animal life got him involved in things I didn't expect.

For instance, although most of the skits I've written were pretty much my own ideas, a great number were derived from jokes I heard. One such joke went like this:

A Catholic priest was trying to get one of his parishioners to quit drinking. He asked him to come to the parish house one night to have a chat. When the man arrived, the priest sat him down next to his desk and pointed out that on the desk were two drinking glasses. One was filled with fresh drinking water, and the other was filled with gin. He then opened a container of earthworms, took one out, and said, "Watch what happens when I put the worm into the glass of water. See how the worm swims around enjoying the cool, fresh water?" Taking another worm out of the container, he told the man, "Now watch what happens when I put this worm into the demon alcohol." Within seconds, the worm in the gin shriveled up and died. "There!" said the priest. "Did you see that? Now what lesson does that teach you?"

"A very good lesson, Father," the parishioner responded. "If you drink booze, you'll never get worms."

St. Paddy's Day was coming up. To make this skit more timely, I made the priest Irish and had him trying to get his brother to quit drinking. I asked our resident Irishman and good friend Tom Bush—a master impressionist who does a great Irish accent—to play the priest. And to make the skit more technically interesting, I decided to use a split screen with Tom Bush doing both roles, the priest and his twin brother.

Now began the work of a TV producer: scheduling studio time and crew, calling Bush, scripting the skit and camera shots, checking out the split-screen effect with the technical director, building the office set, getting costumes, and rounding up the props—two glasses, a water pitcher, a bottle of gin, and, oh yes, live worms.

I have always prided myself on being thoroughly prepared for a shoot, thinking of things that could go wrong, and having a backup plan in case of emergency.

Tape time was set for a Tuesday, 7:30 p.m. to 9 p.m. I had all the props ready at the studio, everything but the live worms. At about 5 p.m., I went to a bait shop just around the corner from TV8 and bought a dozen worms. I called Tom and reminded him to arrive at the studio about 6:30 p.m. Everything was ready. So I went to our cafeteria to get a sandwich to eat while I watched our six o'clock news. During a commercial break, I began to go over production details. I opened the container of worms to make sure they were alive and active. They were.

Then it hit me like a ton of bricks: I needed one dead worm. I didn't have a dead worm. I began to panic, but then I thought, "No problem, I'll kill one." But how? I began to panic again. "I'll cut off his head," I thought. But I've seen worms completely cut in half while fishing, and both ends stay alive. I decided I'd smash it but realized that would be too messy and the worm wouldn't look right. Oh, man! It was about thirty minutes to tape time, and I thought, "What the hell am I going to do? How am I going to kill a worm without destroying its body?" Then I glanced down at my sandwich and a light bulb went on in my head—the cafeteria has three microwaves! "I'll nuke the worm!"

I felt very relieved and very guilty at the same time. I had never deliberately executed anything in my life. But, as they say, the show must go on. I had to hurry. It was about 6:45 p.m., the news would be over at 7 p.m., and the entire shift would be in the cafeteria to eat lunch two minutes later.

I grabbed the worms, ran down the hall, and peeked into the

cafeteria. Perfect. No one was there. My heart was beating faster and faster. I began to feel like a ghoul, about to do something very unnatural to satisfy my selfish needs. "This is not for me," I told myself. "It's for my craft!"

As I placed a worm on a paper plate, another question hit me: How long do you nuke a worm to kill it? I decided to try fifteen seconds. I pressed the start button and began to think of all the old prison movies I had seen as a kid, with the prison guard throwing the switch on the electric chair. I felt really creepy.

I looked out the cafeteria door as the microwave buzzed away. No one in sight. Good! It was the longest fifteen seconds of my life, but it was over. I took the paper plate out of the microwave and gasped in shock. The worm was gone. I looked all over inside the microwave. No worm in sight. Then I noticed what looked like a very faint S-shaped pencil line on the plate. It was the worm. Vaporized. Obviously, fifteen seconds was too long. I grabbed another worm, set the timer for ten seconds, and *zap*. This time, I didn't feel as guilty. When I took out the paper plate, the worm looked more like an "S" drawn with a crayon. I looked at my watch. It was two minutes to seven o'clock. The news was over and the crews would soon be in the cafeteria.

I had one more shot. Would five seconds be enough? No. Still too much. Three seconds? Not enough? I was fast running out of time—and worms, for that matter. I put a new worm in, set the timer for three seconds, zapped, opened the door, and there it was—a perfectly formed worm, dead as a doornail. Whew! It worked.

I grabbed the plate and container of worms and turned to leave—only to find Linda Norman from the camera crew looking down at my plate. "What is that?" she asked. "Is that a worm? What did you do with it?" I tried to think of a believable lie, but drew a blank. "I . . . ah . . . I put it in the microwave." "What!?" she gasped. "You're gross! Why did you do a horrible thing like that?"

"I need it for a skit," I said, and started to leave because others were coming in. She yelled, "Wait! Which microwave did you use? I don't want to use that one."

"I'm not telling you," I teased, and I started down the hallway. "You called me gross!"

"You'd better tell me!" she yelled back. "Or—or I'm going to tell Dick Goddard what you did!"

That really got my attention. But, I figured, what's done is done, no turning back now. We did the skit, and it turned out great. The acting, the special effects, everything was excellent—even the worms. We showed that skit annually every March near St. Patrick's Day.

The next day, when I got to work, a brown paper bag with a note attached was on my desk. I immediately noticed the signature at the bottom, "Dick Goddard," and I knew Linda had blown the whistle on me. "Charlie," the note read, "Next time you need worms for a skit, use these." In the bag was an assortment of plastic worms. To the day I retired, I kept that bag of worms in our prop room as a reminder of the heinous act perpetrated in the name of showbiz.

I later saw a picture of Dick as a young boy on our news show's baby picture quiz segment. Dick was holding a fishing pole, and I thought, "What did Dick do to the worms he used as bait?" A funny line came to me, one that we still use in our stand-up routine in live shows: "You know, people always ask us, 'Is Dick Goddard as nice as everyone says?' Well folks, Dick truly is Mr. Nice Guy, and, believe me, he is the biggest animal lover on the planet. For instance, whenever Dick goes fishing, he tapes the worms to his hook."

A TANK IN YOUR TIGER

The station got heavily involved with the circus one year at Richfield Coliseum. John and I were at every matinee for the whole week to open the show. A lot of TV8 personalities were part of the opening. We were all going to ride elephants and parade into the ring.

Goddard is always last. Somebody has to keep an eye on him or he'll just wander away. We'd be ready to do something, and he'd say, "Ooh, Charlie, look at this . . ."

The rest of us were on our elephants. I turned around and Dick was gone. They were bringing out the tigers, and instead of getting on his elephant, Goddard was looking in the cages. "Ooh, Charlie, look at this magnificent beast," he said. "Come on down, look at this."

I said, "Dick! Get up here! We're holding up the whole thing!" He was oblivious. "Oh, you ought to see this," he said, just fascinated, turning back to the cage.

The tiger, apparently a female, turned its ass around and peed on him. It looked like a blast from a hose hit him right in the kisser. He fell back. His hair was wet, his clothes were wet, and his eyes were burning. He was rubbing his eyes, waving his arms and smiling, not looking upset at all.

But we were at the Coliseum, and he still had to get back to the station to do the weather. So a friend living nearby loaned him a suit to replace his wet, smelly clothes. Dick went on, almost like nothing happened.

Almost, because the friend was about my size. Dick is not. In that suit, it really did look like the circus had come to TV8.

Some other TV8 personalities and I rode elephants through the rings when the circus came to town—except for Goddard, who was peed on by a tiger.

CHAPTER 27

FROM FATS TO TEX

HE ONLY PLAYED FOR KAYSH

Channel 8 was pretty heavily into the commercial production business in the 1980s. They got a job to produce a thirty-second spot for Brunswick pool tables, and they were going to bring in Minnesota Fats to do it. I was already very busy producing specials and other programs, but Tim Iacofano gave it to me.

Busy as I was, I didn't mind this one at all. One of my all-time favorite movies is *The Hustler,* with Cleveland's own Paul Newman as Fast Eddie and Jackie Gleason as Minnesota Fats, and now I was going to work with the real Fats, maybe the most famous pool player in history.

The Brunswick people gave me the script a few days in advance. It called for Fats, whose real name was Rudolph Walter Wanderone, Jr., to do the spot while making some trick shots on a Brunswick table. I said we probably couldn't use a prompter because he'd be moving around too much. We could use cue cards in different locations, or he could memorize the copy. It wasn't much, and we wouldn't have much time to shoot, so I told them to send the script to Fats and make sure he memorized it.

They only scheduled about an hour of tape time, from 3:30 to 4:30 in the afternoon. At five o'clock, the studio would be needed to start taping promos for our six o'clock news. All TV sales departments think you can do anything in an hour, and they'll promise anything to get a sale.

I had the pool table set up, the background lit, the mics checked, and everything ready so we wouldn't waste time. The Brunswick people picked up Fats at Hopkins and brought him to the station about 1:30 p.m. The sales people asked if he had anything to eat and took him out for lunch—a sandwich and what must have been quite a few drinks. They got back about 3:15.

A small crowd of Brunswick people, sales guys, and TV8 people gathered to watch in the studio. Fats started shooting trick shots to loosen up. He won cheers and applause for every shot, and he was eating it up. I didn't interrupt because I wanted him to get comfortable, but at 3:30 I said, "OK, it's showtime." I asked Fats if he memorized the commercial, he said yes, and we got started. He stumbled on the first line. I read it to him, and he kept shooting trick shots and talking. More people gathered, and he started telling one story after another. This was more important to him than the commercial.

I was really interested, too, but we were getting nothing done. He couldn't get ten seconds into the spot. We'd start shooting, and he'd blow it. Nobody but me seemed worried about this, not even the Brunswick people. They were half lit and having a great time, and Fats was still playing to the crowd. But I had to get the spot done. I asked everybody but the Brunswick people to leave the studio.

Fats started telling stories about how Willie Mosconi was not as good as he was. I used to watch pool on TV. Every time they'd play, Mosconi beat him. I asked, "Did you ever bet him?" He said, "No, and you know why? I only play for cash." He said it "kaysh," which was the only time I heard it pronounced like that. "Willie Mosconi doesn't play for kaysh. I only play for kaysh," he said, all the while doing incredible shots. Now he had me doing what I told everyone not to do, leading him into telling stories.

I ran out and frantically started making cue cards. We had ten minutes. Maybe we'd get lucky. It was the last chance. I'd say, "We'll do it again," and he'd try a trick shot, blow his line, and start talking again. More applause.

We ran late, had to stop, and didn't get it done. We had absolutely nothing. Everybody left the studio, and the sales department said they'd try to set up another shoot, but it never happened. Nobody seemed too upset.

So not only did the real Minnesota Fats not shoot pool like Jackie

Gleason's character in the movie, he couldn't drink like him either. But he sure was an entertainer.

I later learned that his real nickname was New York Fats. When *The Hustler* came out, the novel and then the movie, he began calling himself Minnesota Fats and claiming he was the character the movie was about. But Minnesota Fats was fictitious. I liked Fats, but I was disappointed.

My neighbor Joe Dannery used to come over on weekends, and we'd shoot pool and drink martinis until the wee hours. Joe was a great neighbor, a great pal, and an excellent pool player because his father owned a poolroom when he was a kid. He'd do trick shots and call himself Willie Mosconi, and I'd say I was Minnesota Fats. I loved Gleason's portrayal of Fats and the fact that he was good drinker. Even though I couldn't beat Joe at pool, I would outdrink him, which is how I'd win matches. I'd outlast him.

"From now on," I told him after the commercial shoot, because I heard Minnesota Fans was not the real one, "I want to be Fast Eddie."

Joe said, "Well, laddie, I heard you aren't the real Big Chuck either. Rack 'em."

God, I miss those late-night pool games with Joe Dannery.

SMOKING OUT MICHAEL J. FOX

I had another big assignment around then, when the American Cancer Society wanted me to make a musical mini-movie against smoking that could be shown in schools. They told me the society previously had spent all its advertising money to get people to quit smoking and thought just about everyone who could quit had done so. Now they were going to spend their money to deter kids from smoking. They chose me to do this because of the Singing Angels specials I'd done, and the older kids were some of the teens in the movie. It was supposed to star Michael J. Fox. He was eager to do it and would be available when he came to Cleveland to shoot scenes for the movie *Light of Day*.

When the cancer society people met with Michael, however, they learned that he was not only a smoker, he was a chain smoker.

Light of Day, in fact, turned out to be one of the few projects where he smoked on camera. There was no way they could use him. They got a teenage actor from New York City to play the part.

That was my second disappointment in a row. No Minnesota Fats, no Michael J. Fox. It would have been fun. Lil' John knew Fox's bodyguard when he stayed in Cleveland, and he said Fox was a generous, down-to-earth guy who would buy everybody rounds at the end of the day and was easy to work with.

But the mini-movie turned out great. The American Cancer Society loved it, and TV8 loved it.

MISSED HIM BY THAT MUCH

Lil' John booked us for a big Cleveland karate meet that would feature other celebrity emcees like John Lanigan, plus big-name participants like Chuck Norris, who was then middleweight karate champion, and Tex Cobb, who was a kickboxer before becoming a boxer.

They asked if they could come down and do something on our show with Cobb. They weren't sure if Norris was coming to the event. Cobb used to go on Johnny Carson's show, and he was hilarious. He'd talk about the beating he took from Larry Holmes and say stuff like, "I stuck to my plan—stumbling forward and getting hit in the face." Carson would joke around with one of his comments or stories, and Cobb would say, "Does that bother you?" Carson would play that he was backing off, and say "No, no!" They were really good at it.

"That's fantastic," I said. "We can do exactly the same thing Carson does. We'll just keep talking and have him interrupt us, and we'll kiss his butt and apologize."

They were late getting to the show. I remember looking down the hall, wondering when they were going to appear, and saw a bunch of people with one big guy in the middle. That was Cobb. All through the show we had a ball. He would tell his stories, I would correct him, and then I'd back off elaborately. He was really enjoying it.

At the very end, we had the PJ Party closing it out. While we were saying goodbye, see you next week, Cobb whispered to me, "Aren't you going to bring Chuck Norris up?" I said, "What the hell?!" and looked in the audience.

There he was. It was the first time he grew a beard. I didn't know he was there, and he never said a word. He's not tall, so I didn't notice him in the crowd when Cobb arrived. Norris wasn't scheduled to come; he just showed up. He was beaming and smiling all through the show. I started apologizing like crazy, and he said, "Oh man, I had a ball—I've never seen anything like this!" Truly a nice guy who didn't care about being recognized.

CHAPTER 28

ROARING '80S

FRONT PAGE NEWS AROUND THE WORLD

A very special thing happened to Lil' John and me on April 25, 1986. We'd been interviewed by Clare Ansberry, a reporter for the *Wall Street Journal,* who wanted to do an article on our very popular and creative show being the last form of vaudeville left in the country. I was very excited. We'd had a lot of nice coverage in local publications over the years, but the *Wall Street Journal* is sold all over the world.

Any mention from them would have been a big deal. I never thought the story would be on the front page. But it was, and it pictured John and me with the famous dot-sketch portraits the *Journal* used instead of photos.

It was a Friday, perfect for our show, which made it even better. I happened to be at the station early that day, and the phone rang first thing in the morning. "Jesus Christ! You know you're on the front page of the *Journal?*" It was Bill Flynn, calling from Detroit, and he was still a fan of the show. He called the news department to make sure they did a big story on it.

The following week I got calls and letters from all over the world. I told John, "We're now internationally famous." He said, "Yeah—but we still didn't get a raise!"

HOW MUCH SPAGHETTI CAN YOU EAT?

Occasionally I needed to rent a tuxedo, and I went to Pete Petrone in Parma. He had two tux shops. We got to be friends. One day he wanted to meet me about a business deal, and he wanted to come to the station to talk about it. He wouldn't talk on the phone. He and his wife came down—very proper, well-dressed, two of the nicest people you could meet.

He wanted me to produce a commercial for his shops and set it up to run on TV8. I said I would gladly produce the spot, but TV8 had the broadest viewing area and the most power of the local VHF stations and probably charged more for commercials. It would be expensive. I suggested he run it on a UHF station like Channel 43 or 61. It would be a lot cheaper, and all they needed. Our signal went as far south as Dover and New Philadelphia, north to London, Ontario, east to Pennsylvania, and west to Fremont and Toledo. People in those areas weren't going to drive to Pete Petrone's shop, so there was no sense paying for that signal.

Pete was very disappointed. He thanked me and said he would think about it and get back to me. I felt bad, like I'd really let him down. But I had to tell him the truth. He called back in a week or so and said he wanted to meet me again.

This time I said I'd go to his shop. He told me there that he decided not to do the commercial at all. He had enough money, he was living nicely, his house was paid for, and all his kids were graduated from college, married, and doing well. He said, "What the hell was I thinking? I don't need to work, and I certainly don't need to work harder."

He said, "How much spaghetti can you eat?"

That simple line struck home to me like none other in my life.

I would sometimes think that maybe I should have pulled up stakes, uprooted my family, and gone to L.A. with Ernie and Tim and the "Cleveland Clan"—Jack Riley, Ann Elder, Jack Hanrahan, Ralph Hanson, plus more. But I was doing well here and making a nice living, though not nearly what most people think. My family was healthy and well cared for, thanks to my wife, June. Why should I risk changing that? Why should I screw up the family? Why should I chase something else? How much spaghetti can you eat, indeed.

Dom Ortuso left TV8 to go out to L.A., and Tim and Ernie got him jobs directing all kinds of things, from golf tournaments to filling in on Johnny Carson once in a while. A few years ago he retired and came back home. He told me that the first time he had to fill in on *The Tonight Show,* he was so nervous he got there real early and started asking questions. Nobody was really talking to him or paying much attention. He studied tapes of the show. When they were ready to tape and the theme music started, he said, "Stand by to cue Ed McMahon, stand by." *Boom,* Ed was talking before Dom could cue him. He said, "Stand by to take . . ." and *boom,* the switcher took the shot before he could say it. In about five minutes, he learned he didn't even have to be there. He worried all that time for nothing.

Finally he said, "You made the right decision to stay here in Cleveland because you are Cleveland's Johnny Carson."

That meant a great deal to me. It finally erased that question, "Should I do it?" I thought again: How much spaghetti can you eat? To this day I say that.

God bless Pete Petrone.

WILL THE REAL JACK PLEASE STAND UP?

We used many sports guys in skits. One that we got the biggest kick out of was Jack Lambert. He's a Hall of Fame linebacker who was a key part of Pittsburgh's "Steel Curtain" defense, but he's from Mantua, went to Kent State, and grew up watching us. He had a real big summer football camp for kids, and when he said NFL stars participated he wasn't kidding. He had players from all over the league.

He wanted to come down to the show to plug the camp. I asked him to do a skit with us. He had the reputation of being dumb, though he was anything but dumb, and I knew it would be the thing to work with. It was the first image you thought of with Jack Lambert, but I worried about asking him to appear that way in the skit. I said, "There's this thing that you're not very intelligent. Do you care if we do a skit playing on that?" He laughed and said he didn't care.

We did a skit off the game show *To Tell the Truth.* He wore a jersey, and so did John and me. We hit the payoff, "Will the real Jack Lambert please stand up?" and the music starts. John and I look at each other, and I start to stand up and sit back down—copying the way they'd stretch out the suspense on the show. John starts to stand, then sits down. We do it again. Lambert just sits there. The music continues. We start looking at Lambert. It goes on for a good thirty seconds, which is a long time in a skit. John finally jabs his arm and says "You!"—pointing to stand up.

We played his NFL all-stars at the football camp after that. He had some big names, and we never played such a rough game in our lives. They are rough, and they beat the crap out of you. They mauled us. Big Stash brought his daughter, who was a star high school player, and they beat the crap out of her, too. Girl? Didn't matter.

Lambert knew we had postgame parties, and somebody asked in the locker room where we were going. He named a place, and somebody said, "That's a punch palace, man! Guys trying to pick fights! There's one every night!" Don't worry about it, Lambert said. He got us there and said he had to run back to camp to make sure the kids were in bed for curfew. As he was leaving, he said to John, "Don't start anything while I'm gone."

One guy we didn't have to worry about was Joe Charboneau— the American League Rookie of the Year with the Indians in 1980— who was playing with the All-Stars by then. It got too expensive to charter buses for our games, so we'd carpool. Joe rode with me. He'd tell stories, and he'd always drink light beer after games. "I'm half Indian, and that firewater thing is real," he said. "You don't want to get me drunk."

The wildest story he told was about when the Indians sent him to play in the Mexican League one winter. He if you beat their team said the fans would go nuts and go onto the field like a soccer crowd. His team beat the home team at one game, and the fans went after them. In self-defense, the team started decking people on the field. Joe's a brawler. The cops arrested them, beat him, threw him in jail, and wouldn't let him talk to anybody. He said he was there for weeks and saw it could go on indefinitely. So he stopped being a wise guy and got on the good side of the guards by telling baseball stories. They'd leave his cell unlocked once in a while.

So he escaped and had to find clothes and make his way back to the border. He said it was just like *The Fugitive*.

GETTING TO THE FINISH THE EASY WAY

John booked us to do a 5K race in my old neighborhood. The route went down Fleet Avenue, along East 71st Street and back up Harvard Road, my old stomping grounds. We thought we were going to emcee and start the race, but John had it wrong—they had us sign in to run in it.

John hates running. I figured I could tough it out, but it would take two hours. We didn't want to blow it because it was a big event, so we went along. Some of the old people who were watching told the organizers that I once raced and beat Stella Walsh. I never beat her, and she was old, but this somehow got to one or two of the runners. They looked like they were in a panic, keeping an eye on me.

They took off fast when we started running. I told John, "Don't take off with them. We'll blow all our energy in two minutes." Everyone was passing us. We weren't even down to the end of Fleet, and we were fading already. The men passed us, and then the first woman passed us, which I didn't like. So we picked up the pace, and we were dying. John looked back and said, "If the wheelchairs pass us up, I quit."

As he said that, I remembered there was an alley running almost to Harvard. We ran through it when we were kids. I didn't know if it was still open, but we were coming up to it, and it was there. *Boom.* John and I trotted down and came out on Harvard—right behind the leaders, five guys running like mad. They looked back, saw us, and picked up the pace like crazy. I don't know if they would have picked it up anyway, but they were gagging when they reached the finish line.

UP AND AWAY AND TO THE MAGIC KINGDOM

John and I had a much easier time of it when Cleveland had a gigantic balloon launch on Public Square in September 1986. It was an event for the United Way, to set a record for the most helium balloons released at one time. There were more than a million of them, all red, white, and blue, and we emceed the whole thing. It couldn't have been better. The balloons held for a moment, then funneled upward, clustered around the Terminal Tower, and went up together. I'll never forget that sight. What a visual. I have that show on DVD. Maybe I'll include it in one of our "Best of" collections.

We did several shows for Disney. They'd put on celebrity and media events when a new attraction opened at Disney World. We were recognized by so many people from Cleveland down there; someone would be taking a picture every five minutes. John and I would always oblige and sign autographs. A lot of the other celebrities wouldn't, nor would they have as many people stop them.

Somebody at Disney saw this and really gave John and me the celebrity treatment. We got on the plane with other local broadcasting personalities, and everybody was sort of grumbling because John and I were going first class. I turned around, looked through the curtain at our TV8 colleague Jan Jones, and said, "Don't come up here and use our toilet."

When we arrived, there was a sign, "Cleveland media," with a minibus. Another card for "Big Chuck & Lil' John" pointed to a limousine. Everybody else had vouchers for food. John and I had a credit card.

We stayed at the Floridian, and we took a break from shooting for the show to go to a bar at Pleasure Island. The cop at the door was from Cleveland. He was surprised to see us, and I soon wondered about that. John and I sat drinking beer for about fifteen minutes, a little bit above a dance floor, and noticed guys were dancing with guys. I said, "Drink up." The Cleveland cop was gone when we got to the door. Damn it! That's how those rumors get started.

REALLY GETTING STONED

I never took a sick day. Even when Hinckley got snowed in, I'd walk to North Royalton and catch a bus to work. It'd take all day to get there. I had a streak going for more than thirty-five years. Then all of a sudden I had a kidney stone.

When I first had it, it was so painful I fell out of the car in the driveway. June was up at Kelleys Island, so I drove myself to Parma

Hospital, and I don't know how I did it. I went walking in, which took everything I had, trying to be cool because people know me. A young doctor recognized me and said, "Oh my God, heart attack!"

An older doctor was standing next to him. He said, "Stone." That's all he said. That was cool.

It'd come part way out and go back, more painful than anything you could think of, going up and down for two years. The doctors said a kidney operation would be terrible, with a big chance for infection. Operating was the last thing they wanted to do. But the pain would drop me to my knees.

They gave me two tiny little pills. They said if I thought I was having an attack, I should take one and get to a hospital. I carried those pills for two years and was never without them. I was getting ready to direct the noon news one day and felt the tell-tale pain like no other. I knew it wouldn't be long before it was unbearable. So I told the assistant director I'd drive to Southwest General Hospital, and I just hoped I could make it.

On the way out, I took both pills. I got on I-71, and as I got to Bagley Road felt no pain whatsoever. I got off the freeway and stopped at the light. Nothing seemed real. It was like a movie. The stoplight was red against a blue sky, and I thought it was the most beautiful thing I ever saw. I was entranced. It changed to green, and drivers started honking and swearing. Everything seemed to be in slow motion. I got to the hospital and said I felt fine, I didn't think there was a problem. They asked if I took anything for it. Why yes, I did.

They decided to send me home and keep watching it. Then the doctor said they had a new procedure called lithotripsy, where they blast the stone with sound waves. No cutting was involved. They'd put you in a big vat of water with a giant spark plug and focus on the stone to break it up without hurting anything else.

I said I'd do it, and I asked if we could do the procedure—it was so stupid, but I didn't want to lose the sick-day streak—on a weekend. The doctor said we could do it on a Friday, but I'd have to spend a day or two in the hospital.

We were doing a program at that time called *Medical Marvels*. I told Virgil Dominic they could televise the procedure. I'd volunteer.

Running shoes with a tuxedo were my style. This was the publicity shot for the 1988 anniversary special, *25 Years of Friday Nights: The Tradition Continues*.

He was tickled, and they set it up. Rather than knock me out, they gave me a spinal so I could talk during the whole thing. You actually hang in a sling. A track takes you into the next room and lowers you into a vat. There was a very loud arcing noise that reminded me of something from a Frankenstein movie. But I was out of it enough that it never occurred to me that I was completely naked. A doctor ran up with a towel, said, "There's cameras in here!" and threw it over my slinkey. And because this was on TV, someone put a rubber ducky in the water.

It worked, and it was a big success as a program. Storer showed it on their stations, and I got calls from all over the country from people who wanted to have the same thing. Because of the program, they saw how safe it was, so in a small way it helped spur the use of lithotripsy.

Lil' John came to see me in the hospital. I'd always said you have to abuse your body to get the most out of it—not get enough sleep and drink too much. I used to drink seven nights a week, even if didn't want a drink. I'd force myself. "Tonight," I said, "is going to be the first time I didn't have a drink." John left, came back about two hours later, said he was just passing by, and handed me a bag with a Manhattan in it.

That would have been an easy one for him. When my wife was in the hospital, having rough time with our last daughter being born, John came one night to visit. They told him no one was allowed in except me. He called up to the room, and I apologized. Ten minutes later, a cart rolled into the room, and we could hardly see how it was being pushed. John was behind it. He somehow found a laundry basket, took out a scrub suit, put a mask over his face, and pushed the cart to the room.

I told Virgil after the stone was blasted that I did miss one day of work—but since they televised it . . .

He just laughed. I think I ultimately ran my streak up to forty-three years.

EDITING UP TO TWENTY-FIVE YEARS

I was still writing, producing, and directing shows at Channel 8, plus many of the Emmy Awards shows for the local chapter of the National Academy of Television Arts & Sciences. I brought Ernie back for one of them, and we had Phil Donahue, Doug Dieken, Ozzie Newsome, and Norm N. Nite emcee some of the ones I did.

Editing was especially important to me. I learned editing from Bob Soinksi. He was really good. We studied it together, and I learned to shoot to make editing easier. Some of the stuff was fantastic. When I heard that the epic *Ben-Hur* was going to be on TV, about 1965, I called Bob and said we had to watch. It had won a record eleven Oscars, including one for film editing. Within minutes, we were calling each other with glaring edit mistakes. A character would be leaning against a well. Cut to another shot, and he'd be three feet away. We saw that all through the movie. We really paid attention.

Because Ernie Anderson liked the way we edited, he called me in

John and I visit Hoolie at home in Florida for the *25 Years of Friday Nights* special.

the '80s to send some good *Big Chuck & Lil' John* skits for his son, Paul, to study, because he was getting into film. He wanted "anything that's good, any new stuff." I did send the tapes, so I could say I taught Academy Award-nominee Paul Thomas Anderson everything he knew.

John and I went with Casey Kassarda from TV8 to see Ernie in 1988, when we decided to do a twenty-fifth anniversary special for the show. We'd just been moved to Saturday night, after twenty-five years, but I called it *25 Years of Friday Nights* anyway.

We went to Florida to shoot Hoolie, and then to Hollywood for Ernie. We had a ball, and I was happy Ernie liked John. If he didn't like you, he'd tell you, more or less. As cool as John usually is, he was intimidated. Ernie had season tickets for the Dodgers, and Paul Anderson went with us to a ballgame. We didn't have enough tickets, so Ernie had us stop at Harvey Korman's house on the way. Ernie knew everybody, and he still did things his way. Harvey had a huge living room with an L-shaped bar that he'd seen in New England, as long as the room. He had a giant Emmy statue that he saw in a studio back lot. He had the ceiling extended to fit it in and had the statue lowered in by helicopter. Paul remembered he once hired refrigerated trucks at Christmastime to drive to the mountains and haul snow back to his front yard for the kids.

Back home, *25 Years of Friday Nights* was a hit, and also aptly titled. Channel 8 moved us back to Fridays.

CHAPTER 29

FIGHTING MIKE TYSON

Sweat was in my eyes and I was working hard one hot summer day in 1989 on Kelleys Island. There were ants in a tree near our picnic table, and I was gouging the trunk to go after them. I heard something, looked up, and saw two guys walking into the yard.

One looked like George Forbes, president of Cleveland City Council. I wiped my eyes. It *was* George Forbes. The other was Jim Palladino, a Cleveland businessman who has a place on the island.

They had a proposition. Forbes asked if John and I would be interested in fighting Mike Tyson, "Iron Mike," the undisputed world heavyweight champion.

It wasn't as far-fetched as it sounds. Tyson had a mansion outside of Cleveland and was managed by Don King. Forbes made a deal with King to get Tyson to do a voter-registration benefit exhibition for the city and the Urban League.

It wasn't unprecedented, either. We once did a skit with Earnie Shavers, when King was managing him and he worked out in Warren. Hoolie was the ring announcer, King was in Earnie's corner, and John was my corner man. Because I used to fight a little bit, I told Earnie, "It's not going to be funny unless you beat me up a little bit. Just go ahead, I can take it." Ali said that the

After the fight with Earnie Shavers. I told Earnie to really hit me, and got nailed in the throat. From left: Don King, John, Shavers, me, Hoolie.

hardest he was ever hit was by Earnie Shavers. He nailed me in the throat, and I thought I'd never talk again.

But obviously I did, and obviously this was a coup. Of course we wanted to do it. We could have some fun with it for the show.

It was going to be a three-round sparring match, and I started working out really seriously. I was fifty-four years old, figured we had to take our shirts off, and I wanted to look halfway decent. And we had to go three rounds. Boxing is like wrestling—you have to go all out. You have nothing left unless you're in good shape.

Casey Coleman helped the build-up by doing a series on us training. He showed me on Kelleys Island, building piers and swimming and running—"a workout that would kill the average man," he said, "while Mike Tyson vacations in his twenty-six-room mansion, never realizing he had touched a chord deep within the souls of these two men." John did the *Rocky* training scene, with the movie theme playing, running through the Flats and up the City Hall steps. "Hey, John, take it easy on Tyson!" somebody yelled.

TALKING TRASH, SHOWING FLASH

Forbes called me again on the island and asked if we'd come to a press conference. I said sure, thinking it was going to be something for Channel 8. I got back to Cleveland, saw network TV trucks, and thought it couldn't be for us. But it was a real press conference, in a huge room with a long table. Tyson sat there next to Don King, in front of the cameras. I got nervous. I wasn't even dressed for it, still wearing a polo shirt from the island.

I thought: We've got to think of something funny. I'm not good at a spontaneous, on-the-spur comment. I whispered to John: "When we have to say something, I'll say it's a great honor to do this, and a great charity we're fighting for. But if Tyson was any kind of guy, he'd give us more notice than a month to get in shape, we're not going to be at our best.

"We're going to play like we're serious. And when you talk, you're going to get mad."

John was on my left at the table and Tyson on my right. I told John to try to hit Tyson. When John really tries to get somebody, and I really have to hold him back, it's funny. When we fake it, it's

I try to restrain John as he launches himself at Mike Tyson before our exhibition bout in 1989. "That scared me!" Tyson said later.

not funny. Since I told him to go all-out, I'd have to go all-out to stop him.

John, complaining about Tyson giving us little time, said, "Let me tell you something, sucker!" and stood on the table, which I didn't expect him to do. He took a running dive at Tyson. I caught him. Tyson sat back in his chair and laughed, and in that high voice said to King, "That scared me!"

The place went crazy with laughter.

It was a real national press conference. We had to do the thing over because photographers said they missed it, and we'd have to re-create John going for Tyson. Shutters clicked and lights flashed and popped.

THREE ROUNDS WITH IRON MIKE

I decided we were going to go all-out for the fight. We got Baron Aviation to fly us in on a helicopter, and we landed right outside the football field at John Adams High School, where they had a temporary ring set up.

The champ always comes out last. John and I disappeared into the locker room, so they couldn't find us, to make Tyson go out first. He went without a big fanfare and got a nice hand. Once he was in the ring, we came out in boxing robes, taped up and with towels around our necks, behind a chain of big cops with arms linked and with the *Rocky* music blaring.

Kevin Salyer from Channel 8 was the ring announcer in a tuxedo, doing the introductions. He was perfect. He called John "The Italian Stal ... pony!" We clowned around. I put a horseshoe in my glove, and John had a hammer hidden on him. The ref pulled them out, displayed them, and tossed them down. King held up a huge leather jock cup that was called a "Li'l John low-blow protector."

I told John ahead of time that because I'd boxed a little bit, I was going to try with all my might, no clowning, to hit Tyson as hard as I could. He was the world champion—I was sure he could defend himself against me. I said, "When the bell rings, run as fast as you can, right at him. I'll be right behind you. If he's looking at me, punch him right in the crotch with everything you've got. If he's looking at you, I'll hit him with everything I've got."

The bell rang, and we ran at him. It was about two seconds, and it seemed like twenty. I stared at Tyson, and he never took his eyes off me. John got close to him, and *boom*—he flicked John right through the ropes. It seemed like a split second. I started to swing, but he ducked and punched me right in the throat, just horsing around. I could hardly breathe. We were going after him as hard as we could, and he was laughing because he saw how easy this would be. We were really trying to hit him, and he loved that. He liked that a whole lot more than pretending he was fighting.

He pulled John off, started sparring with me, and gave me a pretty good hit from a crouch. He could bend down real low. I'm sure he held up on the punch, but he hit me in the kidney, and I lost my legs and my breath. It took everything out of me instantly. All I could do was try to keep from throwing up. I did not want to barf in the ring. I actually stopped fighting.

Tyson picked up John and held him on his shoulder upside down, spinning in a circle. While in this position, John managed to hit him right in the kisser. The crowd was going crazy with laughter, and Tyson was laughing, too.

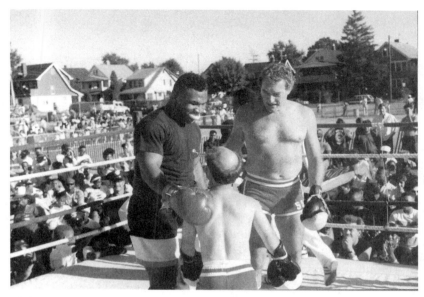
John and I were really trying to hit Tyson, and he loved it. He was laughing because he saw how easy it would be.

I could hardly make it through the next round, but I got my breath back. Tyson jabbed, danced, and clowned the rest of the way. He couldn't have been nicer to us, and he couldn't have been nicer to the kids in the crowd. He talked with them, answered questions, and took time. He didn't have to.

I went in keyed up like we were really going to fight, and everything went perfectly. But I was never so relieved as when it was over, and I was sore for days.

Tyson's next fight after this was with Buster Douglas. He lost. After that, he was in the slammer for three years. After he got out, in 1995, John was doing some errand for his jewelry store downtown and saw him shooting an interview or something outside. John did what he does to everybody: He went up behind and pinched Tyson's ass really hard.

Tyson wheeled around and at first saw no one. Then he saw John, started laughing, and picked him up.

John said, "You know, after you fought us, you really went to hell."

Only Lil' John could get away with that.

CHAPTER 30

CHANGE, BAD ADVICE, AND A FEW PROPS

Channel 8 started going through a lot of changes in the late 1980s and early 1990s, largely because Storer Broadcasting sold its stations, and we had gone through several owners in just a few years. They were people who had no background in broadcasting or media but would buy stations and have no idea how to run them. They'd hire groups to do studies.

One owner hired a group that came to Cleveland and just watched Channel 8, morning to night, in a hotel room. The women couldn't have been more than twenty-two, and a guy with them with was very L.A. in dress and attitude. They were going to study us? They had top echelon meetings with Virgil Dominic, the general manager, who had us number one in news for almost twenty years. They told Virgil that being number one isn't always the best thing. What!? From day one, that was the goal, that's what we're geared for. No, they said—it doesn't mean you're good.

That was their opening. They also suggested we get rid of the old guy doing the weather. Dick Goddard. Virgil said, "Get rid of our franchise." He almost threw them out. And he was gone not too long after that.

Kevin Salyer showed them around the station and brought them to the newsroom. One of them looked out the windows, saw the lake, and said, "Is that the Atlantic?" That was the intelligence of these people.

I still hadn't been notified I was a permanent employee, but I was entering my fourth decade at TV8. To recognize it, John and I were roasted by the Optimists' Club. Bruce Drennan was the em-

cee, and Rick DeChant, Tom Bush, Al "Bubba" Baker, Dick Goddard, and Dennis Kucinich were the roasters. Ernie sent an R-rated
video, and Jan Jones, Michael Stanley, Robin Swoboda, and Tim
Taylor contributed bits. It was quite an honor. I was inducted into
the Radio-TV Broadcasters Hall of Fame the same year.

MR. SMILEY COMES TO TOWN

Ernie called to congratulate me on that, in 1991. While we were
talking, he asked if I'd heard anything about Art Modell selling the
Browns or moving the team to Baltimore. He'd heard something.

That was four years before Modell moved the team. It was also
about the time he hired Bill Belichick as head coach. CBS and Channel 8 were carrying Browns games, so Virgil and the station had a
big welcoming party for him. John and I emceed it. No one knew
anything about him—or at least I didn't.

We were giving away things—trivia prizes like "number one"
sponges and brown and orange pom-poms you put on your finger.
I looked over at Belichick, and he wasn't even smiling. We introduced him and brought him up onstage. Nothing. John presented
him with the kind of beautiful jewelry case he used for his most
expensive items. We had put one of the pom-poms in it. Belichick
opened it. No reaction whatsoever. He looked at me and John, then
back at this thing in the box. The audience was quiet as could be.
We told him, "You put that on your finger."

He didn't. He put it back in the box. Whew.

AND WHERE'S THE STAR OF OUR SHOW

John and I were doing commercials for Ohio State Waterproof-
ing, and we always shot them at Channel 43. We'd do walk-ons on
John Lanigan's *Prize Movie* while we were there, and one time I
noticed the phone booth used by Superhost, Marty Sullivan, on his
shows. I borrowed my son's truck, and a guy who worked at 43 and
used to work at TV8 helped us sneak it out to the truck. We put
it on our set, just to see how long it would take Supe to notice it
was gone—and it took probably two weeks. Marty appeared in skits

with us going back to the 1970s, when he showed up in a "Soul Man" episode, and we had a lot of fun keeping a thing going between us.

Lanigan used to subscribe to a joke service for his show on WMJI radio, and he'd give me the old ones. I'd use them sometimes, especially for "PJ Party." WMJI does a "Moondog Coronation Ball" every March, an oldies show, and one year they asked us to introduce Jay Black. John and I went up, got a nice hand from the huge crowd at the Cleveland State Convocation Center, and a guy in front of us signaled to stretch. I could see where the artists would come on stage, and I didn't see anyone coming. So John and I went into our act. The audience was liking it, so we went on. I saw roadies running around and figured something was wrong with the sound. I still didn't see anybody coming, but they gave us a wrap-up signal, so I went into the intro. I noticed a grubby, gray-haired guy in boots that were actually muddy was standing at the side of the stage, looking at us. We were filling, and he seemed impatient.

It was Jay Black. The first thing he said was, "I thought that little shit would never shut up." He was great—very funny.

CALLING THE RINALDI SOCIETY TO DISORDER

John had meetings at his store on Saturdays of what was called the Rinaldi Society. They got together every week to solve the world's problems. It was really a varied group, and if you missed a meeting you had to pay two dollars.

One member was Dr. Robert White, the famous neurosurgeon and professor, who has a great sense of humor. He appeared in a number of skits on our show and sometimes worked the counter at John's store during the Christmas rush. He was Gorbachev's doctor, as well as the pope's, and one Saturday he was in Russia. I don't know what the time was there, but he phoned in so he wouldn't have to pay the two bucks.

Dr. White would also send postcards from Russia. He knew his mail would be monitored, so he'd write nebulous things like, "See you when the moon is full." I said, "If you keep that up, they're going to wonder what the heck we are." He said, "That's a very real possibility."

I wondered about that later when two beautifully dressed but weird-looking guys with Russian accents came to the station to watch our show. They were really big, and they talked like the "wild and crazy guys" from *Saturday Night Live*.

"You guys are really funny," one of them told us. "I am laughing like crazy."

Another society member was Larry Gogolick, a well-to-do local merchant who also played basketball with the Big Chuck & Lil' John All-Stars, and said so in the greeting on his answering machine. He was "Dr. G." He'd run out to a smattering of applause at games. Then, at one sold-out game, Dr. G was intro-

The Certain Ethnic characters became cover boys when a local magazine did a parody around the same time as the 1990 *Sports Illustrated* swimsuit issue. The photo shoot was actually in Cancun!

duced and the place went crazy, cheering and calling his name. John and I wondered what was going on. He'd bought I don't know how many tickets, gave them to friends, and had a party afterward. He loaded one side of the gym with what must have been hundreds of people. He ran out looking back at us, like "Check this out!" It was really funny.

Doug Dieken was at the store for a meeting one Saturday and saw an old woman, a good customer, standing at the counter. As she glanced at him he quickly took something off a shelf and put it in his coat. She started towards John to tell him. Diek coughed and shook his head "no." He's a huge man. He then put a large clock under his coat and stared at the woman. She started to tell John, and Diek ran out of the store.

THE FUNNY SIDE OF NEWSCENTER 8

We used a lot of TV8 celebrities in skits, including John Telich, Dan Coughlin, Tony Rizzo, Vince Cellini, and Casey Coleman. We also used Vince's brother, Nick, who'd been one of the *Kids World*

WJW's personalities were "Cleveland's Own" when they posed for the TV guide's Christmas cover in the weekly Sun Newspapers. Back row: Chuck, Goddard, Wayne Dawson, Michael Stanley. Front row: Jan Jones, Tim Taylor, Robin Swoboda, John, Casey Coleman.

reporters for me. We used Dick Goddard more than anybody in the station. But I was told not to use news anchors.

The big exception was when I got special permission for Robin Swoboda, at the height of her popularity, to be Cat-Lady in our "Batguy and Rinaldi" skit. It was a big production, a huge hit, and it also featured Kevin Salyer, Joanne Stern, and Lou Gattozzi from the station. Mike Baab, the Browns center, was one of the toughs who worked me over as Batguy, along with Dave Kyle, the Cleveland State basketball great who became a photographer for the Cavs, and Dick Honafshofsky, a big guy and a big fan of the show.

I always wanted to use Wilma Smith in a skit but could never think of just the right stuff. She asked many times. Tim Taylor was always a big fan of our show. He never wanted to be in a skit but would constantly give me ideas, and some of them were really good. He has a great sense of humor. One time we were at some function, and I was talking with a group in a circle—Virgil Dominic, Tim Iacofano, Lou Gattozzi, and Dom Lolli. It never occurred to me that they're all Italian. Tim came up behind me. While they were talking, he whistled in my ear the *Godfather* theme—not the overused "Love Theme," but the main title music. Softly. Did you ever notice how much funnier things are when you can't laugh?

WHO WERE THOSE GUYS, ANYWAY?

I couldn't believe all the things I was still doing in the '90s—things I did in the '60s with Ernie. Personal appearances, taping funny stuff each and every week, working a full-time directing and engineering shift, playing charity basketball and softball games.

We were coming back from a basketball game and party, far east of Cleveland, and it was one of the times we had a bus. It didn't have a toilet. We needed one and saw a rest stop—and let me say that the rest stops in Ohio are better than anyplace else. We pulled in, and one car was there, with Michigan license plates. Somebody looked in the restroom and said a guy was in a stall.

Dave Stacey and Whoopie John got out the accordions, I got the banjo, Mushmouth got out his sax, and we went quietly into the can. John was there with his tambourine, and somebody was wearing a clown costume. We could see the guy's feet in the stall. We started playing "Who Stole the Kishka?," and it shocked me how loud it was. Big Stash, standing six feet seven and wearing a big hat and long black wig, started dancing. He looked over the top of the stall at the guy, who was scared shitless. He came flying out, pulling up his pants, and ran out the door.

He probably thought we were some kind of cheap traveling carnival act, with a midget, a giant, and a clown, and probably he will never stop in Ohio again.

If that guy had a gun, none of this would be written. We'd done so many things like that, but I still can't believe we did it.

Joel Scala, who was called Zipparilla on the All-Stars, would take a shower after a basketball game and get to wherever we were going. No matter how fast I was, he'd be there first and have shots lined up. He'd always say, "Well, we cheated death again."

We cheated death that time.

I could write a whole other book on things I missed with my family and friends and felt bad about. It's just something that happened in my career. It's common in this work. You miss things with your kids and make it up with the grandkids.

One time around Thanksgiving, everyone brought their families on the bus to take them out after a game in Akron. The guy at the restaurant went crazy, calling his wife, taking us into the kitchen, and taking pictures. He had us all go outside and took pictures by the sign.

We used to charge schools and groups just enough to cover our expenses. For this game, the school gave us a check we were going to use to pay the restaurant bill. John gave it to the restaurant owner, and he asked John if he had any identification. I thought it was a hilarious joke, but he was dead serious. I mean, it's not like he didn't know where the hell to find us.

The name became Big Chuck & Lil' John in 1979, and we rode high in the 1980s.

CHAPTER 31

SONG AND DANCE MAN

A DIP IN THE HIP AND A BOOTLEG MOVIE

I like to watch dancing, which is why I like *Dancing with the Stars* and liked the disco era. It brought back good music. You had to learn dance steps, dress up, and dance as couples. It took discipline. People say they hated disco, maybe because it was harder to do. You had to work at it, not shuffle around on a dance floor with a glazed look.

I did takeoff on *Saturday Night Fever* called "Sunday Morning Chills," using the BeeGees' "Stayin' Alive." We did it at Bojangles on West 150th Street, and I met a young man named Bill, who did the choreography. He did a great job of setting up the dancers, who were all young and beautifully dressed. The skit was one of the best we ever did. Bill called me later and said he was going to go out to Hollywood to see if he could get a shot in a dance thing on TV. He wanted a copy of the skit to take with him. I sent it and said I didn't think it'd make much of a resume, but good luck.

That was Bill Hufsey, a great guy who went on to be in a few movies and star very successfully in the TV series *Fame*. He'd come back to Cleveland occasionally and play with the All-Stars. He was not a rock star, but he was somebody the young people could identify with and learn from.

My partner in the skit was Mary Allen, who bid in a Channel 25 auction in 1979 to be in a skit with us. She ended up in a lot of our sketches, and stayed with us to the end.

We were on the floor continuously for about two hours. I was actually getting nauseated from the lighted checkerboard floor and the flashing lights and had to close my eyes. I never forgot that floor.

Then in 1995 we had a good horror movie called *Prom Night*, with Leslie Nielsen and Jamie Lee Curtis. It was made in 1980, but a fifteen-year-old film on our show would be like a first-run. So it was pretty good. I previewed it for air, to find when commercial breaks would come, and noticed the dancing scene in it.

The checkerboard dance floor was exactly the same as the floor in the "Sunday Morning Chills" skit at Bojangles. The background looked identical, and the strobe lighting was the same, too.

Jamie Lee Curtis was dancing, and there were a lot of close-ups of her making eyes at a guy. In our skit, I had a lot of tight shots on me giving the eyes to Mary Allen. I called our film editor, Jim Prunty, and talked him into intercutting me into the dance scene with Jamie Lee.

He cut it in, and it was a perfect match, even the color. I never saw a better match. It took me back to the *Hoolihan & Big Chuck* skits. I didn't mention it in the studio portion of our show when we aired it. I figured it would be funnier if it was a surprise.

Plus I didn't know if it was legal to do what I did. I didn't want any lawyers calling. Movies are "bicycled" around, shipped station to station. We'd get a window from the syndicator in which we'd have to show the movie twice, usually early and late, and then it'd have to go immediately to the next station. I couldn't stress enough to Prunty that on Monday morning he had to restore *Prom Night* back to correct before it went on to another station.

That Monday was when Jim took a very rare sick day, and the film was sent out with me and Jamie Lee Curtis in it. It's still out there somewhere. Prunty would remind me about it—"One of these days you'll be doing your show from Mansfield." I said we'd be cellmates.

Jim was a longtime friend and coworker back to the Ghoulardi days. He'd edit movies, appear in skits, and set me up with some of our best pranks. He died a few years ago at eighty, and he worked full-time at TV8 until the very end. I called his wake the happiest funeral I ever attended. People were smiling and telling stories about Jim. I knelt by his casket and almost laughed out loud. Instead of a suit, he had on a white shirt and his usual suspenders, his Three Stooges tie, and his TV8 ID tag.

His wife and daughters told the story of his last moments. He was dying, and he didn't want to be in bed. They put him on the couch in the living room. It was a Saturday night, and the family was gathered, crying and telling stories. All of a sudden, Jim made a fuss and pointed to the TV set. He wanted them to put our show on, and he died during our show.

I hope he was smiling.

THE MAD DOG AND DREW

Local musician Bob "Mad Dog" McGuire came down to "New Talent Time" in 1983 with a song he wrote. He was a very good singer and an excellent banjo and guitar player, and he wrote the song especially for our show. It was called "Moon Over Parma."

Drew Carey remembered it. He used to come back to town a lot, and he saw it on a rerun. When he got his weekly show in 1995, he and his producer got hold of McGuire, heard him play it at a jazz club in South Euclid, and said they wanted it. Drew sang it, using the same lyrics, and it became the first theme of *The Drew Carey Show* on ABC. Bob made about fifty grand from it.

Drew set his show in Cleveland and loaded it with local props, including a Ghoulardi sweatshirt. A scene in one show had him saying, "Come on over, guys. I got some kielbasy sandwiches and a case of beer. It's Friday night—*Big Chuck & Lil' John!*" But somebody on the crew called Channel 5, the ABC affiliate, which didn't want him to do it because we were on Channel 8. So they took it out. I was told he was upset about it.

He took care of that when the show came to Cleveland to shoot at Jacobs Field. Drew called and asked if John and I wanted to be in it. We did, and we went down in the morning, when they were setting up a crowd shot. We asked where they wanted us to sit, and the assistant director said, "Right there"—pointing to two empty seats, right in the middle, with two empty seats in front of them.

"Who sits in those seats?" I asked. "Drew and Mimi," he said. In other words, they couldn't cut us out.

Drew Carey was a network star and grand marshal of the Cleveland Christmas parade, but he
was more excited about meeting us. He grew up
watching the show.

When Drew's book, *Dirty Jokes and Beer*, came out, I wanted
to get it autographed for my daughter Michelle. Drew was doing a
signing at a mall in Akron. I called ahead, walked to the entrance,
and was met by a guy with a walkie-talkie. I didn't tell anybody
which door I'd be using, so they must have had somebody at every
entrance. He took me to Drew, who said, "Come on, sit down." I
didn't want to stay; he was busy, but I sat down. He was signing and
sweating and smiling and working. People were taking pictures,
and he was talking a mile a minute. I figured I had to get out somehow and started to make my apologies.

He said to me, "You know how you go out locally here, you make
it good, and then you go to L.A. and you hear about the big jump
in money." He was dead serious, not joking around. He said, "I'm
making so much money it's a sin." With the book and the show, he
must have been making a million a week at that point.

He looked at me and repeated, "It's a sin." He didn't have to im-
press me, but that impressed me about Drew.

ALMOST A GRAMMY WITH THE POLKA KING

I dreamed of being a pro athlete, but even more I'd like to be a singer. You can move people emotionally more by singing than by anything else, and you can do it longer. Look at Tony Bennett or Tom Jones, who haven't lost a thing. I like singers.

One we had on our show was Meat Loaf, who was a big fan and came down a couple times. His album *Bat Out of Hell* was released by Steve Popovich's Cleveland International Records in 1977, which is why he'd come to town. He was a big rock star, but we got to talking and he was a down-to-earth guy. He liked Cleveland, wanted to live in Hinckley, and almost bought a home here. I asked how he got into singing. He told me he had a degree in biology and found that all he could do was get a job cleaning fish tanks in a mall. He went to a rock concert and said, "Hell, I can do that."

We knew Steve Popovich as someone who has had a huge career in music, including rock, country, and polkas. In 1986, Frankie Yankovic won the first Grammy for polka with Steve, and a tribute album, *Songs of the Polka King*, was nominated for a Grammy. Its success led Popovich to make *Songs of the Polka King Vol. 2.*

He contacted John about me about being celebrity performers on the album. John told him I could sing and he couldn't. I told him that TV8 program director Bob Huber had me sing in Christmas promos for the station after hearing me sing in a skit.

I dreamed of singing, but of all the things I had to force myself to do, singing was the hardest. I sang "Love Makes the World Go 'Round" for the first promo and taped it after midnight at Channel 8 when almost no one was around. I was so nervous I sat with my back against the control room window so I couldn't see anybody. To back me up, I got a very good local musician I'd heard when the All-Stars stopped at an Irish Pub on the West Side after a game.

People who hear it are surprised it's me. I finished it by saying, "From the Schodowskis to you, peace and love." It was a thirty-second spot. The station liked it so much that they asked me to do it again the following year. For that one I sang "I'd Like to Teach the World to Sing." It wasn't much easier.

Steve said he'd make it easy for me. Only he and the recording engineer would be in the studio. He wanted us to sing Bobby Vinton's "My Melody of Love." I got out the album that Bobby gave me when we did the skit with him, wrote out the Polish lyrics phonetically, and learned them.

When we were ready to record, I said, "John is the only Italian I know who can't sing." Steve said, "Don't worry, we'll fix it. We can fix anything."

We sang on a test recording. Steve got a funny look, took John aside, and said, "Maybe you should just talk."

That's what he did. John yipped in the background, throwing in "Everybody!" and "Eat your heart out, Bobby Vinton!" and "The Italian version! Little Italy! Mayfield Heights! Murray Hill!"

We recorded it, and Steve said it was fantastic. He sent it to Nashville for embellishment with a chorus and more instruments, and it sounded great.

Eddie Blazonczyk is on the track, and musicians on the CD included Joey Miskulin, Don Everly, David Allan Coe, and old friend Roger Martin.

The album was nominated for a Grammy in 1997. It didn't win, but what a rush.

I have a limited range, but when I hear a song I can tell right away if I can sing it within that range and sound fairly decent.

I still dream of being a singer, and I'd like to do an oldies thing, of songs with the word "time" in them. Maybe that will be my next thing. Remind me to call Popovich.

With John in a recording session at Cleveland International Records for the Grammy-nominated second Frankie Yankovic Songs of the Polka King album.

CHAPTER 32

COUNTING DOWN

LAST CALL FOR ERNIE

I was calling Ernie almost every night early in 1997. He'd had a stroke a year or two earlier, and now he had cancer. His son Paul went to live with him, and he answered the phone one evening. He and Ernie were having an argument about a book Paul was going to return to the library.

Ernie yelled, "I'm not finished with it!"

Paul said, "You can't read it anyway!" F-bombs were going off all over.

Ernie could see, but he couldn't scan to read because of the stroke, which meant he couldn't read copy. If he could, he would've worked to the very end.

Paul was working on his movie *Boogie Nights,* and Ernie talked about how he was really into it and serious about editing. "It's going to be a big movie," he said. I didn't realize he was doing that well. When Ernie told me who was going to be in it, I was pretty impressed. I asked what it was about.

He said, "Some porno shit." He was really proud, but he'd never tell Paul that. He would be so proud of him now.

Sometimes a guy with a Spanish accent answered. Ernie would yell that he was the dumbest guy, and the guy would yell back at him. "If I'm so dumb, why did you hire me? You must be dumb!"

Ernie said he was "great, I'm doing great." Then he said, "Uh-oh." I asked what happened. "Oh no! I just shit myself," he said. His days were numbered. He asked me to call him back in about twenty minutes. I did, and we talked for a long time. He asked, "If you come out to see me, how long will you stay?" I said, "Until you shit yourself again." Ernie roared and dropped a couple of F-bombs on me. He was Ernie till the end.

He died in March 1997. It was the top story on the news and in the *Plain Dealer* the next morning, more than thirty years after he left town. It showed the kind of impact he had. In Hollywood, the shrinking Cleveland Clan gathered. I could have gone to the funeral, but I was doing a special for our show and would have to tape another show in advance. I would live to regret it, because Conway was shooting something in Europe and stopped to come back. Ernie and Tim were really close when they moved out there. I dearly miss him.

STARTING TO SHUT IT DOWN

Fox bought Channel 8 early in 1997, after we'd been an affiliate for a couple of years. Bob Rowe came in as general manager, and he didn't like anybody but John and me because we had a lot of energy. But they were looking to cut money.

I took a cut in pay and said I didn't want to direct news anymore. I was too busy and too burned out. I said I would direct promos or something else, and I had a contract that I'd only have to direct news in an emergency. News is the most stressful thing. I was starting to shut it down and would just do the show.

A GUY REALLY OUT OF THIS WORLD

I was phasing out and getting ready to direct the six o'clock news around four one afternoon and got a phone call. "Fox 8, Chuck here."

A man started to speak, hesitated, and said, "Me and my friend would like to invite you . . ." He hesitated again, as though he'd been caught by surprise. "We'd like you to be our guest . . ." He stopped. "Excuse me," he said, "let me start over. I didn't expect to talk to you. My name is Don Thomas. I'm an astronaut."

This was not an everyday introduction. I learned that Don was a local guy who went to Cleveland Heights High School and Case Western Reserve University. He joined NASA after earning a Ph.D., had gone into space twice on the space shuttle, and was scheduled to go up again on Columbia.

Another astronaut on the mission, Mike Gernhardt, was from Mansfield. They'd started talking about the old days watching our show, and they wanted to invite me to the launch. They were allowed one guest in addition to their families, Don said, but next time they'd get more.

I told him it would be an honor. I was a space nut. Still am.

One day a big limo was in front of the station. I walked down the hallway towards the studio, saw an entourage coming in my direction, and recognized John Glenn. He was my hero. Like when I saw Marion Motley, I didn't know what to say and tried to think of something original. Glenn spotted me and spoke first. He said, "Big Chuck!" and hugged me. That was incredible.

And now this. Don sent me a picture of himself wearing a Ghoulardi sweatshirt. He said he watched sci-fi movies growing up and wanted be an astronaut. John Glenn was his hero, too. He sent credentials and a picture of the crew. I was really excited. I went to Cape Canaveral, where they had a family picnic, and I brought "Best of" tapes of skits for Don. His mother said we could meet near the launch area the night before the launch, and it was like a scene from *Apollo 13,* only it was raining. The crew stayed on one side of a fence, we were on the other, and the Columbia was lit up in the background. It was awesome.

Don called me when they were in preflight isolation and said they were enjoying the tapes. I told him I was really honored to watch the liftoff—"but I feel sort of slighted because you're taking Superhost with you."

I guess they hadn't noticed earlier, but another member of the crew, Chief Scientist Roger Crouch, was a dead ringer for Marty Sullivan. Don and Mike cracked up laughing, and the rest of the crew had no idea why.

While they were in space, I got a call from Houston Mission Control. They said they had a special request for a call to me and did all they could to accommodate astronauts. They couldn't use a NASA channel but could arrange through a series of hams across the country for a call from the shuttle, if I was interested. *Abso-*

Don Thomas, far right, and Michael Gernhardt, upper right, with the space shuttle Columbia crew, including astronaut Roger K. Crouch, upper left, who looks a little like . . . say, isn't that Superhost?

lutely, I said. Then the FBI called and said I had an FCC first-class license, which meant they must have done a background check, "so you know you cannot air this conversation."

I didn't know it, but I said, "Yeah, of course I know that."

I got a whole series of calls and was told Don would call during a window about 4 a.m. There was no way I'd get up then, so I just stayed up. The phone rang, the connection kept breaking up and clearing, and Don said, "We're just coming up over Baja California." He described some of what they were doing and seeing, said he'd be coming to Cleveland, and said, "I've got to go now; we're going over Florida." It took about three minutes.

He's retired from NASA now, and we're still friends. I keep his business card, which says "Don Thomas–Astronaut." How many people have that?

Then, just when I thought my "close encounters with the astronaut kind" was only a wonderful memory, Don Thomas called and invited June and me to join him and his wife, Simona, at a spectacular black-tie dinner event on August 29, 2008. Celebrating

NASA Ohio's fiftieth anniversary, the gala at the Key
Center Cleveland Marriott
was emceed by Channel 3
anchor Tim White, a briga-
dier general in the U.S. Air
Force Reserve.

Astronaut Don Thomas proved he was a long-time fan with a boyhood photo of himself, in the middle, wearing a Ghoulardi sweatshirt at Christmas 1964. Grandma approved.

The impressive event
featured nineteen Ohio
astronauts, so I was also
reunited with my other
buddy, astronaut Mike
Gernhardt, who not only
remembered all of our
skits but has the dialogue
memorized. I wanted to
talk about space exploration, and they wanted to talk about skits.
So we compromised!

Now I can honestly say I met and had dinner with nineteen astronauts, and perhaps name drop a few you may have heard of—
Neil Armstrong, John Glenn, and Jim Lovell. So once again, thanks
to Cleveland's own astronaut Don Thomas, my buddy, for getting
us together.

I also learned that Mike Gernhardt has designed a moon-rover
vehicle and may very well be the next man on the moon. Remember—you heard it here first.

What a glorious and exciting night it was. I was on cloud nine.

A NEW CENTURY

In the late '90s, the show got bounced around between Friday
and Saturday nights. We were moved to midnight on Friday, instead of 11:30, so Jay Leno had a running start on us. We almost
never beat him in the ratings like we used to beat Carson, but we
were second only to him, and our ratings would pick up at 12:30
a.m. when he signed off. We always beat David Letterman.

Kevin Salyer had the idea to put us on another show, of skits

Dick Goddard's Woollybear Festival started in 1973 and has become Ohio's biggest single-day festival. John and I, here riding in the 2005 parade, have helped host it every year.
(Rose Costanza)

only, which ran on Friday evening and then at 7:30 p.m. on Saturday. We figured it was good because people getting ready to go out might have the TV on. They tried the skits-only show on Saturday afternoon and then Saturday morning. It didn't have huge ratings, but it was rated number one across the board. And even at night, our commercial time was sold out.

We were still winning awards. John and I received the Cleveland Association of Broadcasters' Award for Excellence in 1999, with Don Webster and Charles Dolan. The show continued to win local Emmys.

Then one day it was 2000, a new millennium. John and I were doing more specials, more trips, and more Cleveland events that Kevin wanted us to do. We served as parade marshals, made appearances, and were doing remotes at least one week out of every month. We were still holding our own in the ratings. Like a candle that burns brightest before it goes out, we got the Living Legends award.

I woke up around then having a dream I'd have every so often. I was playing baseball in it, the way I did when I could really play. I got up, ready to go to Channel 8, and looked in the mirror. The dream was fresh in my mind, and I said, "What the hell happened?" I was old. It was a shock. I was still half asleep.

I thought, "Maybe this whole thing is a dream, and tomorrow I'm going to wake up and go to the foundry. Like a *Twilight Zone* episode. A *Twilight Zone* episode would be old, too.

CHAPTER 33

TV PRIDE AND PALS

There was a guy I worked with at the foundry who worked all the time, a Towmotor driver named Jimmy Hayes. I worked six days a week. He put in seven. He was something, a self-starter who really worked hard. He was always there. Even on holidays, when there was a skeleton crew just to watch the fires so the furnaces didn't go out, it would be Jimmy Hayes. Being prudent and having his work ethic eventually allowed him to get out of the foundry, unlike most people.

I lost track of the foundry guys over the years, but one night I was getting ready to direct the news and met Eleanor, a newsperson TV8 had just hired. She was very, very good, and really a hard worker.

After we worked together a little while, she said she had a surprise for me. "Many years ago," she said, "you worked with my father in the foundry—Jimmy Hayes." I immediately knew where she got her work ethic and her dedication. And I had a link back to the guys in the foundry. Eleanor brought Jimmy to the station a few times. It was just great, and I was even able to call a couple of the guys he kept in touch with. He had done well—I learned from Eleanor he owned several McDonald's franchises. She got into the business, too, after being with TV8 a good while, but she's returned to TV on the Ohio News Network.

I really got a kick out of it when someone I worked with, especially if I directed him, went on to network. Ernie and Tim were the first, and then sportscaster Frank Glieber went on to do golf for CBS. He played on the All-Stars, too. When we played in my Polish neighborhood, I told the announcer to say, "Frank Glieber with the grupa dupa." It's a Polish thing, and means big ass. The place went into a roar. Glieber thought it was for him.

Kelly O'Donnell started as an intern, and she was really good. I used to volunteer to work the news on Christmas morning after my kids got older, so I'd have all day and night with them. It was the barest, minimal crew, with one newscaster and hardly anyone there, and here came Kelly O'Donnell. I said, "What the hell are you doing here?" She said, "Well, you're here." She had that work ethic all the way through. She went to NBC and really made it big.

Bob Franken, Marty Savidge, and Vinnie Cellini went to network news. Tim Iacofano went to Hollywood and now is a producer-director for Fox's *24*.

Virgil Dominic, by the way, is the best reader I ever saw in my life. Herb Kamm, the *Cleveland Press* editor, wrote station editorials for awhile. Virgil delivered them and would never pre-read them. We put it in the prompter, and Virgil came in and read it cold, right through, with emotion, and almost never did we have to re-do it. He was that good. The whole senior gang—Tim Taylor, Wilma Smith, Robin Swoboda—are all great readers. That art has sort of gone away.

TV has changed technically for the better since I started, except for weather forecasting. That's been a thorn in my side. They really can't predict it accurately, and they overrate bad weather because it gets ratings.

Programming in my opinion has not gotten better, especially news. News was once a proud profession, and newscasters had a dignified presence. Now the news is reported by ordinary people who don't speak all that well. Watch the weekend news in particular to see.

It's mainly a way to get more local advertising. Newscasts have more local commercial time than other programming, and ad rates for news are the highest in local television.

Television is not as good, but as I always told John, it beats working for a living.

We tried that once and hated it.

I saw a take-off we did of Channel 5 *Eyewitness News* with John Hambrick and Gib Shanley. People loved it whenever we did something at Channel 5, going back to Dorothy Fuldheim and Captain Penny. I liked them, and they were pretty much like Channel 8, family broadcasters. I loved picking on Gib. He was easy to mimic because he wore loud sports coats and big glasses, and he was also the very popular radio voice of the Browns who called the 1964 championship game. He worked twenty-one years at TV5, from 1963 until 1984, when Ernie told him to go out to Hollywood, where Ernie'd struck it rich. Almost all of Gib's peers told him to stay in Cleveland. He went west; things didn't work out for him, and he returned to Cleveland in 1987 to see if he could rebuild his celebrity status. Nev Chandler had become the voice of the Browns, so Gib was out of that, but he worked at Channel 43 until 1996.

I like to grocery-shop, and I'd see him after he retired at Rego's, now a Giant Eagle in North Royalton. It was sort of awkward in the parking lot, just after he started at 43, because I wanted to ask why things didn't work out for him. I stumbled around, and Gib stopped me and said, "Did you ever shoot yourself in the foot?"

He had a great sense of humor. We started shopping together, and I told him that Linn Sheldon shopped there, too. A few times the three of us were there, shopping together, and Linn was hilarious. He was brilliant. He could take a two-minute joke and stretch it to twenty-five minutes, and it'd be interesting and funny all the way through. When TV first started, he would lip-sync records on Channel 5. It was the first sponsored show on Cleveland television. Time once ran short when he was lip-syncing a record, he remembered, and a floor director gave him a signal to speed it up.

People would avoid us in the store if more than one of us was there—they'd look and sort of duck away. Linn would do a running commentary out of the side of his mouth, in a whisper.

"They're looking to see what we're buying," he said. "Make sure you buy the expensive stuff. Nothing on sale. Whatever coupons you have, don't use them. It'll spread like wildfire."

I said, "Oh shit—tuna fish is on sale." (And it was) That was the trigger for Gib, for some reason. He broke up laughing.

Gib died in April 2008. Linn died two years earlier. Cleveland will forever miss those guys. So will I.

CHAPTER 34

SKITS 2K

Cuyahoga Jones, The Certain Ethnic Six Dollar Man, Pepski-Cola, Slim Whitski. We did movie spoofs, TV takeoffs, and commercial parodies. We did music videos and skits based on jokes and sight gags. We used puppets, animals, and anything else you can think of. We did more than two thousand skits in all. If you came up with one skit an hour for a full work week, it would take you a year.

But a single skit could take longer than that. "The Chase," an extended pursuit that had John, Art Lofredo, and me moving along the ground like we were driving, took us two years to make, frame by frame. Tom Strauss, an engineer who was simply a fan of the show, did the animation that took us from amateur to professional level. He entered it in a film festival, and Ray Harryhausen, the master of movie effects, called it the best amateur animation in the world.

Bill Ward, who did a lot of our announcing, produced skits for the show on his own—edited and ready and good. How great is that? He did a take-off on Clint Eastwood that featured the flute introduction from *The Good, the Bad, and the Ugly.* You saw his boots and poncho as he walked into the scene, the flute played again, and the camera panned up to Bill's face, with a stubbly beard, a cigarette, and a hat pulled way down. He squinted, the music played, and you saw a guy in a tuxedo, playing the flute at a music stand in the woods. Bill started walking, the camera showed his gun, and the music played again. There was a shot, and the flute trailed off. Bill pushed up the hat with the gun. "I hate that music," he said.

Bill is really good—talented and with a nice voice. He reminded me of Hoolie in that. He did commercial parodies for us, too, and

John and I put our feet up for a publicity photo on the *Big Chuck & Lil' John* set at the start of a new century.

some mini-movies for the hell of it. One was "Mel," a touching base-ball story that starts with a kid named Mel and ends with Indians great Mel Harder. Bill got to know him as a neighbor.

Jim Szymanski was another regular. He worked for many years as a late-night DJ for WGAR-FM, and he first came to TV8 to be in the audience of the *Noontime* show I directed. I invited him to be in the *Big Chuck & Lil' John Show* audience, which he immediately did. He attended our weekly tapings, almost without fail, for the next twenty-seven years. I called him our "poor man's Ed McMahon" because he cued our audience to applaud and cheer, and we used him in many skits. When he retired from WGAR, he became an instructor at the Ohio Center for Broadcasting, and he regularly brought classes down to be our audience.

He's a good comic actor with a pro's announcing voice. He added much to the show and now emcees our annual Ghoulardifests. He became a good friend to both John and me.

Bob Kokai was an actor I met while he was hosting one of his outstanding "Murder Mystery Weekends" at a lodge near Loudon-ville. He did the shows dressed in a trench coat and fedora, always smoking a cigarette and doing an absolutely perfect Humphrey Bogart impression, from voice to mannerisms. I had just started a series of skits called "Saturday Night Mysteries," and I asked Bob if he'd like to do one. He did so well that I never did another one without him.

My collaborator, Tom Feran, was in one, and I still wonder how he did it. He played a corpse—a TV critic who'd been murdered—and I figured it would be funnier if his eyes were open. The crime photographer steps in to shoot a picture of him with a flashbulb as big as an orange. You could feel the heat when we shot it off. I said, "Let it go, see what he does." I couldn't believe it. Tom was psyched. I looked at it frame by frame, and he didn't blink, even partially, or flinch. He really looked dead.

Mary Allen started in the transition period from Hoolie to Lil' John, and stayed with us. She had a background in little theater and would do anything.

Carmella Gianpaolo also hung in a long time in many skits. John worked with her at a restaurant in Murray Hill. He'd hide under her skirt, she'd start singing, and he'd emerge. She was great—a very talented singer and a hilarious comic actor, especially when John would play her husband and she would yell at him. Paula Kline and Maureen were outstanding.

Tom Bush, who became a close family friend, showed up in a lot of skits in a variety of ways because he could imitate almost anyone and do any accent.

Tony Carmen was one of the pioneers in the early years. His Kishka and Godfather were probably most notable. He's a musician, and when we started doing *Godfather* skits, he'd go to the union hall and find whoever didn't have a gig. We had better-looking Italian characters than the real movie. They were fantastic. Once we were giving the characters names we'd use, like "Fingers," and he said, "We got a real Fingers! Fingers, come here!" They called him that because he was a piano player.

Mariano Pacetti was a great All-Star and perfect as pizza-fight champion. That's why the bit went so long, because of his loveable personality. Everybody liked Mush.

Dave O'Karma was our champ when he was seventeen years old

because Mush didn't take him seriously. Mush he had to come back to reclaim his crown. Dave was our champ the last few years, and he was over fifty when the show ended.

Bob Ferguson did a lot of the cartoons and artwork we used. He was a fan from day one, since he was a kid.

Dr. Robert White was always game for skits. Good old Tall Ted Hallaman was always there for us. So was Superhost, Marty Sullivan. And I can't neglect Captain Eddie, Roy Lasure, and definitely not the guy in the gorilla suit, Ron Sweed.

I probably shouldn't have started this. When it is published, I'll remember someone I definitely should have mentioned, and I apologize in advance. Just the local athletes and celebrities are too many to mention. I apologize. I love you all.

Some people had limited runs, and it's hard to mention everybody from all two thousand of them. Everyone has a favorite. But they all live again on our DVDs.

People send me photos of stuff I forgot I did. I don't remember being where it was shot, I don't remember owning the shirt I was wearing. Collectors have been sending stuff from the Hoolihan days. Some taped whole shows, including the movies. Show after show. Boxes of tapes.

Dave Stoner in Florida sent DVDs with a complete list of every movie. Rick Edgell's been great. He has the biggest collection of my stuff of anyone in the world. Mike While, Chris While, and Jeremy Maurick have stuff on the Web site, *BigChuckandLilJohn. com*. Even I don't know how they got some of the footage. I've heard from people all over the country—all over the world, in fact, including a base at the South Pole.

Looking back as I put things together, everything was done on film when I began in TV in 1960. The format started changing to two-inch quad tape around then, but mostly for stuff the network sent for news shows. When Ernie began Ghoulardi, everything outside was shot on film. We'd run it on a film projector on the show, or transfer it to two-inch tape. When Hoolie and I started in 1967, and until 1975, the outside stuff was still shot on film.

Then we started using minicameras, recording on ¾-inch tape machines. All of a sudden the two-inch tape was getting phased out.

When Lil' John and I began our show in 1979, I started transferring our old two-inch tapes and film clips onto ¾-inch tape. But I was in no hurry because we still had a film projector and a two-inch tape machine. When those were dumped completely, I worked day and night transferring stuff, the best bits first. I didn't make it. TV8 got all one-inch tape machines and dumped the old equipment before I finished.

I started searching for companies that specialized in tape and film transfers and found one in Florida and another in California. But the two-inch tapes were so heavy, just the cost of shipping would be enormous. I knew the station wouldn't go for it, and I resigned myself to the fact that our older stuff would be lost forever. Then a man called me out of the blue and said if I ever wanted two-inch material transferred, he'd do it for me.

That was Dave Little. No one told him what I was doing, and no one told me about him. Somebody up there likes me. It was perfect. I'd been frantic. Not only did Dave transfer the stuff I had, he said to give him all of our stuff because he could probably make better copies. There are now fifty-one one-hour tapes transferred to beta format. He did that. I don't know how many skits there are. He also transferred the rest of the ¾-inch and film stuff I had.

Single-handedly Dave Little, saved our stuff from extinction. Now he's helping put our beta material on DVD, receiving material that Rick Edgell and Dave Stoner got from all over the country and adding it to our "Best of" series. Thank God for Dave Little.

We're not making a whole lot of money with the DVDs, with postage and all. We probably give away as many as we sell. The reason we do it, and the reason people collect so much of our material, is they tell me they like it. It would be a shame to let it die. I don't want it to die.

AN ALL-STAR ROSTER

Most of the All-Stars were cast in something over the years. A few went all the way from the Ghoulardi All-Stars to the Hoolihan & Big Chuck All-Stars to the Big Chuck & Lil' John All-Stars.

"Big Stash" Russ Cormier, Tom O'Kelly, Phil Fabeetz, Dave Sta-

A burlesque-themed party raised both spirits and money as a benefit for the family of kidnap and murder victim Amy Mihaljevic in 1989. From left: impressionist Tom Bush, me, *PM Magazine* host Jan Jones, John, *BC & LJ* stalwart Julie Ann Cashel, Dick Goddard.

cey, "Dr. G" Larry Gogolick, George Mondock, Whoopie John, Ted Lux, and the flying Arslanians, Ted, Hank, and Armen.

"Corky" Bernie Barabus, Ziparilla Joel Scala from WZZP, Mayor Mark Elliott—we called him Sticks—of Brook Park.

My brother, Paul, my sons, Mike and Mark, and my daughters, Missy, Michelle, and Marilyn. Tim Rossky, Vicky "Rambo," Len Camerer, Bill Russert, Ron Ackerman, Angelo Rodriguez, "Soul Man" Herb Thomas, Casey Kassarda, the Lorius brothers, Harvey Acks, the Loch Ness Monster, Bob Buscher, Soul Woman Alicia, Tom Bush. Even Lou the bus driver played.

Olympic great Harrison Dillard played baseball with us. Olympian Dave Wottle played with us as well.

Gus Johnson played a few games with us. He'd call me up, just because he wanted to. He was fantastic. If the gym had side walls near the hoop, he'd come down the court, run way off to the side, and throw the ball real high against the wall. We'd wonder what he was doing. But the ball would bounce off and hit the rim. One time it went in—great stunt. We'd just feed him during games, and it was like having LeBron. We could beat any team.

A Cleveland undercover cop we called Marvelous Marvin played on the basketball team. He was a guy they'd send in to work with dope dealers by becoming one of them. The other cops didn't even know he was there, so he'd get beaten up and pushed around and thrown in jail. Guys like him hide guns all over their bodies. If someone disarmed him, they'd take away two guns. He'd have four. He put them in his gym bag. A kid picked it up for him once and said, "What do you have in here?" Marvin said, "You'd be surprised." It was heavy.

We'd go to some hick towns I never heard of. It'd look like a scene from *Hoosiers*. The whole surrounding area would come to the game because they never had a show like that. Some had never seen a black man in person before. Kids would get John's autograph and mine, and they'd be knocked out when they got Marv's. He'd write "Michael Jordan." He's a funny guy.

I'd see him on the street, dressed like a ragamuffin, and he'd act like he didn't know me. I'd say, "Hey, it's Big Chuck, look." He didn't like it when he saw people he knew because it might blow his cover, but we knew to be cool. He'd tell stories that would curl your hair.

He became head of security at the Coliseum when he retired, and then went on to become LeBron's bodyguard, the guy that keeps him straight. The stories he must have now.

LOOK WHO WAS WATCHING

We always had Cleveland and its mayors behind us, starting with Mayor Ralph Perk. John knew his wife, Lucille, and he hired us for a lot of stuff in the early years. John played the New Year's baby on Public Square one year. Dennis Kucinich, George Voinovich, and Mike White were all big fans of the show. I don't think Frank Jackson knows who we are.

National show business people with Cleveland ties were behind us, too. Tom Hanks was a huge *Hoolihan & Big Chuck* fan who said that while at Kent State he would not miss the show. Monica Potter, who's been called the actress most loyal to Cleveland, said in a national magazine interview that she'd accomplished everything she wanted except being on the *Big Chuck & Lil' John Show*. She called a couple of times on Kelleys Island to ask about Ghoulardifest, just to say she was going to try to make it.

Joe Benny, who used to be a TV8 producer and now runs Dennis Kucinich's staff, told me that Wes Craven, the great horror director and writer from Cleveland, has a mural in his house of me, Hoolie, and Ghoulardi.

Screenwriter Joe Eszterhas would make it a point to shake hands and tell us he liked the show when we'd see him around.

For a long time, I admit, I didn't know who he was.

We did a benefit variety show in 1989 after Amy Mihaljevic, a nine-year-old Cleveland girl, was kidnapped and later found murdered. John and I were in it. So were Dick Goddard and Julie Ann, and Art Modell's son, Dave, who sang. He was a surprisingly good singer. Art Modell was a big supporter, sitting out there prominently for the cause.

Maybe he wasn't that bad of a guy.

June and I and our family at my seventieth birthday party: five children, fourteen grandchildren, two daughters-in-laws, two sons-in law. *(Tom Bush)*

OUTRO

To accomplish forty-seven years of doing what I did took the support of the people I mentioned and many more—all part of an incredible run of Ghoulardi, Hoolihan & Big Chuck, and the marathon twenty-eight years of Big Chuck & Lil' John.

There were so many at TV8.

I never would have done this if it weren't for Ernie making me go on the air, which is pretty much the story of my career. Ernie made me go on the air and made me be funny. Hoolie gave me the much-needed support to continue when I was down. John gave me the spunk and a whole new attitude, and he made everything funny, which took some of the pressure off.

Hoolie, being from Nebraska, didn't have Cleveland in common with me. Our lifestyles were different. He's outgoing, I'm not. He liked being out and about, I'm a homebody. It's easy for him to perform, and I'm nervous. John and I are both Clevelanders and Cleveland sports fans, with big, ethnic, traditional families and no training for on-camera work. We were like the blue-collar guys who made good. That was our thing.

John's goal in life is to make someone laugh everyday no matter how he feels. He does it. We're still partners and close friends, more like family after so many years. We're still getting booked for personal appearances. We still enjoy doing them and meeting people.

Art Lofredo is a Clevelander, too. He's been with us almost from the beginning to the end, and we were real close in the early days of the show, when we both had young families. He's sort of shy like me but enjoys performing. He gave me the help I needed throughout my career, on- and off-camera—being a good comic actor, making props, even throwing ideas during breaks. I don't think I ever thanked him enough because I saw him every day and took him for granted.

They're so easy to direct. They never questioned anything. They'd just do it, and do it well. You can't get some people to do what you want to do, but I took it for granted with them.

Herb Thomas was the perfect Soul Man. He was so busy as a news photographer that he was hard to get for skits after Soul Man died out, but in later years he became exclusively our cameraman, which was really nice. I'm proud of him.

Special K, Kevin Salyer, was a great fan of the show. He started as a part-time tour guide at TV8 more than twenty-five years ago, became head of promotions, and is now vice president. He and general manager Mike Renda kept our show moving around

Walking the familiar hallway that John ran down during the show's opening each week, I prepare for the last show in June 2007. Longtime announcer and contributor Bill Ward ran in front of me to take this final photo. He said, "This one is for the books." *(Bill Ward)*

the schedule because Fox was sending more and more syndicated stuff they had to run. It was inevitable that the end would happen, but they kept us on as long as they could. We had good ratings, and they were both fans.

Bob Soinski taught me editing and studied it with me. We teamed up for some hilarious bits going back to Ghoulardi, and he'd always make me laugh, even when he shouldn't have.

The man who talked me into being a director, Bob Huber, always had more faith in me than I did, giving me things like the Burgess Meredith movie to produce and direct. He just knew I'd do it.

We got help from Paula Kline and Maureen, crew members Walt Sargi, Dom Lolli, and Ralph Tarsitano, as well as Ralph's father, Papa Tarts. Tim Rossky did several years of stuff with us as a cameraman extraordinaire, editor, and also an actor. He'd shoot

Big Stash, Big Chuck, Lil' John, and Hoolie keep
the laughs coming at Ghoulardifest 2007.
(*Rose Costanza*)

knowing exactly what we needed and where it was. Terry and Phil
and so many good editors at TV8, helped.

Producer Rick DeChant was a big part of the show for quite
awhile and would do voices. Ralph Gertz was a big contributor early
on. It would be hard to name all the directors because whoever was
handy would direct our show. But director Bill Turner was an all-
around ham, writer, talent, and All-Star.

Vicky Benkowski Stracinski was a director who started as an
intern. She would follow me, ask if she could come in and watch
me direct the news, and eventually became my protégé. We called
her Rambo as an All-Star because she had a basketball scholarship
to Miami University. When she would guard you, she'd be all over
you, and you couldn't do anything with the ball. The best thing you
could do was get rid of it. She'd get elbowed in the teeth and knocked
down playing with all guys. I taught her everything about directing
news, and when she started directing our shows she was the biggest

help I had. She'd do the early and late news and volunteer to tape in between. She knew what we needed and just took over. What a huge help she was—more like my daughter than my coworker.

Hoolie's wife, Barb, was dying of cancer before Ghoulardifest in 2007. I talked to them on the phone a couple times. He told me she said that no matter what happened, he was not to miss this Ghoulardifest. She knew how much it meant. He just loved coming back and reuniting. I take it for granted because I still have it all around here. Barb died, and he came two days later, bringing his son and his daughter. He stayed all three days for the whole thing, morning and night. People were lined up to greet him and to shoot us together like a collector's photograph. It was an emotional event for all of us.

The show means a lot to a lot of people. Even when he was dying, Ernie loved talking about the show and stuff we did, and he was not a sentimental guy. If he didn't like it, he'd tell you, in no uncertain terms.

We had something special going on for all those years. It meant something. People relate skits from the show to incidents in their lives.

Someone told me his father had a stroke and didn't talk for a long time. He came from his bed downstairs to the living room, where they were watching Hoolie and me doing a silly takeoff. They didn't even know he was in the room until they heard him laughing, the first sound they heard from him in years. It was emotional. Everyone was crying; he was laughing.

I get story after story like that. People sent me two Purple Hearts, one for a son who'd grown up watching us and was killed in Vietnam. I didn't think it was right to keep them but felt I should hold them for a time and then respectfully give them back.

I've received letters from Vietnam, from Desert Storm, and now from Iraq. The show has been a piece of home to the young men and women serving in the military, a common bond and part of their lives.

Prisoners have written all through my career, too, mostly from Mansfield and Grafton. I'd say the mail came from our captive audience. I never got real friendly with those guys, but they'd tell me all kinds of crazy things and sometimes some heartfelt ones. I once suggested they get together and make a list of movies they'd like to see, a Top 10, and I'd see what I could do. They sent me a list of all prison movies, from *Jailhouse Rock* to *The Birdman of Alcatraz*.

Many people tell me what a family experience the show was, and what they used to eat while watching. They'd almost always send out for pizza or make popcorn. But not always. One guy said he and his sister "always get together and get your show on and eat soup." Somebody else ate Chef Boyardee ravioli out of the can.

I'd hear whispering in the studio audience. Someone would say, "Daddy used to come down here when he was a kid and watch the show." On a couple of occasions it was a grandfather, father, and son who came down. Three generations.

I've always told people, my kids especially, that if you discover you have a God-given talent for anything, it is your duty and your responsibility to develop that talent, and to use it for whatever good it can do, no matter how little you can do with it. If you don't develop it, you're going to regret it someday and catch yourself saying, "Hell, I coulda, woulda, shoulda."

During my career I received many letters from people who enjoyed the show and enjoyed my work, and that's really what kept me going all these years. It certainly wasn't the money, or getting tired of the show. Every time I'd get those letters, I'd feel really good about it. Near the end of my career I'd get well-written, in-depth letters and e-mails saying what the show meant to some people, and how it helped them cope in some cases. Guys with troubled childhoods, people with difficult family lives or trouble on the job. I cherish these letters, and I saved them all.

Hell—I coulda, shoulda, and I did.

And thanks to all of you, I did some good.

More good books about Cleveland and Ohio . . .

from **Gray & Company, Publishers**

Best of Hal Lebovitz / A collection of great sportswriting from six decades, by the late dean of Cleveland sportswriters. *Hal Lebovitz* / $14.95 softcover

Curses! Why Cleveland Sports Fans Deserve to Be Miserable / A collection of a lifetime of tough luck, bad breaks, goofs, and blunders. *Tim Long* / $9.95 softcover

Heroes, Scamps & Good Guys / 101 profiles of the most colorful characters from Cleveland sports history. Will rekindle memories for any Cleveland sports fan. *Bob Dolgan* / $24.95 hardcover

The View from Pluto / Award-winning sportswriter Terry Pluto's best columns about Northeast Ohio sports from 1990–2002. *Terry Pluto* / $14.95 softcover

Cleveland Golfer's Bible / All of Greater Cleveland's golf courses and driving ranges described in detail. Essential guide for any golfer. *John H. Tidyman* / $13.95 softcover

Golf Getaways from Cleveland / 50 great golf trips just a short car ride from home. Plan easy weekends, business meetings, reunions, other gatherings. *John H. Tidyman* / $14.95 softcover

Cleveland on Foot / Beyond Cleveland on Foot / Great hikes and self-guided walking tours in and around Greater Cleveland and 7 neighboring counties. *Patience Cameron Hoskins, with Rob & Peg Bobel* / $15.95 (each) softcover

Trail Guide to Cuyahoga Valley National Park / The complete guide to Ohio's own national park, written by the people who know it best. *Cuyahoga Valley Trails Council* / $15.95 softcover

Cleveland Fishing Guide / Best public fishing spots in Northeast Ohio, what kind of fish you'll find, and how to catch them. Directory of fishing resources. *John Barbo* / $14.95 softcover

Dick Goddard's Weather Guide for Northeast Ohio / Seasonal facts, folklore, storm tips, and weather from Cleveland's top meteorologist. / $13.95 softcover

Ohio Road Trips / Discover 52 of Neil Zurcher's all-time favorite Ohio getaways. *Neil Zurcher* / $13.95 softcover

Cleveland Ethnic Eats / The guide to authentic ethnic restaurants and markets in Northeast Ohio. *Laura Taxel* / $13.95 softcover

52 Romantic Outings in Greater Cleveland / Easy-to-follow "recipes" for romance —a lunch hour, an evening, or a full day together. *Miriam Carey* / $13.95 softcover

Bed & Breakfast Getaways from Cleveland / Great Inn Getaways from Cleveland / Small inns and hotels, perfect for an easy weekend or evening away from home. *Doris Larson* / $14.95 (each) softcover

Ohio Oddities / An armchair guide to the offbeat, way out, wacky, oddball, and otherwise curious roadside attractions of the Buckeye State. *Neil Zurcher* / $14.95 softcover

Cleveland Cops / Sixty cops tell gritty and funny stories about patrolling the streets of Cleveland. *John H. Tidyman* / $14.95 paperback

Amy: My Search for Her Killer / Secrets and suspects in the unsolved murder of Amy Mihaljevic. *James Renner* / $24.95 hardcover

**They Died Crawling
The Maniac in the Bushes
The Corpse in the Cellar
The Killer in the Attic
Death Ride at Euclid Beach**
Five collections of gripping true tales about notable Cleveland crimes and disasters. Includes photos. *John Stark Bellamy II* / $13.95 softcover (each)

Women Behaving Badly / 16 strange-but-true tales of Cleveland's most ferocious female killers. *John Stark Bellamy II* / $24.95 hardcover

The Milan Jacovich mystery series / Cleveland's favorite private eye solves tough cases in these 13 popular detective novels. *Les Roberts* / $13.95 (each) softcover

King of the Holly Hop / #14 in the popular Milan Jacovich mystery series. *Les Roberts* / $24.95 hardcover

We'll Always Have Cleveland / The memoir of mystery novelist Les Roberts, his character Milan Jacovich, and the city of Cleveland. *Les Roberts* / $24.95 hardcover

Truth & Justice for Fun & Profit / Collected newspaper reporting from 25 years by the *Plain Dealer*'s Michael Heaton. / $24.95 hardcover

Do I Dare Disturb the Universe? / A memoir of race and education, this is the story of a girl who grew up and out of the Cleveland projects in the 1960s and '70s. *Charlise Lyles* / $14.95 softcover

Available from your favorite bookseller.
More info at: **www.grayco.com**